D1479061

FOURTH DIMENSION PUBLISHERS

K.O. Mbadiwe

Rebirth of a Nation

Rebirth Of A Nation

(Autobiography)

Dr. Kingsley Ozuomba Mbadiwe

Edited by: Luke Ibekwe Agusiegbe

26769549

Fourth Dimension Publishing Co., Ltd.
Plot 64A City Layout. P.M.B.01164, New Haven
Enugu, Nigeria

DT
515.83
.M38
A3
1991
C.2

© 1991 Mbadiwe

ISBN 978 156 035 5 Pb
978 156 036 3 Hc

CONDITIONS OF SALE

Photoset in Nigeria by
Fourth Dimension Publishing Co. Ltd.

Contents

Part I
The Preparations

Chapter

Part II
The Crusade For Independence

iii

iv

Part V
The Second Republic

Part VI
Vision For The Third Republic

Preface

In writing this preface to the autobiography of our great nationalist and statesman, I have set out principally to portray the background and the character of the author. Also, I have endeavoured to give a glimpse of the issues tackled by him in the book.

Kingsley Ozuomba Mbadiwe, a name which conjures different types of emotion among various people in our national life cannot be fully understood except one is privileged to come into close touch with his ancestral background. To some, Ozuomba Mbadiwe was a consummate actor. To others, he was real, exhibiting his natural behavioural form, be it in politics, business or in social life. A visit to Arondizuogu and a drive into the abode of the Mbadiwe clan, a family that is closely-knit and which carry the obvious badge of a contented group, throws more light into the Mbadiwe story.

Ozuomba Mbadiwe is said to be a reincarnation of a great progenitor known as Okoli Udozuka, who was reputed to be a big trader; a dealer in potassium, tobacco and slaves. He traded as far as Uzuakoli, Arochukwu and some parts of modern Bendel. He was a great fighter too.

A story was told that at one time when Okoli Udozuka sold out his wares of potassium, tobacco and slaves, he locked up all his money and there was hardly any more money left in circulation. That led to a delegation of people from far and near in the villages of Arondizuogu, Uzuakoli and Arochukwu The purpose of the representations to Okoli was that he should start trading again so that currency could circulate. He agreed to the requests made and started his trade all over. Money circulated. He was then styled *Agadagbachiriuzo*, meaning: "the big tree that blocked the way". This title was also bestowed on Ozuomba of our own time.

His penchant **for** creativity **and** innovation was a characteristic he developed during his nine years sojourn in the United States. Professor Hollis R. Lynch, Professor of History at Columbia University, New York, in a recent essay on the American years of Dr. Mbadiwe wrote that "Of all African students ever in the United States, it was probable that Kingsely Ozuomba Mbadiwe of Nigeria made the greatest impact on American society and did more than any other to foster pan-African links between Afro-Americans and Africans as well as general understanding and goodwill between America and Africa".

Mbadiwe spent almost nine years in the United States, during which time he studied at Lincoln University and later Columbia University, from which he received a B.Sc in Banking and Finance in February, 1943. From New York University he received an M.A. in Political Science in 1947. Professor Lynch confirmed that throughout Mbadiwe's stay in the United States, he was a political activist and to promote his goals he was instrumental in founding and playing central roles in two significant organisations - the African Students Association of the United States and Canada, and the African Academy of Arts and Research.

Mbadiwe, like many other African students, had been distressed by the ignorance about Africa in the United States. To attempt to rectify that as well as to give a sense of community and mutual support of African students in North America, Mbadiwe played a leading role in founding the African Students' Association of the United States and Canada in the fall of 1941. Lynch testified that "on the political front, Mbadiwe had begun to think that there was need for an organisation led by Africans which would project Africa favourably and promote its interest". Having conceived the idea he sought distinguished sponsorship for it. In that quest, the bold Mbadiwe wrote to Mrs. Eleanor Roosevelt, the liberal, public-spirited and popular wife of the President, and was granted an audience to the White House with the First Lady on May 10, 1943. The unprecedented event attracted public attention in the nation's capital. At the end, Mrs. Roosevelt had become an enthusiastic patron. That led to the founding of the African Academy of Arts and Research which opened its office on Saturday, November 13, 1943.

On arrival back home, Dr. Mbadiwe plunged into the agitation for self-government for Nigeria which was at a very high pitch. Many leaders had been putting heads together. The upshot of it all was a meeting held at the Glover Memorial Hall on March 27, 1951 where an organisation known as the National Rebirth Committee was proposed. In all the meeting and open air gatherings, Mazi K.O. Mbadiwe established himself as an eloquent and colourful speaker who drew warm applause.

Much as he deplored military rule, Dr. Mbadiwe employed tact, diplomacy and statesmanship to put across his views to the military leaders on a number of issues ranging from depreciation of the naira to the need to end military *coup d'etats* in Nigeria. Again and again he proffered reasonable solutions to thorny issues. He regularly held dialogue with military leaders from Gowon to Babangida.

Dr. Mbadiwe in his autobiography writes about his vision for Nigeria and emphasises the need to terminate military rule. He canvasses five options, citing the arrangements, in U.S.A., West Germany, Switzerland, consideration of military pacts and the possibility of non-cooperation with a military putsch. The place of the military in the Third Republic he affirmed is the pursuit of their traditional duties.

Finally, come his hand-over notes to various sectors of society:

To journalists, he enjoined; 'A Free press does not defame the good name of people or disparage their reputation."

To trade unions he advised: "Raise your productivity that you may justify a rise in wages. Always spend time to study the economy of the country and see where and how you fit in. Only a proper appreciation of your role and responsibility can ensure an egalitarian society."

To professional bodies: "You are the salt of the earth. The standard of achievement of the members of the professional bodies is the gauge for measuring the height of a nation's greatness."

To youths he urges: "All the type of energy, all the type of resources, and all type of talent which we employed to fight imperialism, should now be harnessed and directed by you to fight army take-over of governments in Nigeria."

To the business community, he charged: "Where you have the aptitude, the temperament and the fervour, put yourself up through your political party for any high public office of the land."

To the farmer, he said: "Air, water and food are the daily needs of man and you, the farmer, provides man with food. Your role, therefore, is of paramount importance."

To the artisan, the labourer, the self-employed, he counselled: "One may earn one's living by being a cobbler, a carpenter, a tailor or any other craftsman. An able bodied and strong man, ready on the wings, to render a service for a just pay is also a happy member of the society."

Dr. Mbadiwe in his epilogue sees the new dawn of the Third Republic and a God-send leader who can confidently ask his followers: "Come follow me. The light is lit; be not afraid."

That great apostle of national rebirth confidently opined:"Then both leader and follower will march with optimism and glory unto the Greater Tomorrow of the Nigerian nation. Then, the Rebirth is complete."

Chief Dr Kolawole Balogun

Editor's Note

On 20th September, 1989 , at the Nigerian Union of Journalists' Light House on Victoria Island, Lagos, Dr. K.O. Mbadiwe, in a press conference promised "Hand-over notes" to the next generation after him. Those notes are contained in his memoirs which he was working on. He intended to have them published soon before the elections ushering in the Third Republic in 1992. On 28th July, 1990, K. O. wrote me from Arondizuogu where he stayed back after attending the late Igwe M. N. Ugochukwu's funeral: "By the time I come back (to Lagos) in early August, by 5th, I want all papers typed. All work on the book should be completed by the end of August." Well, that August "ended" on the 29th, when death came calling. However, the book was completed, as he had dictated the last sentence of it, and revised the draft before that fateful event.

Dr. K.O. Mbadiwe reacted with great vision to momentous events in his time. As a student in the US he felt the plight of the blacks and founded the African Academy of Arts and Research and bought the Africa House. At the end of the Second World War which set up a wind of liberation to oppressed peoples, his organisation, the AAAR sent a memorandum to the very first meeting of the United Nations General Assembly, pleading for the dismantling of colonialism, especially in Africa. After the Enugu shooting of innocent miners in 1949, he organised the "National Emergency Committee". When Nigeria's first military *coup d'etat* occurred in 1966, he as the NCNC Parliamentary Leader, together with the Acting NPC Parliamentary leader, Alhaji Zana Bukar Dipcharima, signed the hand-over of power document, in the hope that a military regime was corrective and more patriotic. When he saw it otherwise, he did not close his mouth. Hence Rebirth of a Nation's emphasis is on final military disengagement.

Dr. K.O. Mbadiwe's autobiography offers rare and excellent opportunity for the reader to appreciate his views and actions on some issues that made press headlines, such as the NCNC crisis, the Ijora Causeway land affairs, the Operation Fantastic, the Nigerian Civil War, etc.

The nature of this book, and the modesty of the author, has not fully permitted the reader to know that "*Agadagbachiriuzo*" was more than a politician. Dr. Mbadiwe has written about himself, but it will require other people and other volumes to document his social interaction, his religious life, his business acumen, his press rapport, his campaign speeches, his parliamentary debates and, of course, K.O.'s philosophy of life.

One does not expect the language of *Rebirth* to sound like an address from the soap box. Dr. Mbadiwe is scrupulous, thorough and refined in his writings, press conferences and parliamentary debates . Such is the output in his memoirs.

The book does not need a bibliography. Quotations are acknowledged in the text. However, as the author was dictating *Rebirth* and going down the memory lane, he acknowledged imput from colleagues and writers who reminded or confirmed for him some of the events recapitulated. One such source is Professor Hollis Lynch, who wrote an essay on "Mbadiwe: the American years."

Special mention must here be made of Chief Dr. Kolawole Balogun, a long time friend of Dr. Mbadiwe, who co-edited and assisted to bring this book to its present format.

Greg, the eldest son of Dr. Mbadiwe, and the entire Mbadiwe and Odum family, now headed by Barrister P.C. Mbadiwe, spared no time and resources in seeing that K.O.'s injunction to publish this work is implemented.

Hon. Luke I. Agusiegbe

xi

Part 1

The Preparations

Part 1

The Preparations

BRITISH AND AXIS AIMS
IN AFRICA

A Timely and Challenging Viewpoint and Interpretation of Africa and
Its Relations to the Nations of Europe by an African Student
of Banking and Finance in New York University.

ILLUSTRATED

Cover of my first book, *British and Axis aims in Africa,* published in
New York, 1942.

As President of African Academy of Arts and Research, I here introduce its Grand Patroness, Mrs Eleanor Roosevelt, wife of President Franklin Roosevelt of U.S.A., to Mazi Mbonu Ojike, Executive Director of the Academy, 1943.

On the day Lincolin University, my *alma mater*, conferred the degree of Ph.D (honorary cause) on me, 1956.

On my wedding day with former Miss Cecilia Alisah, at Arondizuogu, March, 18, 1950. A Catholic Sacramental marriage in traditional attire.

Fruit of the marriage: (L to R) Greg, Paul, Francis, Betty and George.

Mbadiwe brothers with family friend/spiritual mentor, (L to R) Chief D.O. Mbadiwe, Dr. K. O. Mbadiwe, Bishop M.O. Unegbu, Mrs, C.N. Mbadiwe and Chief J.Green Mbadiwe).

Mbadiwe Family receives Nehru Family. Front row (L-R) Ogundu (Betty), Eziokwu (Paul), Iheanacho (Greg) and George. Back row (L to R) Mrs Indira Ghandi, former Indian Prime Minister and Nehru's daughter, Dr Mbadiwe, Pandit Jawaharlal Nehru and Mrs C.N. Mbadiwe.

Chapter 1

My Early Years

All of us, Nigerians, are bearing witness to the closing of one epoch of history and the opening of another. We, the first generation of politicians, are transferring the torch of experience and leadership to a new generation, saying to it:

Go ye into the vast field of Nigeria;
Cultivate it with honesty;
Serve your Country with vigour;
And with stronger determination
Hold high that unquenchable torch
Of indivisible, united, powerful nation.

If you turn to ask me what I would want to be remembered for by the people of this country, I will readily answer:

I want to be remembered as
That lamb which voluntarily chose
To be sacrificed for Nigerian unity.

Therefore, with utmost patriotic fervour for my beloved Nigeria, and as one whose services to the country have often been reciprocated, I record in the following pages, the crusade for national unity and independence, my humble roles, and my ideas for a rebirth of the nation.

I wish to start by first recalling my modest background. I was born to the Odum family of Arondizuogu, at Oneh, on March 15, 1917. Oneh is one of the twenty towns which make up the present Orumba Local Government Area of Anambra State. The head of the Odum family came originally from Ogba in Awka, Anambra State, and migrated to Ndi-aniche Uno in Arondizuogu, Imo State. Mazi Odum had six children. The eldest was Chief Igwegbe Odum, a political dynamo, and a

3

colossus of his time. The rest follow according to seniority: Mazi Mbadiwe Odum, Okorie Odum and Anichebe Odum. He had in addition two daughters. They grew close together and they never lived apart.

Chief Igwegbe Odum became leader and spokesman. When he moved, other relations moved together with him. They were bound together by great discipline. They obeyed their elders with that unflinching obedience associated with a united family.

After a while trouble brewed at Arondizuogu. Some said it was over slave trade; others said it was over leadership tussle between Mazi Igwegbe and other leaders of Arondizuogu town Destiny made it that Igwegbe, wherever he was, became so distinguished with dominant influence that he had no rival. He was a star that out-shone all other stars put together.

Leadership was predestined by birth, through traditional inheritance. Whatever you were, and whatever you did, you could not over-step the ordinance and tradition of the town. An effort by Chief Igwegbe to out-shine those who were destined by tradition to hold certain earmarked leadership positions failed. Because Igwegbe could not overstep that tradition, he found himself in a restless position.

It was said that my father was his Chief Political Adviser, to whom he listened very religiously. He convinced Igwegbe that the future was bright for them. A suggestion came that they should all leave Arondizuogu for a while and sojourn in another place. Igwegbe agreed because he loved adventure. He was the legend about whom the book *Omenuko* was written. My father as his Chief Adviser prepared the ground. Chief Igwegbe ordered the exodus of the massive Odum family from Arondizuogu. This involved taking along the five brothers, their wives, sisters and children. The great march soon began. They selected their first destination to be Nkporogwu. From Nkporogwu they moved to Ndikelionwu where they prospered considerably. For want of a large space to accommodate the men and their treasures, they finally left and settled at Oneh where I was born.

The talent of Chief Igwegbe soon became visible in the new abode. The rulers there came to associate him with wisdom. He was a great builder, farmer, and trader. Soon, they adopted him as one of their chiefs. They could not resist the wisdom of Igwegbe. His counsel was sought for in many areas of life. Chief Igwegbe was made a warrant chief, and later became a paramount chief of the twenty villages now called Orumba. Orumba has since grown into a large local government area. Treasured friends of Odum family, such as the late Chief M.N. Ugochukwu, the Igwe of Orumba, hailed from there.

The Naming Ceremony

The eighth-day naming ceremony - the *afa agu* - was a great occasion. Soothsayers were gathered in the village square. Eminent men were invited to hear who was reincarnated in the baby. My father, who told me all these said they were watching with anxiety. One soothsayer proclaimed in a loud voice that he had seen a great vision from his oracle. He announced: "This is no small child. A great man has returned to earth". He looked around. People held their breath. They were in utter suspense He finally proclaimed: "This boy is Okoli Udozuka, the famous and renowned fighter, the warrior and the merchant prince." My parents knew whom he was. The great Udozuka in his life time had many titled names one of which was Ozuomba. The soothsayer said, I must be called "Ozuomba" from that day on. My mother was lost in jubilation because Ozuomba was her maternal uncle. Okoli Udozuka was reputed to be a big trader. He was a dealer in potassium, tobacco and slaves. He traded as far as Uzuakoli, Arochukwu and some parts of the present Bendel State. If anyone disturbed him on his trade route, he would instantly levy war. The other title of Okoli Udozuka was *Agadagbachiriuzo*, meaning, "The big tree that blocked the way against the enemy." A story was told that at one time Okoli sold his wares of potassium, tobacco, and slaves and locked up all the money, leaving the trading community with scarce money in circulation.

That led to delegations coming from far and near to see him.
The purpose was to plead with him to start trading again so that
money could circulate. He eventually agreed to their request and
reopened trade. Money came back to the market. People titled
me *Agadagbachiriuzo* till today, the same title bestowed on
Okoli Udozuka.

One may ask: "Is reincarnation true?" Perhaps not. But the
association of a person's name with a previous ancestor rouses
sentiments and gingers up action in a certain direction. Okoli
Udozuka hailed from Ndi-akunwata. The loyalty of that village
to the first Okoli was passed on immediately to the baby by that
name. Tributes were paid. Gifts were made. The late Chief
L.N. Obioha used to style me "grandfather". The wives of Okoli
Udozuka called me their "husband". Their children respected me
in a special way. The relatives of my mother were happy. My
uncle, Chief Igwegbe, sent a leopard skin to me to form part of
my mat and called me his great "brother-in-law". My father
reserved special presents, and there was jubilation at Oneh and
Arondizuogu. As I grew up, the petting brought me closer to
elderly people than to the younger ones. The scales of shyness
fell off my eyes early and I started to associate with people far
older, wiser, and richer than me.

The Saving Grace: School at Port Harcourt

Chief Igwegbe Odum was a very foresighted ruler. He was so
impressed by the British Administrators that he wanted his
children to be like them. Having gathered a smattering of
English Language, he was able to express and make himself
understood in that language. He made friends easily. He
influenced the establishment of Ajalli Government School. He
used it as his base to bring education to his brother's children as
well as his own children. Some of those sent to school early
were D.O. Mbadiwe and J. Green Mbadiwe. Others were
Francis, Maxwell, Samuel, and Charles Mbadiwe and E.K.
Oruche (one of the sister's sons). They all went to school at
Ajalli.

By the time my father left Oneh and returned to Arondizuogu in 1918, I was only one year old. My elder brothers had finished Standard Six and were preparing for government civil service. Mr. D.O. Mbadiwe was employed as a railway clerk and posted to Port Harcourt. Mr. Green Mbadiwe became a postal clerk.

Mr. D. O. Mbadiwe, my elder brother, was apprehensive that the great pampering bestowed unto me would spoil me and render me useless. Therefore, determined to take me away from home, he brought me down to Port Harcourt and sent me to school. I went to St. Mary's Elementary School, Port Harcourt. He placed me under very severe discipline. He outlined my daily duties. They included waiting at his table, washing plates, seeing that a match box was placed under the pillow at night. Failure would result in caning me. There was no body around to flatter me about the great Ozuomba and shower salutations on me. I wished to return to Arondizuogu, and I had to make plans for it.

It was not easy for me to find my way. I would have to go by train through Ovim, and then on foot to Arondizuogu. And someone would have to carry me for most of the journey. After many restless days in Port Harcourt, I found myself one day in the train. Without a ticket, I got to Afikpo Road Station. As small as I was then, I could speak English, and because of it the train officials excused me for not having a ticket. It was sheer fascination that a small boy like me spoke English.

Running away from Port Harcourt did not let me off school. I was later taken to Aba Government School, where I completed Primary Education. From there I went to Hope Waddel Training Institute, Calabar, a premier educational centre, east of the Niger. The next year, I was in Aggrey Memorial College, Arochukwu.

During my school days at Aggrey, I recall, when my being choosey about food often times made it difficult for me to take the college food; I always had my own solution! I would simply become an uninvited guest at the home of Mrs Ikoku, where I was given the dish which was suitable to my taste. I also recall the warnings by the late Dr. Alvan Ikoku that I should not be spoilt, and that I must take whatever was presented at the school. Mrs. Ikoku's excuse was that she did not invite me, and that whenever I came, and she had anything, she would not deny it to me. Later, I learnt to adapt myself to eating whatever was given at the school. That training has made it possible for me to adapt myself to any condition in which I found myself.

Dr. Alvan Ikoku died on 18th November 1971. *The Renaissance Daily* newspaper, of 10th January 1973 recorded my tribute to this great soul in these words:

At the grave side of late Dr. Alvan Ikoku in Arochukwu last Saturday, were thousands of people from all corners of the town and beyond who had come to watch the traditional "mgbaru" ceremony (paying of homage) by Dr. K. O. Mbadiwe. He was one of the pioneer students of Aggrey Memorial college, founded by Dr. Ikoku. ..." Dr. Mbadiwe said:·

I adore and admire him because he was an incarnate of goodness, an epitome of greatness, and an embodiment of all that is edifying in the life of any single person. The late Dr. Alvan Ikoku in his days towered above his time and age. He saw vision beyond the scope of his immediate environment, and became a pioneer in the modernism which his country has today attained.

Again from Aggrey, I moved to Lagos, and was admitted first at the Baptist Academy, and completed secondary school education at the Igbobi College, Lagos, four secondary schools! But the friends I made in each of those schools were later to have great influence on me and we became colleagues and nationalist fighters for Nigerian freedom and independence.

There were very strong reasons for my attending several schools and colleges. I lived with my brother, Chief D. O. Mbadiwe whom I addressed as "Master" till his death in 1975. After Port Harcourt, where I started primary school, he was transferred to Ehamufu railway station, where there was no school. He had to leave me with another brother, Mr. F. O. Mbadiwe, then a postal clerk at Aba, where I completed primary school.

Because my brothers had the advantage of going to school, they also made sure that those of us after them had the same benefit. The year before me, my brother Maxwell, had gone to the Hope Waddel Institute, Calabar. Chief J. Green Mbadiwe undertook to pay his fees, while Chief D. O. Mbadiwe paid mine. Naturally they wanted me to go to Hope Waddel, not only because it was the most prestigious college then east of the Niger, but also because Maxwell was there to give me protection.

Maxwell was not as subjected to D. O.'s hard discipline as I was. With D. O. Mbadiwe you must have an account book to explain every expenditure and return the change before you were trusted with further money. I resented facing Master for that strict accounting. Rather I would manage whatever little money I was given when I was in the boarding house. Before spending the 10 shillings he gave me as pocket money, I would first set aside four shillings which would take me home when schools closed for holidays.

Maxwell was more carefree. He wrote very good essays and spoke very well. With that flowery language, he got from Green any amount of money he wanted. Green would read his letter and exclaim: "First class." Then he would arrange to send him money that night. Green lived in Minna, as a Railway Contractor, two miles from the station. The train arrived at midnight and sometimes early morning. But to make sure he sent money to Maxwell he would wake up at that time and give the railway guard the money for Maxwell. So as I lived in the boarding house and took whatever food that was served, Maxwell lived outside, and cooked the type of food he wished.

I enjoyed Hope Waddel. The principal, Mr Macgregor, a Scot, was a great man, highly respected by the students. Next to him was one Mr. Lawrence Foster from Jamaica. He was a proud and self-contained man, with great confidence in himself. His style of English and of walking became matters for imitation by students. Many students expanded their arms, in walking like Mr. Foster. But when you could not make the grade he caned you. Most teachers then used the cane, even in secondary schools.

There were some brilliant boys who coached others. In my Number Two dormitory, I had one Ibibio boy who took extra time to coach me in Geometry. He made me love the subject. Those who coached me, I gave some money as gifts, making sure I did not overspend. The discipline from D. O. Mbadiwe (Master) guided me.

At Hope Waddel, we heard about one African who had B.A. Honours in Philosophy, and was opening a school. That was the late Dr. Alvan Ikoku. Hero worship burned through my heart. Whenever we heard that there were people who passed through the secondary school and qualified with B.A., B.Sc, we were elated. So when some of us heard that Ikoku was opening a school, we said: "Good heavens. We must study under this great Nigerian." I was not alone. It was like a revolution. We flocked from Hope Waddel to Aggrey Memorial College, Arochukwu. It was a virgin land. For many years the houses were of mud. We did not care where we were sleeping. We looked up to Alvan Ikoku, B.A.Honours, when he spoke. His English was imitated. His style of walking was imitated. How he wore his shirt was thought the best. So was the position of his neck-tie.

Soon life at Aggrey became unbearable for my brother Maxwell. He was thinking of Igbobi College, in Lagos. It was better than cutting the bush and sleeping in the mud house at Aggrey. I later headed for Lagos merely to join my brother, Maxwell, and breathe the air of Lagos. But there was no vacancy at Igbobi, so I had to stop at Baptist Academy. The Headmaster there was Mr. E.E. Esua, later the Chairman, Federal Electoral Commission. Baptist Academy brought me in contact with Americans. The science teacher, Miss Rapean and some others were Americans.

After one year, a vacancy was made and I joined Maxwell at Igbobi College, also another mission school run by the Presbyterians. It was competing with C.M.S. Grammar School, Kings College and St. Gregory's, all in Lagos. I graduated from Igbobi. Igbobi then produced some of those I had to closely work with later in life, - Hon. T.O. Elias, former Chief Justice of Nigeria, Mr. F.C. Coker, of the Administrator - General's office, Late G.C. Nonyelu, former D.P.P. These were classmates of mine at Igbobi.

Petty Trading
When I was at Igbobi and Baptist Academy my elder brother, Master, was still sponsoring my secondary education. By this time he had been transferred to Jos in Northern Nigeria. My fees and maintenance, he would send part in cash and part in groundnut oil which I would resell when my money ran short. Converting groundnut oil to money was easy because it was in high demand in Lagos. With the ease of exchange he started sending potatoes. I wrote him and said, "In future when you send these, tell me the price". When I compared the price, I found that I made profit. The little labour involved in the sale was an incentive for me. When I went on holidays to Jos, I tried the exchange in a bigger way. I added beans to the goods. On return to Lagos they were easily sold to Mr. Saka Tinubu who was a prison contractor. Then I requested that my brother send no more money to me but commodities for sale. They were sent by train and I would go to the railway station to collect them. So when I finished secondary school, I was already engaged in gainful employment as a petty trader. I immediately engaged in this form of importing and employed people to be stationed in Jos. I am still an importer till today.

I expanded my petty trading and stationed another person in Kano. These agents of mine brought down groundnut oil, beans, potatoes, and dried fish in commercial quantities. The commodities when brought down from the North to the East, also paid well. I invited a younger brother of mine to enter Baptist Academy and to take charge of the beans in Lagos; part of the profit was used to pay his school fees and a portion left in the bank. I then went to Port Harcourt to handle the east trade myself. In addition I tried my hands in of palm produce trade.

That business inclination made me found the African Insurance Company Limited in 1950 and run the "Greater

Tomorrow" Transport Service. Later, after the Nigerian civil war, I established the Afro Engineering & Construction Limited, Afro World Merchants Limited, Afro Foods Limited, and Afro Motors Limited.

Newspaper Agency

Some time in 1937, Dr. Nnamdi Azikiwe came to Port Harcourt and delivered a lecture. I attended and was very fascinated by his eloquence. When he was billed to speak at Aba, some forty miles away, I also travelled there to listen. His address was brilliant and captivating. It was the kind of thing my senior brother, J. Green Mbadiwe liked to hear. I sent Green a telegram, telling him that I had heard a voice that was rare and capable of bringing great changes in our country.

He replied that he was a very busy man, but that if I could arrange a reception for Dr. Azikiwe, I should then proceed to the North and take charge of the reception. So I left for the North. On my arrival at Minna, I explained to, Green, then a financier and contractor in the North, more about the wonderful man, Zik, and his speeches, and his hopes for the people of Nigeria. He was very excited and happy to hear all these things about a Nigerian and invited Dr. Azikiwe who readily accepted. I took over the arrangements. My brother gave me great latitude on things like that.

Dr. Nnamdi Azikiwe came, delivered a crowd-pulling lecture, and was given the most lavish civic reception which Minna had ever witnessed before. The next morning, before Dr. Azikiwe left for Lagos, my brother called him and they had a meeting at which I was present. Green asked what Zik wanted him to do. Zik requested him to take up shares that would qualify him to be a Director in a newspaper, the *West African Pilot*, which he was then organising to publish. Green asked what the shares would amount to and he was told. He immediately drew a cheque for that amount, handed to Zik, and said, "You have my blessing. Go and speak to the whole country through the medium of that paper." My brother, Chief J. Green

Mbadiwe, did not care to ask Zik what would be the profit, who would represent him on the Board and other conditions for running the paper. My brother did not ask for any conditions. He simply said, "Go and do what your talent can for the country". Zik gratefully left, returned to Lagos and established the *West African Pilot.*

For the circulation of this newspaper, agents were advertised to cover the East. I applied to represent the paper in Port Harcourt, Aba, and Onitsha. Zik readily accepted my offer. I employed two friends, one to stay at Aba and the other at Onitsha. Port Harcourt was under my direct charge. After one month of operation, I despatched my report and returns of finances. The accounting system which I devised and the way in which I reported was such that on one chart you could see the whole operation. I got a telegram of commendation from Zik saying, "Most satisfactory work carry on". Later he summoned me to give him the format of accounting and report which he ordered as a pattern for other centres.

I was not only an organiser of sales of the *West African Pilot*, I also sent stories as a correspondent. I took time to build the circulation of the *Pilot*. In a bid to promote the paper, I organised all night dances, at which I made Mr. (Now Chief the Rt. Hon.) D. C. Osadebay, a Customs Officer in Port Harcourt at that time, the guest of honour. Mr. S. U. Nwokedi of the Resident's Office, Dr. Erukwu and Mr. Aduba, later Chief Superintendent of Nurses, were made masters of ceremonies. At the party, we would read sections of the *Pilot,* particularly "INSIDE STUFF' by Zik. I got vendors and educated them on how they would sell the papers to homes and offices. The circulation grew and so did my commission. Added to my Kano trade, I would not say I was doing badly.

Chapter 2

The Argonauts.
Landmarks Of American Years

Between 1936 and 1937, a new wave of nationalism was raging on the West coast of Africa, sparked off by the powerful pen of Dr. Benjamin Nnamdi Azikiwe. Through his crusading paper, *The West African Pilot*, published in Lagos, Nigeria, a new era of nationalism started. A new breed of men and women accepted the credo of nationalism and took the challenge, as its apostles. The battle cry was "Down with British imperialism, Nigeria must be free".

Dr. Azikiwe who led the crusade, had just returned from the United States of America, and everyone who dreamt of a new dawn of political emancipation looked towards America as the ideal country from where to imbibe the needed knowledge, and from where one could be fortified spiritually and morally for the struggle. Zik, as he was called, encouraged young men's aspiration and furthered it by practical demonstration of encouraging his *alma mater,* the Lincoln University, to offer admission to aspiring Nigerian students.

Before then, the grounds had been watered by the courageous fight against imperialism by the late Herbert Meelas Macaulay, and later joined by members of the Nigerian Youth Movement.

Their activities encouraged the exodus to America of several young Nigerians. The first team to leave our shores for the U. S. may go down in history as the Nigerian Argonauts in search of the golden fleece. I was in this team of eight. We left the shores of Nigeria on December 31, 1938, for the United States of America. The team was led by the late Mazi Mbonu Ojike, (the oldest of all). He had been a tutor at the Dennis Memorial

14

Grammar School, Onitsha. Others were Dr. J. B. C. Etuka Okala, Engineer Nwankwo Chukwuemeka, Dr. Okechukwu Ikejiani, the late Mr. George I. Mbadiwe, the late Dr. Nnodu Okongwu and my humble self. Dr. A. A. Nwafor Orizu joined us in the U. S.

My elder brother, the late Chief J. Green Mbadiwe, a gold miner and railway contractor resident in Minna, who financed the exploits of quite a number of these "Argonauts", could not come to see us off. He requested Dr. Nnamdi Azikiwe to do so. However, he sent me a most touching letter through Dr. Azikiwe. It read in part:

> We send you our farewell to the United States. We are confident you will come back with the Golden Fleece. In sending you to America, we send you with great sacrifice. I am called a Nigerian millionaire; do not be carried away by this, for I am the best judge of my worth. Do not therefore live in the hope that your brothers are millionaires, for it is not what the hand fetches that matters, but what the hand is able to keep.
>
> When in tne States whatever your hand findeth to do, do it with your might. Prepare yourself adequately and the.. return home to face the task ahead.

Another great son of Nigeria who joined in making arrangements for our journey in quest of knowledge was Sir Mobolaji Bank-Anthony, KBE, CON, LL.D. He took us to the American Consulate for visas and to the Medical Officer who gave us Medical Certificates of fitness. He later saw us off to the boat. Dr. Azikiwe and a host of other friends and well-wishers were there by the shipside.

We arrived in the United States on February 8, 1939 and entered the Lincoln University, a leading black college. After a year, I transferred to Columbia University, one of the nation's most prestigious private universities from where I graduated with B.Sc. in Banking and Finance in 1943. I received an M.A. in Political Science from New York University in 1947.

I was fully conscious of my purpose in the United States to prepare myself for a struggle for the political emancipation of my people. I employed my time not only for academic work, but also towards acquiring the experience necessary for the task.

First, Mazi Mbonu Ojike, Dr. Nwafor Orizu and I undertook the task of organising the Africans we met in the United States to form an association. We requested Dr. Kwame Nkrumah who was the oldest African student we met to organise an African Students Movement so that we could have a rallying ground. He declined the invitation and advised that we pursued our education first.

We however, proceeded with our plans. We organised the first African Students Association in 1941. Mazi Mbonu Ojike was elected the President while I was elected its Executive Secretary. A year later, Dr. Kwame Nkrumah joined, and out of deference for his seniority, Mbonu Ojike stepped down for him to become the President of the association. The association served to give us a sense of belonging in a community of sixty or so African students in North America. Through its journal, *The African Interpreter*, we pressed for the complete economic and political independence of Africa.

On my twenty-fifth birthday in March, 1942, I published my book, *British and Axis Aims in Africa*. I condemned Nazi Germany's aggression and allied imperialism, calling for an end to colonial rule in Africa.

In order to widen the sphere of the struggle for freedom, I founded the African Academy of Arts and Research in December 1943. I intended to involve American liberals. I organised and staged African Dance Festivals under the sponsorship of Mrs. F. D. Roosevelt, wife of the President of the United States, at the famous Carnegie Hall between 1943 and 1946. The President's message was read at an interval of the performance.

I was invited to be the guest of Mrs. Roosevelt at the White House on May 10, 1943. A negro friend who knew I was going to the White House took me in his black Cardilac Limousine.

At the gate the security men were already informed that I was coming, and so the gates were thrown open. I alighted, dressed in a gorgeous African attire, carrying my ivory walking stick. My visit was announced and I waited in the large reception room for a few minutes. Mrs. Roosevelt soon walked down. I greeted her and we sat down for talks. I said: "I know you are a very busy woman. I have come to thank you for your graciousness in welcoming African students to your country. I thank you for replying to my letter. I have come to tell you more than I could write down concerning my interest in Africa, its future and how I want America and Africa to be friends. That is why I have come to your country to study and learn your ways, and your methods."

I then told her more of my great interest in culture and my plans of staging African music and dance festivals. I wanted an exchange of music and dance with America and concluded: "My single purpose of coming is to respectfully request you to sponsor it". We stayed for about one hour. Until I finished what I had to say, she listened unruffled; then in reply she thanked me for my efforts and promised to give me all assistance and to be present at the show. The date for her to attend Carnegie hall for the dance and music festival was fixed before I left her.

It was a significant successful venture. My success stunned our other fellow students. My friends could not believe it till Mrs. Roosevelt appeared on the appointed date and donated $500.00. She attended subsequent shows.

The lesson the visit to Mrs. Roosevelt taught me has been a guiding principle, namely, if you are in any high office, open your doors to receive both the big and the small person. With Mrs. Roosevelt, the power behind the President was already with me. I needed not meet the President, for anything which I wanted. She would get it easier and faster from the President than I could ever get directly.

It was during the festivals that I made the *Walden Wilkey Awards* for persons who had "one world conception". We adopted Walden Wilkey because he was a man who was imbued with broad-mindedness and an expression of one people and one human race. The recepients included Governor Baldwin of Connecticut, who got an elephant carving as a souvenir, and Emperor Hàile Sellasie of Ethiopia, who was given a round-world radio as a memento.

I was not the only African student burning with African nationalism. But my approach was different. Most sophisticated African elite of that period thought that the best reaction to the humiliations of race prejudice was to build their own walls of prejudice and teach Africans retaliations at home (in Africa). As preliminaries to this line of thinking, Africans should be awakened to the appreciation and pride of only things African. This trait is manifested in such nationalistic writings as *Studies in. Akan Peoples* by Dr. J.B. Danquah, *Facing Mount Kenya* by Jomo Kenyatta, *Presence Africaine* Journal edited by M. Alione Diop, and in the African dress of the Boycott King, Mazi Mbonu Ojike. I thought slightly otherwise.

I saw that the best way to break the racial barrier was for all races to share in the abundance of one another's culture:- playing together, singing together, dancing together, working together, as the children of one family, God's great family. I saw ignorance as the real great obstacle to racial harmony.

Then I hit upon the idea of an organisation which could not only be a meeting ground for mutual exchange of views between the peoples of Africa and other races, but also one that would create an awareness of what Africa can offer, given liberty and freedom. This is how and why African Academy of Arts and Research was born, and the Africa House established.

In 1945, I established the Africa House as a meeting centre for Africans and Americans. It turned out to be a shelter for African students who had no residence in the United States, due to lack of sufficient funds to pay their rents. It was at first patronised by Liberia, the only Independent African State then.

During the United Nations' first sittings at San Francisco, the African Academy of Arts and Research sent on 18th October, 1946, its then Secretary, Mazi Mbonu Ojike, to lobby the delegates for freedom for Colonial Africa. The Preamble to a nineteen-page memorandum from the Academy is worth quoting in full. It reads:

"WHEREAS the achievement of universal peace, the progress of mankind and the promotion of fundamental freedoms for all, are the primary concern of all the peace-loving peoples of the world, without distinction as to race, sex, religion, economic or political organisation; and WHEREAS European nations have for centuries been engaged in the exploitation of the natural resources of the continent of Africa and have by force and violence seized, annexed and otherwise converted the ancestral homelands of the African peoples to their own use as colonies; and WHEREAS the African peoples, in the various colonies thus established by these imperialist Europeans powers have been, and continue to be, oppressed, subjugated, degraded, discriminated against and denied the most elementary human rights and fundamental freedom, including the right to govern themselves, to plan and develop their own education, commerce and industry; and WHEREAS the continuation of colonialism and imperialism in Africa constitutes the most complete negation of the noble aims of the United Nations and greatly endangers the efforts of the peace-loving peoples of the world to establish an enduring peace;

We, the delegated representatives of the African Academy of Arts and Research, Incorporated, 55 West 42nd Street, New York 18, New York, an organisation having among its objectives the promotion of international brotherhood and the dissemination of vital information on Africa, hereby direct this appeal to the United Nations.

We believe that the United Nations under the provisions of its charter, has a direct role to correct the disgraceful plight in which the indigenous population of nearly the entire continent of Africa today finds itself. The following references, in part, define the relation and give direction for its fulfilment:

i. *Preamble to the Charter of the United Nations*:

"We the people of the United Nations determined to reaffirm faith in fundamental rights, in the dignity and worth of the human person, the equal rights of men and women of nations large and small..."

ii. *Article 1 - Section 3 - Charter of the United Nations:*

"The purposes of the United Nations are: To achieve international cooperation in solving international problems of an economic, social, cultural, or humanitarian character, and in promoting and encouraging respect for human rights and for fundamental freedom for all without distinction as to race, sex, language, or religion."

iii. *Article 13 - Section 1 (b) Charter of the U.N.*

"The General Assembly shall initiate studies and make recommendations for the purpose of promoting international cooperation in the economic, social, cultural, educational and health fields, and assisting in the realization of human rights and fundamental freedoms for all without distinction as to race, sex, language or religion".

iv. *Article 73 - Chapter XI - Charter of the U.N:*

Functions of the United Nations Regarding Dependent Territories:

(a) "To insure, with due respect for the culture of the peoples concerned, their political, economic, social, and educational advancement, their just treatment, and their protection against abuses:

(b) To develop self-government, to take due account of the political aspirations of the peoples, and to assist them in the progressive development of their free political institutions according to the particular circumstances of each territory and its peoples and their varying stages of advancement;"

Therefore, the officers and members of the African Academy of Arts and Research, after careful deliberative studies and conferences in the search for the approach to be used in bringing to African colonials the human rights and fundamental freedom which they fought for suffered and died to secure for others during the two world wars, most respectfully appeal to and call on the United Nations to use its authority now, in order to restore democratic peoples' governments to African dependencies, by abolishing colonialism and imperialism throughout Africa. To that end we submit herewith for your information and action the following memorandum of facts pertaining to this age long twin inhumanity with certain recommendations on the present intolerable situation which, unless promptly remedied, must continue to hamper not only the peace and progress of all the African peoples, but also of all the rest of the world".

Respectfully submitted on behalf of the
African Academy of Arts and Research, Incorporated.

Rev. James H. Robinson
(Chairman of the Board of Directors)

K. Ozuomba Mbadiwe
(President)

Mbonu Ojike
(Executive Director)

While in the United Sates I did not lose sight of what took place at home. I was closely identified with several movements and organisations in Nigeria. I also gave publicity to Nigerian events and movements in the U.S. During the 1945 general Labour Strike, for instance, I raised money in aid of the workers. When the *West African Pilot* was banned, I recorded my support for its crusade and gave it succour. Equally, my activities were given due coverage in Nigerian newspapers, especially the *West African Pilot*. For instance, when I announced in December, 1947 that I was leaving the United Sates for Nigeria after nine years of absence, the country was agog with the news, and everybody looked forward with excitement to the day I would set foot on our soil.

Chapter 3

The Home-Coming: The African Academy Of Arts And Research

Before I left the United States, I had produced a motion picture - *The Greater Tomorrow* - depicting major events of my activities in the United States. It was principally dedicated to Dr. Nnamdi Azikiwe's 1947 delegation to London. The delegation had gone to press for Nigeria's Independence and to protest the contents of the Richards Constitution and thereafter visited the U. S. where I received them and later introduced Zik to Mrs. Roosevelt at the Hyde Park, home of the late President Roosevelt. There he paid his condolence to the late leader and laid a wreath.

Leaving New York on December 26, 1947, I sailed for England arriving in London on January 1, 1948. Here was my first visit, lasting six weeks, to the capital of the world's largest empire, in the process of tumbling, in the aftermath of world war II. In London was an anti-colonial ferment; a myriad of groups, representatives from Britain's far-flung empires, working feverishly for political independence; or in the case of the Indians and the Pakistanis, exulted in their countries' new-won freedom. Of course, I associated myself closely with those political organisations which concerned themselves with West Africa: the West African Students' Union (WASU), the Nigerian Students' Union of Great Britain and Ireland (NSU), and the West African National Secretariat (WANS).

The West African Students' Union was of course, the oldest and most active African student organisation in Britain. Its leaders had been in communication with their counterparts in the Nigerian Students' Union and the Academy in the United States, and this relationship had been strengthened by the active role played within WASU. by Nkrumah and Jones Quartey, both of whom left the United States for further studies in Britain. The Nigerian Students' Union was one of several African territorial students' organisations which began to proliferate after World War II. WANS was founded in early 1946, following the Pan-African Conference held in Manchester in October 1945, and sought to maintain the impetus towards West African independence and unity. During this visit, I participated in a mass anti-colonial rally organised by the WANS Secretariat.

In late January and early February, I was given two major receptions, the first jointly organised by WANS and NSU, the other by WASU. Both were well attended. Among outstanding future political colleagues both attending were Dennis Osadebay and G.C. Nonyelu, (lawyers) and Okoi Arikpo, an anthropologist. At both meetings I propagandized on behalf of the Academy and the Africa House. I emphasized the need for West Africans to forge strong links with the United States given its pre-eminence as a world power, its democratic institutions and its vast educational opportunities. I also attended scores of private meetings with African and Carribean anti-colonial leaders.

I spent most of my time in London seeking to arouse interest in, and support for, the Academy and the Africa House. Here I had a great trump card in my film, *The Greater Tomorrow*, which I showed on several occasions. It was billed as the first film ever made by an African. It showed major activities of the Academy and featured all its principal officers and supporters, including Mrs. Eleanor Roosevelt, Mayor William O'Dwyer, Joe Louis, the heavyweight champion, and Dr. Nnamdi Azikiwe. It also included still photographs of such major West African figures as Nana William Ofori Atta of the Gold Coast and Herbert Macaulay of Nigeria.

My major goal in London was to persuade the Colonial Office to give substantial and regular support to the Africa House in New York. I knew that WASU's London hostel had received such assistance since 1937. Moreover, the British Government, under the Colonial Development and Welfare Acts (1940,1945)

had committed itself to accelerating its programme of training
Africans for self-government. Further, the Colonial Secretary of
the Labour Government, Mr. Arthur Creech-Jones, the founder
and former chairman of the Bureau of the Fabian Society, was
known to be highly sympathetic to African aspirations for
political freedom.

On January 9, I met with Mr. Creech-Jones "over tea" at the
Colonial Office and presented him with a long memorandum
which essentially requested support for the Africa House to the
tune of 25,000 pounds ($124,000 US) and permission for
African students with means, who wished to study in the United
States, to transfer funds there. I further informed him that the
Board of Education of New York City had granted the Academy
forty tuition-free scholarships tenable at its vocational high
schools and requested an additional $32,000 to pay for the
transportation and up-keep of the students over four years. *The
West African Pilot* which regularly reported my London activities
editorially backed my proposals to the Colonial Office thus:

> "**Mbadiwe** intends to verify how far concrete Britain's plans for the
> development of her colonies are ...
> Mr Creech-Jones has to augment American dollars by yielding to the
> Mbadiwe proposals or give away the labour Government as being
> insincere in its claims".

The Colonial Office was not ready to make such a
substantial outlay through a private organisation controlled by a
colonial. And it still doubted the suitability of American
education for British Colonials. But no longer could it ignore the
problems which students from its African colonies faced in the
United States. Indeed a few months after my visit, the Colonial
Office sent one of its officials to work with United States
officials in conducting an investigation into African student-life
in the United States.

As a colonial committed to democracy, I took special
pleasure in a tour of Parliament, in late January. I was conducted
into the House of Lords by Lord Seabury, and in the Commons
by the Rev. Reginald William Sorenson, a left wing colonial

expert of the Labour Party. Although I won no financial support for the Academy or the Africa House, my trip to England was important in making new political contacts, among both colonial rulers and African nationalists, who would later aid my own political career.

I left England, and then proceeded to Sierra Leone where I was warmly welcomed. The late Ben Okagbue, who later became a Federal Permanent Secretary in Nigeria, was on hand and accompanied me wherever I went in Sierra Leone.

I moved from Sierra Leone to Liberia. There, I was honoured by the government as its special guest. The late President Tubman issued a special proclamation designating a special day for my official reception.

I moved to the Gold Coast, now Ghana, as special guest of late Dr. Kwame Nkrumah, (leader of the defunct Convention People's Party) and Mr. Ako Adjei. I arrived there at a time of great crisis. There was a popular uprising against Association of West African Merchants (AWAM). Mercantile shops owned by foreign interests, comprising big firms like the UAC, John Holt, CFAO, G.B. Olivant, SCOA, etc., were looted and some of them burnt. The irony of it is that during the rioting, the generality of people played the part of vigilante group, guarding and protecting shops and properties of A.G. Leventis and Company Limited. I asked my host why he thought the Company was spared. He narrated the cause of the uprising. People were bitter against some companies which conspiratorially charged exorbitant prices for their commodities but strictly controlled the prices they (the firms) paid for cocoa and other commodities produced locally for exports. They singled out Leventis as not belonging to the foreign commercial business houses which offended the national interest.

That was my first time of knowing the A.G. Leventis company. I was told it existed also in Nigeria. I made up my mind to know more about the firm which had so ably identified itself with the aspirations of the people among whom it lived. When I returned to Nigeria, I met Mr. C.P. Leventis, he introduced me to the most senior of the Leventis family, the late A. G. Leventis. We became good friends.

Home to Nigeria

I moved from the Gold Coast to Nigeria. As early as January 1948, a committee was formed to plan an elaborate welcome-home celebrations for me. *The West African Pilot* editorial of April, 23rd emphasised that "nothing but a tremendous welcome was due this great son of Africa".

In early May, even when it appeared that there was no news about the date of my arrival, *The Pilot* continued to heighten the anticipation of my return home. Two of its issues carried large photographs of mine in the United States with supporters of the African Academy.

At long last, in the afternoon of Thursday May 27th, I disembarked at Customs Wharf, Apapa, and was welcomed by a large cheering crowd of family, friends and well-wishers. The group included Chief J. Green Mbadiwe, Mazi Mbonu Ojike and Dr. Nnamdi Azikiwe. The next day the *West African Pilot* added its own editorial welcome:

> "The metropolis saw him (Mbadiwe) disembark yesterday, a citizen whose services to humanity in these ten years have catapulted him to a height of unique magnitude. As a unique go-getter, Ozuomba is a proud feather in our cap... We welcome him whose coming is destined towards liberty, recognition and prosperity".

On the evening of Friday 28th May, 1948, one day after my return, a well-attended reception was held for me at the Wayfarers Hotel in Lagos. I emotionally and eloquently reported my triumphs abroad, as well as my tribulations which included the premature death of Dr. Nnodu Okongwu and the goals of the African Academy and the African House. I saw myself as a crowd-pleasing speaker, as I counselled "If you want to be great, you must finance greatness". The crowd yelled in applause. I saw that the stage of hope was set; it remained to build the stage of action. Ever since, I had deliberately (often outside a prepared text) coined words to make my points stick. My first movie was titled *"The Greater Tomorrow"*. Political campaign strategies were baptised "operations" (totality, number one, muzzle down, clean the way). The memorable PAN-AM/Nigerian Airways first joint flight venture direct to New York became "Operation Fantastic". And when an accord snaps and sticks again in a new formation, it became "Accord Concordialle".

The *West African Pilot* again gave editorial support to the sentiments expressed in my address. It said:-

"We see in this clarion call to action and self-help enormous possibilities for cooperation and national progress".

On the afternoon of Saturday May 29, the All Nigerian Dance Committee, a cultural creation of Mazi Mbonu Ojike, put a lavish and well attended show of songs and dances in my honour at the Lagos African Tennis Club. In fact, it was repeated the following Saturday June 5th, this time under the patronage of the new Governor, Sir John Macpherson.

Meanwhile, in the evening of Tuesday June 1, I began a role symbolically pointing to a major Nigerian politician when I was the featured speaker at the Glover Memorial Hall, Lagos, along the main arena of Nigerian nationalism. Befittingly, the lecture was presided over by Nigeria's leading nationalist, Dr. Nnamdi Azikiwe. An overflow crowd of 3,000 from all walks of life attended, including Sir Hugh Foot, the Chief Secretary to the Government.

My speech focused on my activist years in the United States, my future plans for the Academy and my dream of a strong, united, independent Nigeria. As part of the popular protest against western cultural imperialism, I was attired in a resplendent blue Nigerian "boycott dress". My speech was greeted with frequent and prolonged applause. I felt that the event had highly stimulated the patriotism of those who attended. These representatives of the Nigerian nation left the hall with a new determination and a new zeal.

The Chairman, Dr. Azikiwe, had earlier spoken highly of me. He said: "Ozuomba Mbadiwe has scaled the ranks of the apostles. He is the evangelist of the Lord's work, a promoter of African dignity, a practical internationalist in art, business and education".

The scene at the Glover Memorial Hall was virtually re-enacted the following evening. This time, I spoke on *"The Nigerian Political Theatre."* I explicitly joined the call for early political independence for Nigeria. I demanded the immediate extension of press freedom. For the freedom to express oneself is a political right not a privilege. I was very deeply concerned about the lack of unity in the struggle for Nigerian independence. I suggested that a committee be set up to iron out differences among the major political parties. I cried out loud: "I belong to all the people of this nation. I call for nationalist unity in order to promote the redemption of our country".

My third lecture at the same Glover was on June 10. This time the topic was *"Our Economic Strategy"*. I sharply criticised the colonial policy of inhibiting African economic democracy. I advised Nigerians to pool their resources together for investment instead of "burying" their limited wealth or engaging in "one man business".

Following my exposure to the public, I set out to mobilise major community leaders and organisations in support of the Academy and the Africa House. After extensive discussions, a campaign committee of the Academy was established on June 24 at a meeting at the Glover Memorial Hall, attended by representatives of twenty four ethnic, cultural, labour and political organisations. The elected Chairman was the Jamaican-born "Bread-King of Lagos", Mr. Amos Stanley Wynter Schackleford, while the Secretary was Barrister H. U. Kaine. Members of the NYM and Egbe were conspicuously absent from the committee membership which comprised senior government officials, merchants and professionals.

I did not cherish the press war which existed between the Nigerian Youth Movement (N. Y. M.) and their organ, the *Daily Service* on the one hand, and the National Council of Nigeria and the Cameroons (NCNC) and the *West African Pilot* on the other hand. After observing that ugly situation for four months, I issued a statement titled "*Nigeria Faces Grave Crisis*".

It is worth quoting extensively:

> The political temperature of this country has soared far above normal. I sensed this unhealthy atmosphere on my return from the United States now going to four months. The political cloud was then gathering thick and fast, I tried as far as it is humanly possible to retard or otherwise dislodge the outburst.
>
> In spite of all attempts, the storm let loose and has not only succeeded in drenching all of us, but is making desperate effort to engulf all our intellectual and physical energies.
>
> This nation must now realise that a grave situation exists. I sense a philosophy of hate and suspicion permeating our social fabric. If such philosophy thrives and triumphs, we cannot repair the damage which will be done to our national life for the next fifty years. Worse still, all our dreams for a Greater Tomorrow, for a happier and better life, would have been doomed for many years to come.
>
> Dangerous seeds of malice and bitterness are now being sown. It is our innocent youths who will suffer most. They are constantly exposed to a most devastating policy of hatred, malice and suspicion, with the spurious aim of being pawns in selfish politics. The present tumult and press controversy have offered this country and its peoples nothing but a road to national suicide. It is tragic that we have not learnt from history. It is calamitous that as a people we have definitely refused to be great, to think big and act big. We have definitely refused to prove to the world that we are not born to be perpetual hewers of wood and drawers of water.
>
> As a people we have refused to achieve and conquer, and we have determined to drag down those among us who dare to attempt and to achieve. We refuse to think, but we are ready to obstruct those who dare to think among us..."

Yet I had faith in a Federated Nigeria with a strong central voice that would cede authority to regional governments. I was then, as now, persistent in working for national unity and saw myself as a conciliator and mediator among Nigeria's various peoples.

During my five months stay in Lagos, before reaching my home town and Eastern Nigeria, I had successfully launched the Academy's fund raising campaign. The reluctant Nigerian Youth

Movement (NYM) by September 8th, had recommended that its members individually support the Academy. The Nigerian Government, like the Colonial Office, was non-committal. In words and action we showed that money collected publicly for the Academy was put to proper use.

In August, 1948, the Academy offered three well qualified students, Messrs C. Okoye, P. Onyekaba, and B. Osaye Rotimi, tuition-free scholarships at American Universities to study education, engineering and medicine respectively. A sparkling send-off party for these students was held on September 10 at the "Zoological Gardens" of Chief Biney's Estate and was attended by a galaxy of Lagos leaders.

As a result of my participation in numerous private and public meetings whose goals were political independence and an improved standard of living for Nigerians, I had emerged fully to the frontline of the nationalist struggle.

On October 27, I left Lagos for the East. Before departure, I announced publicly that I had sent $1,000 ($4,000.00) raised from my campaigns to the Academy headquarters in New York for the renovation and running of the African House. This represented a dramatic and unprecedented reversal of America's missionary and philanthropic aid to Colonial Africa.

After four days of road travel from Lagos and almost ten years absence, I returned to my home town, Arondizuogu, on October 31st 1948, to the grandest reception ever accorded any individual at that time. It began with a three-mile procession headed by twenty cars, amidst booms of canon shots, traditional dances and songs. I briefly addressed the surging crowd which over-flowed the large premises of the Stone Palace, the home of the Mbadiwes. The entertainments, the merriments and the celebrations continued for many days.

I spent ten days with my family and towns people. In fact it was the first opportunity for relaxation since my return to Nigeria from the United States.

Later, I went on a tour of the entire country with the film, *The Greater Tomorrow*, starting of course with the East.

Between November and December, I organised and toured Eastern Nigeria. I received great support for the Academy programmes from the Easterners, who were proud of my successes. The tour took me to the major towns, including Port Harcourt, Aba, Umuahia, Enugu, Calabar, Okigwe, Uzuakoli and Orlu.

The tours were carefully planned. Key figures were contacted at each centre before hand, and asked to form a local Academy campaign committee. Next, a small advance guard of the national campaign committee would visit and ensure that proper arrangements were made for public meetings, accommodation and publicity. Finally, I and the rest of the entourage would appear to a well planned and exuberant welcome which generally included a motorcade, dances, songs and addresses of welcome. Everywhere the film, *The Greater Tomorrow*, proved a major attraction and was enthusiastically received.

In the same way, I planned and toured the North from January 1949, visiting Makurdi, Lafia, Kafanchan, Kano, Jos, Zaria and Nguru, the last railway stop in the North-East. In Kano and Zaria I first obtained audience with the Emirs and briefed them about the Academy and showed the films. The Northern trip was a huge success netting some $3,970.00, but it was also there that I suffered a great physical and nervous exhaustion due to the arduous and sustained work of the Academy. In fact, for five weeks I was inactive. I was forced to rest in bed for one week in Zaria and one month in Jos, where I came close to dying. In my weakened condition, I had contracted the dreaded "cerebro-spinal meningitis, which was a major cause of death in the North in those days. I give credit to Dr. Onyemelukwe for saving my life.

After my recuperation and a ten-day visit to Lagos in early June, I resumed the fund-raising campaign in the West and the Mid-West. I visited Ibadan, Benin, Sapele and Warri. A large crowd greeted me at the Mapo Hall, Ibadan, and the following day the *Western Echo* endorsed the tour. By August 27, 1948, I returned to Lagos to finalise plans for sending sixteen Academy-sponsored students to the United States that year.

I was received with hospitality by Nigerians everywhere I went. Is it any wonder, therefore, that I came to love these people who received me with open arms, showed me such affection and the warmth of their hearts. My message to them from the beginning was for unity. I urged them to close ranks. They were fascinated.

Whether in the far North among the Hausa/Fulani, or in the Igbo heartland, or the Yoruba of the West, or the mid-west, among the Binis, the Ijaws, the Itsekiris, the Urhobos or the Ogojas, the Rivers people, it was with the same warmth that I was received. Those were the impressionable experience which made me accept the need to pay any price or make any sacrifice for the cordiality of contemporary and the new generation.

For many young Nigerians, my movie, *The Greater Tomorrow*, was the first encounter with the marvels of modern science and technology. Many swore to find out more, and to explore the riches of "horizontal education". Hence there was the great quest for a westward movement, in spite of British propaganda against United States standards. Within a decade 1948-1958, young Nigerians in United States Universities and Colleges were counted in hundreds. By 1968 when I toured North America in search of peace and relief during the civil war, the population of Nigerians had grown to thousands, and many had been highly qualified.

In addition to *The Greater Tomorrow* film, I launched other ventures aimed at improving the standard of life of the people. These included:

(a)   The *Greater Tomorrow* Transport Company, It operated two buses, plying between Onitsha and Enugu. They were the first luxury inter-city buses ever used in Nigeria.

(b)   The African Academy of Arts and Research, Nigerian Sector. This organ effectively sponsored Nigerian students to the United States universities and colleges. Its able secretary was Mr. Simon Nduka Okolo.

Decline of the Academy in Nigeria

A combination of factors helped to stifle the life of the Academy in Nigeria. The most devastating was the rivalry and hostility of the Colonial Government. Government functionaries had been taken into confidence and had participated in the activities of the Academy, initially. But rather than support it, the government, in 1949 as a follow-up to Mr. Foot's tour of America, set up and financed the Committee on African Students in North America (CASNA) which in effect was imitating and duplicating what the Academy was doing for Nigerian students. I saw it as a deliberate attempt to destroy African initiative. *The West African Pilot* took a similar view in an editorial:

> As a result of CASNA, Nigerian Academic plans in United States universities are being curbed by rules and regulations, enforced through the power to grant or refuse dollar exchanges.

Then in a letter dated October 16, 1950, thirteen Academy students at Lincoln wrote complaining of late remittance of money and "undue restrictions in the handling of slender pocket money" which for thrift and security, they were to draw on account from the Institution. I was naturally stunned by the spurious charge of the students, I wrote them:-

> Since my whole existence, I have never received a letter from friend or foe such as you have written me. If I had been your house-boy, I would have expected to be better treated.

At a meeting at the Glover Memorial Hall, I fully explained and defended the activities of the Academy.

Some of the students said they were coerced to sign the letter and apologised. The Secretary of Ohafia Union wrote the students, informing them that "Mr. Mbadiwe has not given anybody cause to suspect his sincerity of purpose" and in a public apology on their behalf stated, "from these facts and figures, one can judge that these students are properly cared for and that Mr. Mbadiwe is doing all in his reach to help them." In clearing the air further, the President, Board of Lincoln University, whose opinion was sought by Nigerians, said in reply, "Lincoln's relationship with the Academy has been marked only by the highest trust and integrity." He went on: "Now you can imagine that I was considerably irritated when you sent me the clipping (with the complaints of the students, from the *Eastern Nigerian Guardian* of December 30, 1950. I was the more irritated by memories of my own sacrifices as a student and the hard times I had to eat, clothe myself, have shelter through menial work which I performed to get these necessities. I have knowledge that these five gentlemen are not required to raise one little finger in work for the assistance that is given them."

A committee headed by Mr. O. Ajibade (Chairman) and Mr. Abiodun Aloba (Secretary) reported favourably that the "Academy has performed a useful public service in sponsoring students at a time it could have otherwise been impossible for them to get to the United States to better their education". It however sympathised that "frustration could develop in most of them a feeling of suspicion and bitterness".

The press also had its share in the controversy. While the *Daily Service* saw nothing good in the Academy, *The West African Pilot* regarded government intervention as "political". In the process, government withdrew the Academy's power of raising funds publicly, an action which led to the organisation's quick decline. Moreover, other national events took over from 1949, beginning with the crisis brought about by the massacre of the Enugu miners. However, the activities of the Academy and Africa House continued in the United States, but the dynamism was no longer there because of my departure.

Chapter 4

My American Years Re-Dramatised in Nigeria.
The Bond Visit.

To enhance the educational role of the Academy I invited a renowned Afro-American educator, Dr. Horace Mann Bond, to visit Nigeria. There could not have been a better choice. Bond, whom I knew during my long stay in the United States, was a distinguished scholar who in 1945 had become the first black President of Lincoln University, the oldest and one of the most prestigious of the black American Colleges. He was deeply interested in Africa, highly approved of Lincoln's ties with the black continent, and especially proud of prominent Africans, including Azikiwe, Nkrumah and my humble self, who had studied at his institution.

I sent Bond the invitation in March with the promise that I would pay half of the cost of the educator's airfare and be totally responsible for his support in Nigeria. Bond accepted and the visit originally set for August, took place from October 13th, to November 1st, 1949. Delighted with the opportunity to visit his "homeland" for the first time, Bond spent an additional three weeks in the Gold Coast, Liberia, Sierra Leone and Senegal.

The visit turned out to be a phenomenal public relations success for me and the Academy, and a triumphant "home-coming" for Bond. It had, indeed, been carefully planned. Anxious that it should not be partisan, I had sought the support of colonial officialdom, the American Consulate and the whole spectrum of the Lagos African elite. A reception committee was established in Lagos with branches in all the towns and villages that Bond was scheduled to visit. And, of course, Zik's

35

newspaper, *The West African Pilot,* gave the visit maximum publicity.

Bond flew into Lagos from Accra in the afternoon of October 13th, and was lavishly welcomed by a large, distinguished, representative committee headed by me. He rode into the city in my new stylish Hudson Commodore as part of a twenty-car motorcade. In the city he was the guest of Chief Biney who owned a large, beautiful home in Yaba, set on extensive, landscaped grounds, known as the "Zoological Garden." The first public reception for Bond was held on Saturday afternoon at the historic Glover Memorial Hall. For Bond and for Lagos it was an unforgettable grand affair. On the six mile route from Chief Biney's home to the Hall, there was a 150 car motorcade, several troupes of dancers and singers, and a high-spirited, welcoming crowd of about 100,000. The first part of the reception consisted of a garden party hosted by Governor Sir John Macpherson. Here there were troupes of wonderful traditional dances which prompted Bond to remark "that no European pageantry ever had a culture so rich in aesthetic and artistic expression as what we watched." Bond was, indeed, overwhelmed and exultant at the occasion.

In a letter circulated to his faculty, friends and professional associates, he wrote from Lagos:-

> "I am having a tremendous experience, the more so, because before I came, it was quite inconceivable to me ......
> I have received a welcome that all, even the Governor, tell me is the most remarkable outpouring of national feeling ever witnessed here. Not the Governor, with all the pageantry of British power and pomp, indeed, not even the prince of Wales, when he came to visit, was the recipient of such a spontaneously enthusiastic reception".

His racial patriotism profoundly stirred, Bond confided to the wildly excited crowd at Glover Hall that "of this land can I truly say, that this is my own, my native land;" and he vowed to "work harder for African emancipation". On Sunday afternoon, there was another spectacular display of African dances and songs for Dr. Bond, again with the Governor present, on the grounds of King's College, the leading secondary school in the nation. In the evening Chief Biney gave another cocktail party for Bond which was attended by the leading elite of the African and European community.

Bond and I left Lagos by road on October 17 and over the next ten days visited the following major towns:- Ibadan, Ilesha, Benin, Sapele, Onitsha, Nnewi, Arondizuogu, Port Harcourt, Calabar, Aba, Umuahia and Enugu. We also made brief stops at a number of villages along the way. Everywhere Bond went, he was given an incredibly rousing reception and awarded honours and gifts. In Ilesha, the Oba made Bond an honourary Chief and Councillor, and gave him chieftaincy robes and a wooden foot stool, traditionally used by the royalty. In historic Benin City, he was similarly grandly received by the Oba. Bond, who saw himself as a symbol of blood-brotherhood reported to friends and associates that his trip to Nigeria "can best be described as fantastic, utterly fantastic".

Bond's trip was so hectic and so tiring that, fearing he would collapse, he begged off from visiting Northern Nigeria, as had been originally planned. Everywhere he had been, he took a special interest in the educational facilities and needs of the area. He had spent an entire day as a special guest at the new Ibadan University College and was particularly impressed by the highly qualified Africans in the faculty, while noting that there were not many of them. At Arondizuogu, Bond witnessed a crowd of 10,000, lay the foundation stone for the construction of Iheme Memorial Secondary School.

Bond and I returned to Lagos on October 28th. On October 30th, he gave a well-attended public lecture on "Negro Education in the United States", doubtless as part of the campaign to completely dispel the view that American education, particularly at its black colleges, was inferior. At a final press conference, he averred that Afro-Americans were developing a strong interest in Africa and he pledged to promote it further.

Dr. Bond's visit certainly served to advance two causes of special interest to me and the nationalists, namely the acceptance by the Nigerian Government of American education as suitable for Nigerians and the development of stronger ties between the Nigerian and Afro-American elites in mutual interest.

Early in 1950, the Nigerian Government publicly endorsed the idea of Nigerians studying at American universities, but indicated its concern about the wide differences in standards among them; it announced that it would offer a limited number of scholarships for the study of Agriculture and Engineering to be tenable only at the best American universities. But before implementing this policy, the Nigerian Government decided to make its own independent investigation of conditions of study for Nigerians at American universities. Thus, for five weeks in June/July 1950, Sir Hugh Foot, Secretary to the Nigerian Government, made an extensive tour of the United States.

On Mr. Foot's return to Nigeria, the government announced the award of five scholarships, two were tenable at Cornell, and one each at the Massachusettes Institute of Technology, Harvard and Swarthmore in the fields of Engineering and Agriculture. It decided to give financial aid to Nigerian students already in the United States who could not continue their studies because of the 40 percent devaluation of the British and Nigerian pounds since September 1949. It provided a suitable office and adequate secretarial assistance for the Lagos-based CASNA Committee. And it appointed to the British Embassy in Washington, D.C. one Dr. Barrett as a full-time liaison officer for Nigerian students in the United States.

I was far from happy with the new Nigerian policy and practice. I would have preferred that the Nigerian government recognised degrees from all accredited United States universities and colleges. Moreover, I saw the Government's recognition of CASNA, rather than the Academy, as a deliberate attempt to destroy African initiative, as I mentioned earlier.

The NCNC nationalists and I were resentful that Mr. Foot, a colonial advocate of a cautious pace towards Nigerian independence, had been so warmly received in official circles in the United States. We were concerned that the anti-communist cold war atmosphere prevailing in the United States in 1950 precluded that country from championing the drive of colonial territories towards independence. Through our organ, *The Pilot*, we began to see the United States as a "villian with a smiling face". We castigated "Anglo-American diplomacy" as devoid of "morality and good sense", and threatened "to cooperate with any country, even the USSR bloc, which would accelerate our pace towards national freedom".

My concentration on the activities of the African Academy of Arts and Research, more than anything else, placed me within a short time, as one of the better known figures, not only in Nigeria but in other areas of West Africa and the Camerouns. The *"Greater Tomorrow"* film, the Greater Tomorrow mass-transit buses, and the AAAR joined to bring me into instant national prominence. When in 1951, therefore, I organised and summoned all known political leaders for a "National Rebirth Conference", the response was massive. When I sounded a clarion call for a "National Emergency Committee" to react to the Enugu shooting of 1949, I was heeded. And when I contested the 1951 election, it was an easy win.

Happily, one can say with pride that the eight Argonauts' mission was accomplished. Unfortunately, however, we lost one of us during our sojourn in the United States. Among the remaining seven, three found their places in politics; the late Mazi Mbonu Ojike rose from the office of Managing Director of the *West African Pilot* (he wrote the famous "Weekend Catechism") to be elected Deputy Mayor of Lagos, and finally became the first Minister of Finance in Eastern Nigeria. Dr. Nwafor Orizu rose to the office of President of the Senate. He was destined to hand over the reins of power to the first military government during the January 1966 army mutiny when he acted as President of Nigeria. My humble self rose to the post of second in command in the NCNC-NPC coalition government of the Federation. Professor Nwankwo Chukwuemeka is recorded in Nigerian history as the first Nigerian to make cement out of Nigeria's clinker. Dr. Okechukwu Ikejiani, a medical practitioner, also became the first Nigerian Chairman of the Nigerian Railway Corporation. Dr. J.B.C. Otuka-Okala, an academician, became a Professor at the University of Nigeria, Nsukka.

And the late George Igbodebe Mbadiwe, who for ill-health did not complete his education in the United States, returned home and became the Editor of the *West African Pilot* before he died in 1948, a few months before my return home. Late Dr. Nnodu Okongwu, was a brilliant student. He had a Ph.D. in Education, but on the eve of his return to Nigeria, he took ill and died. He was accorded a very colourful burial by members of the African Academy of Arts and Research. Mazi Mbonu Ojike and Dr. Nwafor Orizu each authored books before they returned to Nigeria. Ojike's book was titled *I have Two Countries*, while Dr. Orizu's book was titled *Without Bitterness*.

My United States education and my early contact with the inmates and occupants of the White House (the seat of the United States Government) made me always to dream of greatness for Nigeria and Africa. They formed the power-house for my "operations" whether they be "Operation Slum Clearance", or "Operation Fantastic", for the greatness and glory of Nigeria.

Chapter 5
Family And Business Base

Marriage

Ever since my student days in America, I had been so immersed in organisational activities, that I had had little time for dating women. In 1949, I was thirty-two and there was still no prospect of a wife. This, of course, was of deep concern to my family who decided to find me a bride. In January 1950, I reported to an American friend my family's successful quest:

> "On March 18th, I will be married. I have been so busy since my return that my family had to go and look for a girl. I met her for the first time in November (1949) and approved of her, and incidentally, she approved of me (laugh)."

The girl was Cecilia Chidozie Alisha, an elegant, charming, petite, and demure young teacher on the staff of the Immaculate Heart Primary School, Onitsha. The daughter of a policeman, she, too was from Arondizuogu. She had attended Secondary School at the Holy Rosary Convent in Enugu and trained as a teacher, a high quality western eduction, rare for women in those days, in our area. Although both she and I, were Catholics, I, as a nationalist, decided on a basically traditional marriage, making concessions to my Catholicism.

The first major step of the marriage ceremonies took place on New Year's day 1950 when both families met and performed the traditional oath of concord. Thereafter, Cecilia lived for three months in the compound of Chief D.O. Mbadiwe, my brother, and the head of the extended family.

The marriage celebration itself was a spectacular affair. It was held on March 18th, three days after my thirty-third birthday, first in Chief Mbadiwe's courtyard and then at

41

St.Philips Catholic Church, Akeme. Mr. Stephen Okafor Agbaji spear-headed it. It was attended by 3000 people, 500 of them were visitors to the town. There was a representative cross section of the Nigerian elite as well as of Europeans. Colonial officialdom was represented by Mr. Harold Cooper, the Government's Public Relations Officer, who had become an admirer and friend of mine. Symbolic of my desire for inter-territorial cooperation was the presence from the Gold Coast of Mr. K. Barakatu Ateko, a retired Master of Achimota College, the leading Secondary School in the Gold Coast, and a member of the African Academy Committee of Accra.

Because of the difficulty of travelling then, and the extended time needed for it, many invited guests did not attend. However, we received hundreds of congratulatory messages from resplendent friends in Nigeria and other parts of West Africa, the United States and Europe who couldn't attend.

Both Chidozie and I wore resplendent African robes. In his capacity as traditional ruler, the Ogbuefi of Onitsha, Dr. Nnamdi Azikiwe was vested with the authority by the two leading local rulers, Chief Aniche and Nwafor Odum, to officiate at the traditional ceremony. Zik accepted gratefully. He poured libation, invoking the blessing of God. Soon after, five cannons boomed, signifying the sanctity of the union.

The traditional ceremony was followed by the Catholic rites later. A fleet of forty cars, led by the new Bethel Brass Band of Onitsha, escorted my wife and I to the St. Philips Roman Catholic Church, where Rev. Fr. Edward Nwafor administered the Sacrament of Matrimony. On its way back to Chief Mbadiwe's home, the festive wedding procession was greeted by cannon-shot salutes from the surrounding villages. The last of the traditional marriage rites was concluded on March 21, and on the following day, my wife and I left Arondizuogu for our private residence, "The Greater Tomorrow Lodge", 113 Hundred Foot Road, Aba.

The Christian marriage marked a new beginning for me, a new beginning founded upon a rock. On return from the United

States the Argonauts had, in their war against Christian religion, almost misfired the target which was imperialism, till I broke away and celebrated a Christian Catholic marriage. It was a timely counter balance of the negative effect of some doctrines against "imported religion" as written in the "Weekend Cathechism" of the *West African Pilot.*

By my action, I had distinguished religion from imperialism. Through my christian marriage also, the conspiracy of the church and government to discriminate against American education became dismantled. Not long after, churches were sponsoring their priests to study in America. Rather than being an opponent, the churches became companions in the fight against injustice, inequality, exploitation, segregation and domination which were the tools of imperialism.

My Catholic inclination in a predominantly protestant family, was the great handwork of the late Mazi Stephen Okafor Ogbaji, an ardent catholic of Akeme-Uno, Arondizuogu, and father of Reverend Dr. Festus Okafor, a Professor of Education, University of Nigeria, Nsukka, himself a Catholic Priest.

When I returned from Port Harcourt as a small boy and stayed briefly at home, I was fast in speaking English. This attracted the white Reverend Fathers who visited Akeme.

But I was nearly refused baptism. They were not too sure of my constancy, because I came from a ruling family of Odum and from the home of Protestants. Mazi Stephen had to intervene. He first interviewed me and got a promise that after baptism, I would be married in the church. That was about 1930, well before I travelled to America for studies. I gave him the assurance. He then approached the Reverend Father and asked him to baptise me. He did and I took the name Gabriel.

Before my marriage in 1950, Mazi Stephen reminded me of my pledge. I keep my word always and respect my seniors therefore I prepared for Catholic christian marriage which he arranged. My continued membership of the Catholic Church, apart from conviction, is strengthened by that backing of Mazi Stephen Ogbaji and my wife's faith and devotion to the Church.

Establishing A Financial Base

During 1950, I first took major steps to establish a financial base for myself. This was necessary because of my new family responsibilities and also because of the need for funds for the Academy and my future political career. In seeking to establish my own business, I was fortunate; I had both academic and practical experience in business administration. I was doing so at a time of tremendous urbanization and commercial expansion in Eastern Nigeria.

I could count on the cooperation of successful businessmen, especially among the Igbos, as well as the financial support of my own family, especially that of my wealthy elder brother, Chief J. Green Mbadiwe. I established two limited liability companies:-

(a)   The African Insurance Company Limited

(b)   The Greater Tomorrow Transport Company.

The latter was of course, named after my film of the Academy which was widely seen in Eastern Nigeria. It was a private company capitalised at £50,000 with twenty-five shares each worth £200. The company began to operate in November 1950, and within a year it owned five de luxe buses. They served Enugu, and in particular its mining community, running daily from Asata to Coal Camp. On Sundays, it plied between Enugu and Onitsha. The buses met a felt need. As the nation's coal-mining centre, and the administrative capital of the Eastern Region, Enugu had experienced phenomenal growth in the decades of the 1930's and 1940's and by 1950, with a population of 60,000 was the third largest city in Eastern Nigeria after Onitsha and Port Harcourt. This growth created a need for increased public transport facilities in Enugu and Onitsha. The bus service between Enugu and Onitsha also made good sense for the latter was a great magnet of educational and commercial centre of Eastern Nigeria. Moreover, many of the workers in the Enugu mines came from the city.

The African Insurance Company was also capitalised at £50,000 with such well-known Nigerian political figures as Ojike, Orizu, Amanze Njoku and Dennis Osadebay among its major investors. A limited liability company, it aimed at insuring motor vehicles, primarily lorries. Lorry transport had proved a great commercial success. Introduced into Nigeria in the 1920's, it had expanded greatly, competing successfully with government subsidized rail transport. But in forming an Insurance Company, I was also breaking the monopoly which Europeans hitherto held in that field.

Indeed, the expatriate insurance companies initially sought to hinder the incorporation and operation of the new indigenous insurance company. But nationalist pressure on the Government prevailed in my favour. Thus in my insurance venture, I had secured the political support of venerable and highly influential Sir Adeyemo Alakija who actually accompanied me to a meeting with top government officials on the question of incorporation. Its headquarters was then in Aba. I wrote to a friend in the United States: "the old English commercial establishment was amazed at my company's sturdy start. In the African Insurance Company the intellectual giants of Nigeria got together." African Insurance still stands today and competes favourably with others in that sector of the economy.

Both ventures were successful as would be expected from ventures with small capital investment.

Part II

The Crusade For Independence

Members of the National Emergency Committee meet with the Colliery Workers after the Enugu shootings of 1949. Fifth from left sitting is Dr. K.O.Mbadiwe, sixth is Chief H.O. Davies and ninth is Chief M.A.O. Imuodu.

Members of the Council of Ministers pose with Queen Elizabeth II of England on her maiden visit, 1956. (L to R): Financial Secretary, Hon. Aja Nwachukwu; Hon. Muhammadu Ribadu, Chief Secretary to Govt, Hon. Sir Abubakar Tafawa Balewa, Hon. D. S. Adegbenro, Sir James Robertson, Hon. R. Amanze Njoku, The Queen, Hon. Kola Balogun, Dr. K.O. Mbadiwe, Another expatriate ex-officio: Hon. M.T. Mbu. Chief Hon. F.S. Okotie Eboh and the Press Secretary.

With Oba of Lagos, Adeyinka Oyekan II

With Sir Abubakar, the Prime Minister, 1957.

With Dr. Kwame Nkrumah on Ghana's Independence day in 1957.

With close colleagues at a reception. (L to R): Dr Mbadiwe, Engr. Isaac Iweka, (the Igwe of Obosi), Chief Dr. Kolawole Balogun, and Chief Dr. M.T. Mbu)

As Minister of Communications and Aviation, riding on a horse on the way to commission the Kano International Airport.

As Leader and National President of the D.P.N.C, a party formed in reaction to the N.C.N.C crisis..

Chapter 6

The Political Stage Before 1949:
The Enugu Shooting: The National Emergency Committee.

My return, like that of my colleagues of the Argonauts, was rather at an auspicious moment of Nigeria's history. The Second World War had just ended and there was a cry for freedom all over the place. Those soldiers who fought in other lands for "world freedom" joined to ask why, Nigeria, their country was not yet free. An association of the war veterans was formed and it joined the vanguard for Nigerian freedom.

The National Council of Nigeria and the Camerouns (NCNC) had just toured the country, agitating against the Richards Constitution.

Young men became aware of their rights. More received secondary education. Some fought through their town or tribal unions to go to universities overseas.

The *West African Pilot* and other Zik group of newspapers became the bible cf the political struggle.

However, there was no single cohesive front to which the different forces combined. The most vocal and dynamic body was spearheaded by that indefatigable champion for equal rights, on the platform of the Nigerian National Democratic Party (NNDP), which he founded in 1923. I refer to the doyen of Nigerian nationalism, Mr. Herbert Macaulay. Even the peasant farmer who saw the man's aggressive face in calendars and almanacs, watched with admiration his stance as a freedom fighter.

The songs of praise composed for his lofty crusade resounded in every nook and corner of Lagos. In content the NNDP was national because it aimed at a nationwide audience with its aims and objectives which were meant to achieve nationalistic purposes; but territorially, the NNDP was not nationwide as an organisation. Its membership did not extend beyond Lagos Colony, with activities restricted to Lagos Island and Mainland. The party, with its organ, the *Lagos Daily News*, however, became the authoritative spokesman for Lagos and far beyond.

Herbert Macaulay was a political colossus. He was an uncompromising critic of white rule, and a ruthless pamphleteer. He became the idol of the on-coming youths throughout Nigeria. A significant stage was reached when, still under the platform of the NNDP, some distinguished lawyers, doctors, journalists and leading businessmen played prominent roles in the politics of nationalism. Such men were Sir Adeyemo Alakija, Mr. Eric O. Moore, Dr. C.C. Adeniyi-Jones, Mr. Ernest Ikoli, Mr Egerton Shyngle, Mr. Wynter Shackleford and Mr. J. Clinton.

Newspaper Evangelism

No account of Nigerian nationalism could be complete without the record of the role and power of the Press in the struggle for the attainment of Independence for our country. The nationalist ferment was everywhere, especially in Lagos. That rising consciousness was being transmitted systematically up country through the newspapers, especially the Zik Group of Newspapers that included the *West African Pilot*, the *Southern Nigerian Defender*, the *Nigerian Spokesman,* the Daily *Comet*, the *Eastern Nigerian Guardian.* For that contribution of Dr. Azikiwe towards the freedom struggle, the common people of Nigeria made him their hero.

The Nigerian Youth Movement

The Nigerian Youth Movement was born around 1934. It became an embracing political organisation by 1937. Dr. Azikiwe, Chief Awolowo, Chief H.O. Davies, and many other leaders were members of the movement. It challenged the supremacy of the NNDP and of Mr. Herbert Macaulay. In 1941, Dr. Azikiwe and Samuel Akinsanya broke away from the NYM, and Zik later joined Macaulay to lead the National Council of Nigeria and the Camerouns (N.C.N.C.). Students and Trade Unions played major roles in the quest for freedom for Nigeria. the Yaba discussion group and the Union of Nigerian Students in Great Britain and Ireland were aggressively active in the quest for freedom from colonial rule.

Trade Unionism

The following trade Unions were forces to be reckoned with in the progressive march towards freedom and independence:-

(a) The Railway Workers Union of Nigeria led by Micheal Imoudu.
(b) UAC African Workers Union.
(c) The Coal Miners Union.
(d) The Railway Permanent Way Workers Union.
(e) The Post and Telegraphs Workers Union.
(f) The Locomotive and Footplate Workers Union.
(g) The Railway Station Staff Workers Union.
(h) The Civil Service Union.

Most of them were affiliated with the Nigerian National Federation of Labour (NNFL) with Mr. Michael Imoudu as President-General. The 44-day general strike organised by Mr. Imoudu in June, 1945, shook the British administration and helped to emphasise that the days of colonialism were numbered.

Liberation Literature

The few available books and newspapers by Nigerian authors became a source of inspiration to Freedom Fighters. In the *West African Pilot* were:

"Inside Stuff" - by Zik
"Weekend Catechism" - by Mazi Mbonu Ojike, and
"Despatches" -- by George Padmore.

Books included:
"Renascent Africa" - by Zik,
"Without Bitterness" - by Nwafor Orizu,
"My Africa" - by Mbonu Ojike,
"British and Axis Aims in Africa" - by K.O. Mbadiwe.

World War II (1939 - 1945)

The explosion of nascent nationalism dated from, and in fact was a by-product of, World War II. Discussions centred often on the experiences of the war and its impact on the world community. The war theme was "fight for world freedom", when Nigeria was still under serfdom. Nigerian soldiers for that freedom, made exploits in the Middle East, Burma and the Mediterranean. On return home, these demobilised soldiers formed an association of ex-service men. The stories of the national liberation movements in India, Burma, Malaya and East Africa filled the patriotic air.

Formation of the NCNC, 1944

At the instance of the Nigerian Youth Congress the National Council of Nigeria and the Camerouns (NCNC) was formed. It was a Council comprising many unions, groups and associations. NNDP became a member of the NCNC. Herbert Macaulay became the first National President.

The first programme planned by the NCNC was the Pan-Nigerian Delegation to London. It first toured all sections of Nigeria and the Camerouns to seek a mandate for going to London to ask the British for a democratic Constitution for Nigeria, and for her Majesty's government to abrogate certain obnoxious laws which militated against the interests of the people. For the first time in Nigerian history, the people contributed funds to foot the bill of a delegation and prayed for its success.

The NCNC delegation, by sheer obstruction of the British, failed to gain much in London. The then Secretary of State for the Colonies, Mr. Creech Jones told the delegation: "Go home and cooperate". What the delegation failed to achieve in London, it made up in Nigeria. It organised a mass tour of the country and succeeded in rousing popular anti-colonial feeling all over the country. Nigerian nationalism had changed from the elite discourse and occasional public lectures in Lagos to a mass movement country-wide.

Meanwhile, during the country-wide tour before the London delegation, Herbert Macaulay took ill in the North. He returned to Lagos and died. Dr. Azikiwe became the leader in his place and continued with the delegation as planned.

The Zikist Movement

No historical sketch about the struggle against imperialism will be complete without mention of the impact of the Zikist Movement. This was a radical, revolutionary body that was affiliated to the NCNC. The youths were unsure about the pace and commitment of the elders to immediate self-government, and founded the movement on February 16, 1946 at the suggestion of three young men namely, Mr. M.C.K. Ajuluchukwu who became its Secretary-General, Mr. Abiodum Aloba, and Mr Kolawole Balogun, the first President.

What is the Zikist Movement? The answer is found in their aims and objectives:

i.   Zikism holds that self-determination constitutes the inalienable right of the people, and that colonialism is wholly incompatible with this right.

ii. Zikism accepts the Marxist thesis that the economic factor conditions the moral, legal and political aspects of development in any society, and therefore urges the need for a just distribution of national wealth.

iii. Zikism strives towards the establishment of "the Zikist Way of Life" and to make the Movement an effective organ of expression for the revolutionary youth.

iv. Zikism represents the revolt of the youth against the desecration and vicious influence of imperialism in Africa, and against the complacence and reactionary tendencies of old Africa in a fast changing world."

A Call to Revolution

A lecture entitled "A Call to Revolution" was delivered by Chief Osita Agwuna under the chairmanship of Chief Anthony Enahoro. It called for a positive action which included:-

(a)   Boycott of British goods.

(b)   Boycott of schools and employment (including the Police and the Army).

(c)   Non payment of taxes to Government but instead to the NCNC and other nationalist organisations.

(d)   Mass violation of every law and executive order that negates human rights.

(e)   The flooding of the prisons with protesters in the mode of India under Ghandi.

(f)   The programme of non-cooperation with the authorities and civil disobedience as a means of liquidating imperialism in Nigeria.

For this type of public call and similar activities, Zikists were arrested and tried. The trial came to an end on February 2, 1949. The five men who were sentenced to various terms of imprisonment were:-

> Anthony Enahoro
> Osita Agwuna
> Raji Abdallah
> Oged Maçaulay and
> Smart Ebbi.

Finally, on April 12, 1950, the Zikist Movement was banned.

Zikists' agitations were directed against two quarters, namely, the British colonial administration and agents of British Colonial rule in whatever form. But it did not appear that their extremist stance had the blessing of the NCNC or its leadership. Zik in his INSIDE STUFF in the *West African Pilot* had described them as "fissiparous lieutenants and cantankerous followers".

In a Presidential address at the Annual Convention of the NCNC in Lagos on April 4, 1949, Zik, in an obvious reference to the Zikists, said:

"We must inculcate a sense of discipline and responsibility in our cadre. An unprincipled and irresponsible army is a liability, and not an asset, to any nation. Individuals must realise that membership of a national movement is neither a permit for licentiousness nor a warrant for irresponsibility. Lastly, the rank and file of our national movement must rely on the leadership to develop its own techniques, strategy, tactics and logistics. This requires implicit obedience, loyalty and tact. A disobedient, disloyal and tactless followership is just as suicidal to the national cause as an unprincipled and cowardly leadership. When the followership becomes impatient of its leadership, the course to follow is not to lose faith and become confounded, sullen and disillusioned, rather it must trust those at the helm of the ship of state, remembering that 'true courage is always mixed with circumspection', this being the quality that distinguishes the courage of the wise from the harshness of the rash and foolish...

We must make allowance for the bold and timid, hoping that this will vindicate the correct perspective. When, therefore, the militant elements among us feel that the time of positive action has arrived, they must ponder deeply that for such action to succeed, there must be, first, a mobilisation of forces; second, a disciplined army, third, a well-protected general staff, fourth, a line of communication; and, lastly, a cause worth fighting and dying for. Failure to plan any warfare, totalitarian or unitarian, on a detailed basis as above, is not only folly of the highest degree, but it is an invitation to disaster."

It is debatable to what course events would have taken if the NCNC had declared full support for the Zikist Programme of Action. Perhaps, independence would have come earlier than 1960. Perhaps, the Action Group would not have been born. Perhaps, there would not have been the NPC (Northern Peoples Congress), and the spokesmen of the Northern Nigeria would have been Aminu Kano, Raji Abdallah, Saad Zungur and Zana Bukar Dipcharima. Perhaps, too, there would have been shedding of innocent blood, which I abhor by temperament.

Certainly, I did not share the ideological or tactical inclinations of the Zikists.

However, I attended, on invitation, a major Zikists' function in February, 1950. The occasion was the ordination in Port Harcourt, of the first priest of the National Church of Nigeria, Mazi J. N. Egbuche. Such an occasion lent itself to further excitation of nationalist sentiments. The church had already "canonized" the slain Enugu miners as "Martyrs of Nigerian Freedom". On the occasion, it gave out three categories of certificates to Nationalists:

 (a) Defenders of Nigerian Martyrs (DNM);
 (b) Victims of Nigerian Freedom (VNF); and
 (c) Champions of African Freedom (CAF).

I was one of the eleven National Emergency Committee (NEC) delegates who were awarded DNM certificates. The jailed Zikist leaders were honoured with VNF awards, and only three men, Paul Robertson, Kwame Nkrumah and Nnamdi Azikiwe merited the CAF's.

I have already given a catalogue of the nationalistic forces at work before my return to Nigeria in 1948. They were the Nigerian National Democratic Party led by Herbert Macaulay, the Nigerian Youth Movement, the Students Unions both of Yaba College and of Great Britain and Ireland, the Trade Unions led by Michael Imoudu and the NCNC founded by the Students and led by Herbert Macaulay and Nnamdi Azikiwe. Finally there was Zikist Movement that supplied the revolutionary vanguard to the nationalist struggle. All these bodies were on their own, they were not co-ordinated, they were not combined; each was pulling on its own. That was the scene before my return to join the vanguard of the struggle in 1948.

On my return to Nigeria, I did not immediately join any political party. I kept a neutral stance. I was friendly to all sections of the Nigerian political leadership. I had always cherished the idea of fighting imperialism under a unified front. I therefore insisted on unifying all interest groups into one massive combat force.

It was not going to be easy. I was faced with a nationalist front which was already broken into bitter ranks, each faction fighting fiercely to subdue or eliminate the other. The political parties, led mainly by wealthy lawyers and influential journalists, kept the harshest of words in their arsenals, not for the British imperial lords, but for brother nationalists. Based mainly in Lagos, the nationalist credo was yet to secure a strong foothold among the people in the interior where representation in the Nigerian legislatures remained nominative, not elective. Even in Lagos and Calabar where periodic elections were held to send representatives to discussive 'parliaments', politics became activated only during such elections. And such campaigns were so unhealthy and gruelling that Britons felt relieved of nationalist agitation, at least for that period.

During that period, Nigeria lost its sense of oneness in its aspirations to fight for freedom. The nationalist front was split, as leaders began teaming up behind their own tribesmen. The Nigerian Youth Movement was balkanised into two, one faction led by Yoruba Lagosians, the other by Dr. Azikiwe. The latter soon joined the NCNC.

It was just then that my colleagues and I arrived on the scene with our determination not to join any one of the forces or factions but to strive to unite them as one indestructible, anti-colonial army. I waited for an opportunity to come. Meanwhile the stage was being set for a review of the then Richards Constitution which divided Nigeria into a semi-federal unit of three regions, the Northern, the Eastern and the Western Regions.

Though, all Nigerian nationalists protested against the constitution for its refusal to allow Nigerian participation in government, they were not altogether speaking with one voice. Because Dr. Azikiwe had condemned it outrightly, Chief Awolowo would give it a test. Such was the bitter antagonism, and disharmony among the elite politicians in Lagos. For instance, Dr. Azikiwe mounted a heavy nationwide campaign against the "obnoxious package" in 1946 and 1947, yet late

Chief Ladoke Akintola, former Premier of the defunct Western Region, who agreed that the Constitution was "one rotten fruit of imperialism", appealed: "We shall have to adjust ourselves to it as best as we can."

The Enugu "Massacre" and the National Emergency Committee

The Enugu "Massacre" of November 18, 1949, in which twenty-one demonstrating African miners were shot dead and fifty-one wounded, as a result of an order from a white police officer, helped to resuscitate the somewhat flagging Nigerian Nationalism and brought me into its mainstream. Other nationalist leaders and I seized on this overt demonstration of the essential violence of colonial rule to show our aggressive nationalism. But more than most nationalists, I clearly saw the Enugu tragedy as a major opportunity to unify the Nigerian nationalist movement . I was in the forefront in organising the first mass meeting in Lagos held at Glover Memorial Hall on November 23, which protested the Enugu Massacre and demanded a full official enquiry into it. At the meeting, leading members of the major nationalist groups of the South did close ranks. A National Emergency Committee (NEC) was formed with Dr. Akinola Maja as Chairman, and Mazi Mbonu Ojike, Secretary of the new organisation. Dr. Azikiwe was in Britain at the time of the incident and did not return until December 8. He sent a message of solidarity from there. It read:

"Ozuomba Mbadiwe care Francis Mbadiwe Enugu Nigeria you have our Hearty Cooperation in the stand you have taken on the Enugu Massacre stop we wish you and H O Davies success in your endeavours to investigate causes of this shocking and barbaric act stop most people here have been asking what is Nigeria's Answer". **Zik.**

I was one of a six-man delegation appointed by the NEC to go to Enugu to conduct its own enquiry into the shootings. Other members were H. O. Davies, Bode Thomas, S. O. Gbadamosi, Chief Michael Imoudu and Rotimi Williams. The Commission of

Enquiry headed by Mr. Fitzgerald was the outcome of the N.E.C. agitation.

An interesting experience H. O. Davies and I had (as the first set of members of the delegation) that comes back vividly to my mind is what happened at the Onitsha side of the Niger on our being ferried across from Asaba. There we were met by an European Police Officer who suspected and questioned us. In the ensuing dialogue, he concluded: "you are up to no good." I roared: "you are the one up to no good. You must be up to something sinister." When the dust raised by the fiery exchange of words died down, the late H.O. Davies wanted to know from the police officer what his name was. He replied that his name was Mr. Davies. H.O. Davies retorted: "I, too, I am Davies."

Though excited, the police officer was apparently not flattered by the joke and the coincidence of name. However, he allowed us to continue on our journey to Enugu.

As events turned out, the same police officer happened to be one of those cross-examined by Chief Davies as Lawyer for the miners during the Fitzgerald Commission of Inquiry.

Ever since, whenever I met H.O. Davies, I would humour him by saying "you are up to no good." He would laugh and reply "K. O., you are also up to no good." That was the Onitsha ferry incident.

At Enugu we were welcomed by the local sub-committee of the National Emergency Committee, one of such which had sprung up in many other towns in the country. The next day we called on the Lieutenant Governor, Mr. Pyke Nott, and informed him that we were going to address the miners at the Enugu coal siding. He naturally objected vehemently and warned us not to do so. Chief H.O. Davies and I defied his order and told him we were going ahead. We did. Despite his threats of using force against us, nothing happened.

Some NEC officials did give evidence before the Fitzgerald Commission. Mr. F.R.A. Williams and several NEC lawyers represented, free of charge, the workers and union officials before the commission. Appearing before the commission on

Saturday, December 24, 1949, I stressed the political implications of the incident. It demonstrated that the time had come for Nigerians to rule themselves. I characterised the union leadership of the colliery as "responsible", though inadequately trained.

In addition to my testimony, I submitted to the commission a memorandum, written by me, which had the approval of the NEC. It was essentially a nationalist brief. The memo demanded a more equitable distribution of the resources of the society by the narrowing of the large gap which existed between the standard of living of Nigerian workers and European colonial officials. Specifically, this memo called for the downward revision of salaries of white officials; the abolition of "Expatriate allowances"; and the introduction of the principle of equal work for equal pay, whether Africans or Europeans. I reiterated the nationalist's credo that "political independence was the only solution to Nigeria's problems."

The National Emergency Committee had succeeded. It had made its impression on all, and we hoped it would evolve into a permanent political party, but it did not. It was not until June 10th, 1950, that the White Paper on the Report of the killing of the 21 miners at the Coal Mine (1949) was published. It blamed the Police Chief for "high handedness." Our agitation had been vindicated and the miners justified.

Chapter 7

The Committee On National Rebirth. Entry Into NCNC.

In furtherance of my dream of a massive force against the British, I sought the support of Mazi Mbonu Ojike and Chief Kolawole Balogun, who had just returned from the United Kingdom where he qualified as a lawyer. Both men shared my belief that there was need for the closing of ranks by all the competing nationalists in order to give a tough fight to the British. With their support, I called a meeting of all political party leaders under the umbrella of the "National Rebirth", at the Glover Memorial Hall under the chairmanship of Sir Adeyemo Alakija. On the high table were Dr. Akinola Maja and Dr. Nnamdi Azikiwe. I acted as Secretary.

The West African Pilot on April 10, 1951, published a report of the proceedings. It reads:

"The long expected meeting of the Committee on National Rebirth came off successfully in the Committee Room of the Glover Memorial, on Tuesday March 27, at 5 p.m. Before the scheduled time, the hall was packed full with enthusiastic members of the public who, despite the fact that the meeting was not announced in the papers of that day, were anxious to listen to the deliberations. At 5 p.m. prompt, the meeting was declared open and a roll call of the invitees was taken. Sir Adeyemo Alakija, Dr. Nnamdi Azikiwe, Dr. Akinola Maja, Mazi Mbonu Ojike, K.O. Mbadiwe, Magnus Williams, S.L. Akintola, S.O. Gbadamosi, H.U. Kaine, Fred Anyiam,M.A.O Imoudu, Nduka Eze, Chief Bode Thomas, Kolawole Balogun, A. Ogunsheye, Lewis Agonsi, Rotimi Williams, T.O.S Benson, Mr. Lawanson, Mallam H.R. Abdllah, Mallam Abubakar Zulogi, E.A. Cowan, Ralph Aniedobe, H.P. Adebola, J. Marcus Osindero, S.G. Ikoku, N.A. Cole, S.O. Maduike, E.C. Nkemadu, Ejim Agwu and J.N. Ojile. Others were Messrs A.K. Blankson, Aniegboka Amobi, Peter Jackson, Mallams Salihu, Yahaya Adda Abubakar, Ani Dina, Alhajis Sanda, Mutari, Magaji, Alichindo, Ali Ahamadu, Inuwa Majar, and Messers Okafor Nwani and M.O.

Awoyinfa. From Onitsha came Dr. Chike Obi, while Mrs. Margaret
Ekpo and Chief Gogo Abbey attended from Aba and Mr. M.C.K.
Ajuluchukwu from Port Harcourt. Mr. Obafemi Awolowo, Ayo
Okusoga and Dr. Okechukwu Ikejiani attended from Ibadan. Three
delegates, Mallams Magaji Danbatta, A.K.H Dangayi and I.S. Dan
Sekondi attended from Kano."

After the roll call, a Chairman was called to direct the affairs of
the meeting. At this point, Sir Adeyemo Alakija opposed the
election of a Chairman, giving as his reason the presence of the
uninvited crowd and the failure of the conveners to hold a prior
committee meeting, both of which would make it impossible, in
his opinion, for the Committee on National Rebirth to hold that
day.

After a heated debate on the matter, the circular letter
distributed to all invitees was read. It revealed that the original
was signed by all the conveners in their own handwriting.

After an appeal by Mazi Mbonu Ojike the crowd filed out,
and the conveners of the Committee on the National Rebirth
present met in private for a few minutes, at Chief Bode Thomas'
suggestion, before the full house resumed.

Sir Adeyemo Alakija was elected Chairman, and I,
Secretary. After a while, Sir Adeyemo took permission of the
house to attend to another meeting and appointed Dr. Azikiwe to
act as Chairman. Dr. Azikiwe, in a humble and polite speech,
said that it was an African tradition for the youth to vacate a seat
for the aged, and he was therefore declining in favour of Dr.
Akinola Maja. Sir Adeyemo insisted that Dr. Azikiwe acted for
him and so Zik took the chair amidst thunderous ovation which
also greeted Sir Adeyemo as he bowed out.

I outlined the object of the meeting. I stated that the
Committee on National Rebirth was no political party but was
simply a vehicle for assembling nationalists from all over the
country in order to air their views on the nation's future, and
decide from past experience what is best for the country and the
way to achieve it.

I believed, I said, that this was the time to agree or disagree "on the larger content of self-government. Drawing analogy from the fundamental unity of purpose of the United Nations, with the divergent views and ideologies which characterise its component sovereign states, I felt that the people of this country with identical heritage, with a common tradition of suffering and living within a definable geographical boundary, should unite for the liberation of Nigeria and the Camerouns.

I asked for the formation of a strong organisation on a countrywide basis. I opposed regional and separate political bodies which would never serve the country's purpose. I concluded my speech by outlining a five-year programme of action.

Councillor Nduka Eze opened the debate and felt that the country must unite against the common foe. Chief Bode Thomas agreed on what I thought were the ills which had prevented national leaders from uniting on a common platform, namely, belief in regionalisation, and the thought that political organisations should function on a regional basis.

Mr. Obafemi Awolowo believed that the organisation of the country had been inefficient and that the leaders lacked mutual confidence. He suggested that if the formation of a countrywide organisation was to be a reality, the existing political organisations, NCNC, NYM, etc, must be dissolved and a strong new one created.

After the debate which lasted for over four hours, Mallam Magaji Danbatta, one of the Kano delegates, moved a motion calling for the immediate inauguration of an all-embracing countrywide organisation which would fight for self-government for Nigeria and the Camerouns. The motion was seconded by Mr. M.C.K. Ajuluchukwu, the Port Harcourt delegate.

Amendments by Chief Kola Balogun were accepted by the mover. A further amendment by Mr. Awolowo was accepted in part. The motion was carried unanimously by an overwhelming majority.

The following is the text of the motion as amended:-

"We the people of Nigeria and the Camerouns, conscious of our duty to
retrieve our noble heritage, assembled under the auspices of the
Committee for National Rebirth, for the purpose of bringing about our
renaissance today, Tuesday March 27 at Glover Memorial Hall, Lagos,
agree and declare as follows:-

(1) That we shall achieve self-government for Nigeria within five
years hence.
(2) That we shall build immediately a national political organisation
as distinct from regional or ethnic political organisations to
achieve this objective.
(3) That we shall ultimately evolve into a socialist commonwealth in
the event of our achieving home-rule, in order to enable self-
government have meaning to the common man all over Nigeria.
(4) That we shall immediately promote a national platform to achieve
the above aims.
(5) That we shall contest the forth-coming elections on the said
national platform."

A Committee to plan the programme of the new organisation was
elected and comprised the following:-

Mrs. Margaret Ekpo, Mazi Mbonu Ojike, K.O. Mbadiwe,
Kola Balogun, H.O. Davies, Obafemi Awolowo, H.U.
Kaine, Mallam H.R. Abdullah, and M.C.K. Ajuluchukwu.

The Committee was to report back to the general body. After a
closing speech by Dr. Nnamdi Azikiwe, the meeting adjourned
sine die at 10.45 p.m.

Following deliberations at four meetings, the Sub-Committee
recommended that a national party be formed, having the
fundamental features listed. The Committee further strongly
recommended that in order to achieve our objective more easily
and quickly, one of our existing national organisations should
adopt a recommended constitution and manifesto and publicly
announce such adoption within fourteen days. The constitution
and the manifesto of the proposed central political body are of
great interest in the emphasis they laid on such issues as *national*,

as opposed to *regional* set up, a socialist commonwealth, one man one vote and technological education.

Nigeria's problem is not lack of knowledge of the nation's priorities, rather it is the absence of the will-power to prosecute and achieve those national objectives.

Adoption Of The Report.

The detailed minutes of the meeting of the CNR for the adoption of the Report is equally of interest. It read:-

1. The recommendations of the Organising Committee appointed on March 27th to devise ways and means of implementing the resolutions of the National Rebirth Assembly were adopted after a lengthy debate on Saturday April 7th at 5 Ibadan Street, Ebute-Metta. As Glover Hall was not available on the 7th and as there was a felt need for quick decisions and for channelling of operations, Mazi Mbonu Ojike offered 5 Ibadan street, Ebute-Metta free, for the Saturday debates.

2. When therefore, the Assembly resumed debate at 5 p.m, the Chairman of the Sub-Committee, Mr. H.U. Kaine, Barrister-at-Law, and his Secretary, Mr. Kola Balogun, read out the recommendations; Mazi Mbonu Ojike, member of the Committee formally tabled the documents for discussion. Mr. Marcus Osindero, opening the debate, said that regionalisation has come to stay; he wanted the new organisation given a new name.

3. Mr. C.D. Onyeama, who was in favour of forming a new party to which he may want to belong, suggested that the socialism clause should be deleted in order not to alienate the cooperation of capitalists and natural rulers who may not want socialism now.

    He felt that "Freedom Everywhere" might not be acceptable to all religious denominations as a national song because it appears to have been taken from the Hymn Book and Prayers of the National Church of Nigeria and Camerouns. He did not want paid officers because he did not receive any allowance or salary for being an officer of an ethnic organisation.

4. Mr. J.A. Wachuku, Barrister-at-Law, wanted a clarification of intentions of the conveners. "Is a new party contemplated?" he asked. Mazi Mbonu Ojike categorically stated:

    "We are not out to build or found any new political party but to rebuild, retrieve and invigorate existing ones as was intended by the title,

"National Rebirth" - as clarified in Mazi Mbadiwe's statement of purpose on March 27, 1951. "Rebirth" Ojike argued, connotes that a birth had already taken place. He drew an analogy from the Tom Jones Memorial Library which is now undergoing a rebuilding and renovation physically by adding a third storey and altering the features without starting an altogether new building on a new plot of land. There-upon Mr. Jaja Anucha Wachuku said that one must get into a party before renovating it. He said that there are political parties such as the New African Party and the Nigerian Youth Movement, for one to join. He was emphatic that the NCNC is not a political party but a conglomeration of organisations.

5. Mr. Kola Balogun, Barrister-at-Law, explained, as the Secretary of the Organising Committee, that the recommendations under discussion were merely a skeleton of aims and methods which could be filled in later with details in a purely constitutional form. He wanted a dynamic action on a nation-wide scale towards our objective of National Independence immediately. He denounced chronic arm-chair critics and seekers after personal fame who multiply political parties in our country.

6. Mr. E.C. Nkemadu suggested that the NCNC should be requested, being a most competent body, to undergo the rebirth by adopting the recommendations to carry out the programme for Independence within five years. Mr. Onwu supported Mr. Nkemadu.

7. Mr. O.F. Beyioku suggested sending the documents to all the existing political parties, and that as many as adopt them should form a coalition to operate as one new entity. Here Mazi Ojike empasised that he was convinced that coalition is impossible in a dependent country. Mr. B.B. Salami supported that the NCNC, being most representative and having international reputation, be asked to carry out the recommendations. The Assembly decided that no new political party should be formed, and called for a formal motion.

8. Mr. E.C. Nkemadu moved, and Mr. B.B. Salami seconded, and it was overwhelmingly carried, "that the NCNC be requested to undergo a Rebirth and adopt and carry out the programme recommended."

9. Mr. Beyioku's counter motion that all political parties be given the documents to operate together in a coalition, for those that adopt them, and Mr. Ojogun's counter motion that NYM and the NCNC alone be given the documents, were lost.

10. The house adopted the documents, ordering them sent to the NCNC without delay, for study and reaction.

11. It was finally decided to call a mass meeting on Thursday, April 12, 1951, to report to the public the conclusion of the work and the resolutions of the Committee on National Rebirth.

12. The meeting was adjourned *sine die* at 7.30 p.m".

Acceptance Letter From National Council of Nigeria and The Camerouns:

The Protem Secretary,   April 10, 1951
Committee on National Rebirth,
23, King George Avenue,
Yaba Estate.

Dear Sir,

I am directed by the Cabinet to acknowledge with thanks receipt of your letter dated April 7, 1951, with its enclosure.

I am to add that in view of the fact that the NCNC Cabinet has already issued a statement to the press, vide the *West African Pilot* of March 17, to the effect that it had decided to embark on an intensive reorganisation, and taking into consideration that the principle of your recommendations coincides with the present spirit of the NCNC, I am further directed to convey to you the following decisions taken on a motion adopted by the Cabinet last night.

"That the recommendations made to the NCNC by the Committee on National Rebirth be accepted in principle subject to modifications by the cabinet".

While realising that an emergency exists in our national affairs today, which makes it necessary for quick action to be taken, the NCNC cabinet assures your committee that all efforts will be exerted to speed up the implementation of the recommendations as modified by the cabinet, but the NCNC would regret any precipitate action by anyone as this will seriously embarrass the NCNC.

You will realise that an organisation of the size of NCNC must be very tactful in the way it handles a major problem in order to keep intact the goodwill of its valued supporters.

My organisation therefore pledges itself for the onward march of Nigeria, and I here express appreciation of the gesture made by your committee.

I further assure you that the cabinet will do all that lies in its power to justify the trust that the people of Nigeria has placed in the NCNC.

Yours faithfully,

Signed: F.O. Ebuwa, Federal Secretary.

Dr. Nnamdi Azikiwe's Address On 12 April, 1951.

The following is the text of Dr. Azikiwe's acceptance speech on that occasion of the mass meeting of the CNR:-

"This is a supreme moment in our national history and we must prove ourselves equal to the occasion. Determined as we are to be free, not to be distracted by meaningless wrangles about who is right or wrong, we are convinced that the true path to national emancipation lies in doing what is right for our country. To be realistic, the time has come for us to admit that the attainment of unity in a country whose heterogeneity of culture, language, traditions, folkways, mores and conventions has baffled the best sociologists and anthropologists, is an idle dream. Union is desirable in our country and it is materialisable, but unity is not. To continue in quest of unity is a figment of the imagination.

As I see it, no useful purpose can be served by further efforts towards political unity in this country; rather we must draw an ideological line on the basis of partisan politics, put all our energy and resources into battle, with the sole aim to gain political power and use it for the greatest good of the greatest number, and if we fail to attain our objective, then like good sportsmen, we must give way to those who are able to do so.

In our march towards national rebirth, we must gather in one fold all who hold identical political beliefs, then we must mobilise our forces, promulgate our articles of faith, plan a programme of positive action, proceed to make our dream come true, and damn the consequences which must inevitably follow our action.

Now that the committee on National Rebirth has entrusted the realisation of a positive programme to the National Council of Nigeria and the Camerouns, I hereby call upon all supporters of the NCNC, throughout this great country, who believe in our cause, to join hands with us in carrying out this sacred task dedicated to the emancipation of our country from foreign rule.

No crumbs, however tempting should distract us from our legitimate aspiration, which is the attainment of independence for Nigeria within five years. No impediments, however formidable, should deter us from our goal. No person, however powerful should dampen our ardour in a way so as to demoralise and frustrate us in the pursuance of our natural ambition.

Fellow Nigerians, I have been authorised by the NCNC Cabinet to say publicly that, in view of the fact that the recommendations of the Committee on National Rebirth are consonant with our beliefs and aspirations, we accept same with an iron will which knows no defeat until victory has been achieved.

Join our colours, fellow crusaders of Nigerian freedom; on to battle with us, fellow bondsmen of alien rule!.

Forget the disappointments of the past, overlook the misunderstandings of yesterday. Discount the recriminations which might well in your breasts.

Come forward, compatriots, let us smash the ramparts of imperialism and establish an independent state of Nigeria, so as to redeem this continent from the obloquy of its slanderers and the rapacity of its exploiters. Let us organise ourselves in the West, in the East, and in the North. There is no reason why we should not contest the next elections and expose in all its nakedness the deception hidden under the cloven hoofs of the Macpherson Constitution.

We must give battle to the forces of reaction and conservatism, and by the God of Africa, there is no force on earth to stop us in this grim struggle to emancipate our race from oppression".

Mbadiwe Joins the NCNC

The next official move by Dr. Azikiwe on assumption of the responsibility was an invitation to me to join the NCNC as now reconstituted. The text of Dr. Azikiwe's letter reads as follows:-

Mazi Ozuomba Mbadiwe,   April 17, 1951
c/o Mazi Mbonu Ojike,
23, King George Avenue,
Yaba Estate.

Dear Sir,

As a result of the reorganisation scheme of National Council of Nigeria and the Camerouns, it has become necessary to invite more nationalists to serve on our Cabinet of Executive Committee.

I am wondering whether you will be good enough to accept this invitation to serve with us on the Cabinet.

Notices of meetings will be sent to you from time to time and we should be happy to have you present with us whenever it is convenient to you.

I should be obliged to hear from you as soon as possible.

Yours for the cause of Nigerian Freedom.

Signed: **(Dr. Nnamdi Azikiwe)**,

Federal President.

I replied accepting the invitation. The text follows:-

Dr. Nnamdi Azikiwe,   April 18, 1951.
Federal President,
NCNC,
Yaba, Lagos.

I accept your nomination to serve in the Cabinet of the National
Council of Nigeria and Camerouns without reservation.

I have faith and conviction in the cause we have dedicated ourselves to
champion. I am happy to join you in this crusade for freedom.

Yours in the service of the Nation.

Signed: (K. Ozuomba Mbadiwe).

Chief Obafemi Awolowo And His Attitude towards National Unity

One will note here that Chief Obafemi Awolowo attended all the
sessions of the National Rebirth Committee and participated
fully. In one of his motions in the Committee, he moved for the
dissolution of both the Nigerian Youth Movement and the
NCNC and suggested the establishment of a new political party.
This motion was, however, rejected.

Meanwhile, Chief Gogo Abbey (a journalist at Aba), who
attended the National Rebirth Committee meeting had, in an
article published in the *Daily Times* of March 26, 1951 a day to
the National Rebirth Conference, captioned, *"Towards Nigerian
Unity: Who is Right, H.O.D or Awolowo?"* brought out
forcefully the philosophy of Chief Awolowo towards Nigerian
unity. It contradicted the principle behind his motion for a fresh
new party. This was contained in a lecture Chief Awolowo gave
to members of Egbe Omo Oduduwa at Aba. According to Chief
Gogo Abbey:-

"..... Awolowo's opinion is that advocating mass unity for Nigeria is
mere dissipation of energy, and would entail many years of futile toil. The
easier way is to start from the bottom, for Nigerian leaders to educate the
peoples of their respective tribes into the real meaning and practice of
unity.

In other words, Awolowo wants Zik, Nwafor Orizu, Ojike, Mbadiwe and others of the noble band, to see to it that all Ibos are taught to appreciate fully, their common stock and interest, while he, Davies, Maja, Rotimi Williams, and their other Yoruba colleagues would see to it that the Ijebu man who settles in Ibadan is made to feel thoroughly and completely at home. The same must apply to other tribes.

When these tribes begin to enjoy the benefits of united action which, assuredly, must result, they will, by themselves, begin to aspire to the greater benefit of a country-wide unity.

That, according to Awolowo, is the "bottom medium" of achieving national unity. Awolowo's "bottom medium," is miserable mediocrity, and vulgar half measure, if "unity must be achieved, , it must be country-wide."

Chief Awolowo was not convinced that Nigerian leaders were serious. If political leadership would mean anything in Nigeria, it must be a full-time affair, he insisted.

He forgot that a political party of people with a common ideology, can have that cementing influence that is essential to unity. In other words, that the Igbo, Efik, Yoruba, Ijaw and Hausa who belong to the same school of political thought, could be more united than members of the same tribe who have different political views.

Having failed to achieve the purpose of his motion, namely, to break up the NCNC through the medium of the committee, Chief Awolowo announced the formation of his Action Group based upon his Egbe Omo Oduduwa doctrine.

That doctrine became an important development in Nigerian political scene at the time when we were ushering in the new Macpherson Constitution. But in pursuance of the policy of creating political climate healthy enough to make one a citizen wherever he lived, Dr. Azikiwe contested and won, the general elections in 1951 into the Western House Assembly. To stultify this policy of one Nigeria in favour of his tribally-based philosophy, Chief Awolowo got some elected members to "cross the carpet" from the NCNC to his A.G. side. Zik, the victor, lost. And Awolowo's party was able to form the government of the Western Region.

That was the beginning of rigid tribalism and carpet-crossing through the purchase of political party members. That incident shook the advocates of one Nigeria to the marrows. And the politics of Nigeria has never recovered from the tremors of that vicious manouvre ever since.

Chapter 8

The Macpherson Constitution
1951; Carpet-Crossing

Nigeria was a mere geographical expression till 1914. The year 1914 marked the beginning of Nigeria. It was at this period that Lord Frederick Lugard, merged the Northern Protectorate and the Southern Protectorate into one administrative unit.

In 1923 came the Clifford Constitution. For the first time it provided a common platform for the discussion of national problems with the establishment of a *Nigerian Council* in which nominated people served, though in an ad hoc capacity. The body was of course purely advisory. Because the provisions did not go far enough, the late Herbert Macaulay founded the Nigerian National Democratic Party (NNDP) the same year to fight its shortcomings.

In 1939, one significant development took place. That was the division of the Southern Protectorate into Eastern and Western groups of provinces. The North was not, however, split on the excuse that Kaduna was central to all the provinces in that Protectorate. This incident inflamed nationalism in the Protectorates to a new height. A revolutionary spirit with the banner and warcry of "One Country, One People, One Destiny" rent the air as Macaulay's image soared well above the horizon. No one thought about ethnic differences.

Then in 1946 came the Richards' Constitution which created three Regional Houses of Assembly and Houses of Chiefs for the North and West. The composition of elected members in the Central Council remained as under the 1923 Clifford Constitution. It gave a very limited franchise, and Dr. Azikiwe was dissatisfied. He took up his provocative pen against the Richards' Constitution. He also toured Nigeria, soliciting support for the delegation to be sent to London to press for a more dynamic and purposeful reform.

The colonial administration simply provided a new Constitution, based on some what popular representation of the people, without supplying them with power. That was the political situation in Nigeria when the shooting of the miners in Enugu occurred, and a wave of agitation was sparked off. By that time, I had returned from the United States and had helped to organise the National Rebirth, as recorded above.

The Macpherson Constitution of 1951 represented the British reaction to:-

(a)   the prolonged and sustained agitation of the nationalist fronts represented by the Pan Nigerian delegates led by Dr. Azikiwe to the U.K. and the United States;

(b)   the Fitzgerald Commission of Inquiry into the shooting of the 49 coal miners of the Enugu Colliery which prompted the establishment of the National Emergency Committee, and finally,

(c)   the far-reaching National Rebirth deliberation organised and promoted by me which resulted in a Constitution and manifesto of the NCNC party charged to champion the cause.

Following on the heels of all the above agitations and representations by the Nigerian National fronts, it could then be said that the Macpherson Constitution was the best that the British could offer the country at that material time. It was its boldest attempt since colonial rule began in Nigeria. The Macpherson Constitution provided for Regional Houses of Assembly, a House of Representatives and a Council of Ministers. It, therefore, decided to bring into one hub all the various elements and sections that made up Nigeria. The Regional Houses were made so attractive that they provided for a leader of government business, and later the Premiers of the Regions. But the Centre was still dominated by British administrators because there was a large number of them in government, and in the Cabinet, known then as "The Council of Ministers".

They included the Governor-General, the Secretary to the Executive Council and the Financial Secretary. These were all British officials. In the Council, each region was represented by three Ministers. Southern Camerouns had one Minister.

The NCNC Consolidates its Rebirth Mandate

The NCNC since receiving the mandate of the National Rebirth in April, 1951, to spearhead the country's Independence struggle, saw the Macpherson Constitution as a challenge. The party saw the whole of Nigeria as its constituency, even though the Macpherson Constitution emphasised regions. The NCNC contested the election throughout Nigeria under its banner of one nation, indivisible and indissoluble. In the North, the NCNC decided to contest through its ally the NEPU,(Northern Elements Progressive Union), led by Mallam Aminu Kano.

In the Western Region, the NCNC won the elections over the Action Group, by a handsome majority. Here began the great innovation and surprise in Nigerian elections, hinted earlier. A most dangerous practice in the electoral process of Nigeria was introduced for the first time, namely, carpet-crossing and open bribery, which were brought into operation by the Action Group. Overnight, successful NCNC members were bought over by the Action Group and the majority was reversed in its favour. Embers of tribalism were fanned by the Action Group leadership. Successful NCNC men who were not Yoruba were scared away. Dr. Azikiwe who won a seat to the Western House of Assembly from a Lagos Constituency, decided to resign. Since membership of the House of Representatives was by an electoral college in the regional house, no NCNC from the west came to the House of Representatives in Lagos. That was how Awolowo and his team qualified for the Federal House and Zik was therefore excluded.

That event of carpet-crossing marked the very first tragic scar on Nigerian political process from which Nigerians have never recovered till this day. Tribalism scored its greatest ugly victory. Chief Awolowo reaped its fruit temporarily, but the strategy branded him a tribalist till his death in 1987. Regionalism as created by the Macpherson Constitution achieved its objective of divide and rule. It seemed a defeat for those who preached the unity of Nigeria, and a triumph for the Action Group which never pretended its stand for Regionalism. When the late Chief Awolowo launched himself into a national, as against a regional leader, Nigeria did not forget. All his virtues as a leader, and they were many, would have won him the Presidency, but for tribalism. On death he was described as "the best President Nigeria never had".

Yet, Zik was undaunted with his mission of one Nigeria, despite the setback. In the East, the NCNC also fought the election and won. The NCNC installed the Government under the Leadership of Eyo Ita as Leader of Government business. The leadership of Professor Eyo Ita was weak and the rank and file of the NCNC membership felt it did not reflect its philosophy or its will. The Government was asked by the Party to resign, but this directive was resisted.

Eyo Ita and his other colleagues, for their failure to resign, were known and called the "sit-tight" ministers. They reacted and formed the National Independence Party led by Eyo Ita, Udo Udoma, Alfred Nwapa, Okoi Arikpo and Eni Njoku. The formation later fused with the United National Party (UNP) of Alvan Ikoku and Marcus Ubani, to constitute the United National Independence Party (UNIP) which was based almost wholly on the ethnic minorities of Eastern Nigeria.

The NCNC gave them a fight and had their Government dissolved. In the election which followed, a new government of the NCNC came into being in the Eastern Region with Dr. Azikiwe as the leader of Government business.

The Northern People's Congress (NPC), led by Ahmadu Bello,the Sardauna of Sokoto, and prompted by the British

dministration, quickly rose to political eminence and indeed
ominance over all Northern Nigeria. Opposition to it in
Jorthern Nigeria came from the Aminu Kano-led Northern
lements Progressive Union (NEPU) and the Joseph Tarka's
Jnited Middle Belt Congress (UMBC). Those Northern
pposition groups were allied with the NCNC and the Action
Jroup respectively.

When the Macpherson Constitution was put into operation, it
evealed without doubt the masterstroke of the British strategy in
ts fight against the rising tide of the Nationalists, agitation for
reedom and independence. By its counter-attack, it threw the
ationalist forces into disarray. It regionalised the country into
iree - the North, East and West. Each Region had its dominant
olitical party and its leadership. In the Central Legislature, the
Sritish entrenched themselves because that was where the power
iy. The problem created was how the three leaders would make
: to the Centre. If all three came to the centre, how would they
gree to appoint one of themselves as the leader? The British
ully calculated all the implications and felt satisfied that its
nasterplan had worked. Before those three regional giants could
olve the problem thrown to them, the British consolidated and
ontinued their dominance.

Before I was made a Federal Minister, the extent of my
ontributions is better assessed from my very maiden speech at
ie floor of the House of Representatives. I was contributing to
ie Budget debate for fiscal year 1952/53. It reads:-

"Mr. President, this is a momentous occasion as we gather here in the
New Nigerian Parliament to consider the first appropriation Bill under
the New Constitution Order in Council of 1951.

For the first time in all our constitutional struggle we have our first
African Ministers both in the regional and central Houses. It warms our
heart at the reflection that the struggle of many decades is bearing fruit.
We congratulate our Ministers, and we are confident that they will carry
out the policies of this Legislature to the best of their ability, bearing in
mind that they owe their position not by any benevolent disposition of
any Governmental action but by the expressive desire of the people. The
will of the people is therefore supreme. The thought that some who first

sounded the freedom bell and led the Constitutional fight have died, and the fact that there are others living but not in this chamber, should all the more make us humble in the great national service before us.

Mr. President, the Constitution has a great bearing on the financial policy of the government. Infact the constitution determines the financial structure of the state. That being the case, it will not be out of place for me to make a little observation on our constitutional instrument that has a great bearing on our financial policy.

I have listened carefully to the messages of goodwill sent from overseas to this Honourable House, whether from Her Majesty the Queen, or from the Secretary of State for the Colonies, or from Parliamentary delegates from U.K. - they convey one thing, among all others, a wish for unity among the peoples of Nigeria. Unity in diversity. His Excellency in his speech from the throne during the opening of this Parliament called for Unity. I am particularly happy to note that the Honourable Members from the North who spoke before me without exception have sounded a clarion call for Unity. I am proud of this gesture.

I wish to make it clear that my Party, the NCNC stands for the Unity of this Country. Whatever is propounded for this country, be it from the North or the West or the East, if it is for the good interest of this Country shall have our solid support. We shall guard jealously the greatness of this country, nationally and internationally. In the pursuit of this greatness for our country we must be frank to one another. Our country has been divided into three Regions. The Capital of Nigeria,Lagos, which has been sustained and built by all and which for decades has offered a focal point for Nigerian unity has been incorporated with the West. Mr. President, it is fruitless to cover the uncoverable. Neither the West nor the North nor the East is responsible for this unhappy state of affairs. The responsibility for this gravest political blunder rests on the shoulders of the British government and the Advisers to the Secretary of State. We pray that God shall help us to resolve this matter so that those imperial agents who sought to throw an apple of discord among brothers would have failed in their most aggressive attempt.

Mr. President, I now turn to the economic aspect of the country. The estimated revenue for the year 1952 - 1953 is £42,582,880. This amount for a population of 30 million people works out roughly to #1.11.8d per head of population. Sir, Gold Coast with a population of under 4 million has an estimated revenue of slightly over #33,000,000 this works out to #8.5 per head of population. This figure compared to our #1.11.8d shows clearly that all is not well with our economy and we have been all the time living in fool's paradise. Our economy needs a radical transformation from the old system of waiting to reap where we did not sow. The old government is guilty of planless economy. It is alarming that for years we have depended for our revenue on the Export - Import trade. Any Nation whose economic structure is founded solely on this type of trade is bound to meet economic disaster sooner or later, especially during a period of international conflict when exchanges of goods and services between countries become almost impossible. In the Budget before us, our Customs and Excise accounts for #27,100,000. Colonial Development and welfare grant accounts for #4,132,670. These two items total #31,132,670. If we subtract this amount from the gross revenue, we have a balance of #11,150,150. This works out to about 8/ -per head of population. Our internal trade gives a sad picture. Something is wrong. It represents a woeful economic planning. I am convinced that if we employ efficient staff with correct "know how" to man our present departmental establishments, there is no reason why our internal trade cannot account for #22,000,000 that is 100% increase.

1.   The Marine Department revenue is estimated at £844,700. The total expenditure is estimated at #1,691,230 of which £494,490 accounts for personal emoluments. It is curious that a department with great potentialities like the Marine should be run at a deficit. This department can easily earn a revenue of over £2,000,000. Why not operate a regular ocean passenger and freight service between Lagos and Port Harcourt. The demand for such service is high. Why not open up the Opobo port? These are definite revenue projects.

2.   *Post And Telegraphs*

     We are called upon to approve an expenditure of £1,633,150 for this department with an expected revenue of £775,000. This is another revenue getting department, if its facilities could be extended and its operations under efficient hands. This department should bring a revenue of £2,000,000 if soundly administered. The same arguement holds for other departments.

3.   Compare the aforementioned departments with the Custom and Excise department. We are called upon to approve an expenditure of only £278,470 which includes personal emoluments of £212,410 in return for an expected revenue for £27,100,000. While in the Marine Department the personal emoluments amount to £494,490 in return for a deficit. The Posts and Telegraphs calls for personal emoluments of #696,771 in return for a deficit. What economic analogy could we draw from the above?

1. Our past government is collector of revenues but has never been an efficient producer. The reason is that colonial territory has been a traditional ground for dumping pen pushers and brains of marginal utility from the mother country.

2. The entire civil service of this country needs total overhauling if we must intensify and expand our internal trade which is a *sine qua non* of a sound economy. We must expunge from this country the army of European pen-pushers who are dumped here in exchange for experts and efficient administrators. We must go to the world market and buy brains.

   Our Ministers have it as a very important duty to see that the Civil service comes under the jurisdiction of Nigerian Legislature. This does not mean interference, but the right to determine and hire qualified men for the task ahead.

3. The revenue of the country is drained by personal emoluments of European civil servants most of whom consume wealth but cannot produce wealth. Customs and Excise Department deserves congratulations. It is our desire to see more Africans promoted to Senior Service posts.

This new constitution has served as a medium of increasing the pay of civil servants, and creating more lucrative posts. We maintain today three Lieutenant Governors in the three Regions and these offices cost us £9,760 each a year. The office of the Governor has jumped from £17,452 last year to £23,080 under the New Constitution. The New Constitution has become a boom to civil servants without corresponding benefits to the people of Nigeria. Our Ministers have it as a sacred duty to see to it that only the best men and women in their respective vocations are imported into this country.

Agriculture and Industry

No review of our internal trade will be complete without touching on Agriculture. His Excellency calls it in his address as a primary industry. The Financial Secretary agrees, but unfortunately gives us no clearcut agricultural policy. Honourable Awolowo gives agriculture top priority, but speaking on industrial development says that only a small measure of industrial development should be introduced. Honourable Awolowo's fear is that large scale industrialization will mean doom for agricultural enterprise, and that in such an industrial race, many Africans will be displaced by European fortune seekers. The Honourable Gentlemen's fear reduces itself to an economic fallacy. Industrialization does not hamper agricultural progress unless there is no sound agricultural policy. Even if there is no industrialisation and a country is without a sound agricultural policy, agricultural enterprise will not improve. What we desire in this country is a sound agricultural policy along with scientifically planned industrial enterprise.

1. The rural areas must be improved with adequate social services and recreational facilities.
2. Unless the rural communities are improved people will continue to desert the farms for the Urban towns.
3. The Nations Schools must have curricula to reflect agricultural environment.
4. Cooperatives must be introduced in rural communities, credit cooperatives, marketing and consumer cooperatives. These under the supervision and guidance of the government.
5. The agricultural department must energetically introduce new methods and new techniques. In this way we could hold together our farming communities. The United States is a highly industrialized country, but still its agricultural pursuit accounts for the major part of its revenue. Its cooperative societies have grown over the years. In 1915, US had 5,424 cooperative associations which did a volume of business of #154,000,000. In 1938 it increased to 10,900 associations which did a volume of business of #600,000,000. In 1913 Japan had 14,000 rural cooperatives. Cooperatives have found strongholds in India, Korea, Canada, Scandinavia and Czechoslovakia. These countries are industrialized, yet their agricultural enterprise has grown tremendously because of sound agricultural policy.

Industrialization

The Government announcement of industrial programme for the country is welcome. Whether the Policy behind the programme is sound or not is another question. It is however happy to note that a New Government manned by our Ministers has arisen with new blood. As the legislature, it is our duty to help in shaping the policies. It is unfortunate that neither the Budget address of His Excellency nor that of the Financial Secretary has given us clearcut policies on what forms this industrialization will take. Government must assume direct responsibility to give a lead. The plan to merely attract investors to develop new industries and call such "industrialization" will be sheer economic madness. The country will suffer because its citizens have not been given the right type of functional and industrial education to enable her cope with large scale industry. Colonial education has at its very best produced 5% thinkers, 10% who think they think and 85% who'd

rather die than think. The government must assume responsibility unt
the avenues for education are widened .

The first stage of our industrial development will be:-

1. To improve without delay communication and transportation. It is
    shame that a huge country like Nigeria could not boast of any we
    built trunk road. The roads are narrow, crooked and dangerous. The
    should be first class trunk roads running from Lagos to Asab
    Onitsha to Victoria via Manfe thence to Calabar. Another fro
    Lagos to Kano, Jos to Maiduguri etc. Water transportation must b
    improved and expanded. Old Railway engines should be discarde
    and new ones imported. Transportation and Communication are
    must. The construction must be placed under construction enginee
    as it will take the public works more than twenty years
    accomplish that task.

2. The Niger River connecting Asaba - Onitsha should be bridged th
    linking the East with the West. Industrial Bonds should be sold f
    this purpose maturing 20 years from now. Toll should be collecte
    when the bridge is completed. In twenty years, the tolls will mo
    than pay for the cost. These are industrial projects which a
    investments for the future.

3. Internal trade should be intensified by encouraging small Africa
    Companies to grow. The principal aim of the Bill to aid pione
    industries should be to protect Nigerian industries. It should be a
    African protective tariff.

4. The Central Government should engage in basic industrie
    beginning with textile industry, shoe manufacturing, and then iro
    industry. In the later case, we can begin with scrap iron. In this w
    we can turn out iron for our buildings, bridges, marine equipmen
    etc.

5. No industrial programme can be effective without skilled labou
    The Financial Secretary in his address puts it ably this way. "Goo
    machines are useless without the skill to work them; and the be
    organization will fail if there are no trained executives an
    administrators capable of directing their activities." I agree, and ca
    upon the government to undertake an extensive scholarshi
    programme of granting within the next two years 100
    scholarships, 500 of these to be awarded to students already oversea
    pursuing studies in fields which will aid rapid industrialization.Th
    programme calls for functional education; that is, training for
    purpose.

6. Again we must lay a strong financial structure to cope with th
    above enumerated industrial programmes. Mr. President, this cal

for the government to establish within two years, a Central Revenue Bank. The Bank will act as the fiscal agent of the government, and will become the banker's bank of Nigeria. This bank will receive the reserves of African banks and will issue its own currency. It will receive the reserves of all our marketing boards, and will solve the problems of Marketing Nigerian Securities which the Financial Secretary is now finding the best way to solve. The revenue Equalization Fund which will reach an impressive figure of #12,750,000 will serve as a foundation for this bank. With this bank in operation, it will be easy for the government to borrow as well as loan money through the money market of the world. More than this, it will aid in the industrialization programme we now envisage.

Ten-Year Programme

The results of the ten-year programme are poor. For the remaining five years, I call upon the government to set up a five-year development board to carry out the remaining portion of this programme. It beats me hollow how the government proceeded to handle a project of #55 million pounds without a board. It requires the invitation of experts.

Public Relations Department

The function of the Public Relation Department should be clear. It does not require detailed investigation. It should be an Information Department - maintaining a well stocked library of the House of Representatives with a well-trained librarian who could give information to the Legislators and Executives without delay. It should issue factual information on the accomplishments of the government. It should be utilized for propaganda purposes. The Engraving Department should be retained to serve the public. We have confidence in Mr. Harold Cooper, and we think that he has done his best to understand the people he works for.

Military and Defence

Mr. President, I want to sound a warning that any country without adequate defence especially at this time of international tension is not secure from any sudden invasion. Time has come for the government to provide military training for our youths in the best military academy of the world. Our aim is to gain immediate self-government for this country, and when the time comes for England to say goodbye to us, we would not become vulnerable to outside attack. Thousands of our ex-servicemen who could have played a prominent role in the military

affairs of this country have been disbanded and disillusioned. Ou
military training has become a matter of great urgency.

Sir, we are called upon to vote £1,052,420 for the military an
defence. I must warn that in the future it will be necessary to oppos
any more vote under this head unless a definite programme for trainin,
future African Officers of the army is undertaken. Sir, the office o
Minister of Defence is essential and the creation of one should be
considered.

The Press

Mr. President, the press is an important instrument in the disseminatior
of information. It will be in the interest of this country to give the
representatives of the press from various parts of the country free
transport to enable them to attend the sessions of this House. The press
is not viable in this country and consequently many newspaper owners
could not afford to send reporters. What is happening here is of interest
to all communities of Nigeria, and information can only reach them
though the press.

Mr. President, the ship of Nigeria is afloat. It has the vigor and the
vitality. Goodwill prevails all over. In it brothers of Nigeria have come
to dream together and worship together, Sir we are ready to sail. The
objective is common crusade for freedom and the pursuit of happiness.

I support the appropriation bill.

When I went over that speech again, I confirmed my belief that
my present message for a rebirth of the nation will not be ignored
by my audience, namely, the present and next generation, as well
as the new crop of leaders. What I proposed in the said address, I
followed up in motions which were carried in Parliament and
implemented. And so the government in which I served and
subsequent administrations adopted my vision and put into
practice the steps which I outlined in my maiden budget address
delivered some forty years ago.

Chapter 9

The Test For Nigerian Nationalism:
The ".Self-Government For Nigeria" Motion

Between the two participating parties in the Central Coalition Council of Ministers, the Northern People's Congress, representing the North, had only recently been initiated into the struggle for freedom. The other party, the NCNC was already a veteran in the struggle. Since the mandate from the "National Rebirth", it emerged more united, indestructible, indivisible and freer to act. It adopted a course of action which would result in independence within five years. It had a manifesto which it was compelled to implement. Hence, the NPC had a competent partner in the Federal Government. However, the NCNC, having realised that the NPC also had a tradition to keep, decided to be cautious and understanding in its piloting role, otherwise the British could intervene and upturn the peace and cordiality between both parties in power. Colonial masters were notorious for the diabolical machinery of divide and rule.

The Parliamentary Leader of the NPC was the late Sir Abubakar Tafawa Balewa, while that of the NCNC was my humble self. With time, the two of us became very close friends. Before long, we discovered that we shared common beliefs and aspirations about the way to pilot Nigerian affairs.

However, it did not start with all that smoothness. For when Nigeria attained nationhood in October, 1960, not very many were in a position to realise how deeply we were divided in the Central Legislature, or how Nigeria escaped a return to bitter internecine politics which featured seven years earlier. This can only be narrated now.

It all started with the entry on the Order Paper for March 31st, 1953, in Parliament, of that famous motion on "Self-Government for Nigeria". It stood in the name of Chief Anthony Enahoro, a prolific writer and highly talented debater. The motion urged that "This House of Representatives accepts as a primary political objective the attainment of self-government for Nigeria in 1956".

One will recall that one of the cardinal policies enunciated by the Committee on National Rebirth in March, 1951, was "That we shall achieve self-government for Nigeria within five years hence" - that is in 1956. It was, therefore, a happy augury when the motion appeared on the Order Paper, although it was listed the last of seven private motions.

It was feared that the House might not wait to deliberate on the motion by the time the Members were half-way through the business of the day.

But very soon the motion gathered storm, and controversy was built around it. Northern representatives would not accept the date 1956. To them, the South was being too much in a hurry because they had sufficient skilled manpower to run government affairs in a free nation. The North feared they lacked such manpower. Hence, leader of the NPC, Alhaji Ahmadu Bello, the Sardauna of Sokoto, tendered an amendment motion which read:-

> That this House accepts as primary political objective the attainment of self-government for Nigeria as soon as possible.

As would be expected, Governor Macpherson would not subscribe to this kind of motion, for he was not prepared to jettison the then colonial constitution for anything. For sometime, he had been made the focal point of attack by the Action Group to which Enahoro belonged.

An open dissension followed the introduction of the issue in the Council of Ministers before the House met. There, a majority of Ministers signalled their opposition to the motion. They would rather support the amendment. The four AG Ministers, Chief Bode Thomas, S.L. Akintola, Arthur Prest and the Oni of Ife, Oba Adesoji Aderemi, remained staunch and adamant in their support of the original motion.

Meanwhile, the NCNC crisis of the Eastern House had affected our solidarity in the Parliament. We were split into two factions, one led by Dr. Azikiwe and the other by Mr. A.C. Nwapa, the Central Minister of Commerce and Industry. Those who held allegiance to Dr. Azikiwe followed me in the House. I fully realised the impact of the motion which had its forerunner in the National Rebirth resolution of April 7th, 1951. Hence my group supported it.

On the day the motion was to be debated, I created history. I approached Chief Awolowo and solemnly promised him my party's support for the motion. That bold step was unthought of the relationships between the NCNC and the AG. Of the six motions listed before the "SGN 1956 motion", three each were to be moved by members of the AG and NCNC. Awolowo and I agreed to convince our members to drop their motions so as to enable the "SGN 1956 motion" come up earlier.

And so, contrary to the expectations of all opponents of the motion in the House, and among Ministers, the motion for self-government was left the only one to be debated. It was moved and seconded. The Sardauna of Sokoto also moved his amendment. It was seconded. But all of a sudden, Alhaji Ibrahim Imam, a member of the NPC rose up to move the adjournment of the debates. This was disappointing.

Chief Awolowo took umbrage at the suppression of the motion. He got up and said:

> We should be free to say our minds on this issue without being fettered, and the North should be free to say its mind without being fettered. At division time we know by the look of things that we (proponents of the motion) will be beaten. But we are not afraid. It will go on record that A B C and D once voted for freedom for their country and that E F G and H once voted against it.

..... We are prepared to be voted out any time, in a spirit of sportsmanship. But we are certainly not going to submit to a situation in which we are being muzzled into the bargain.

I would like to say, Sir, on behalf of the Western Region that we will not stay here to continue this debate.

Chief Awolowo and his colleagues in the AG, including the Ministers, trooped out of the House. Immediately, I rose up to support the AG stand, we walked out too. Both Chief Awolowo and Dr. Azikiwe ran into an embrace for the first time. But that incident brought us to a crisis of confidence with the NPC, our partner in government.

This issue which seemed to be a setback was however, short-lived. Again, I went into action getting the nationalist fence mended. In a short while, Alhaji Abubakar Tafawa Balewa and I became very good friends. Earlier on, there was so much suspicion that when Northern Ministers were leaving the Council of Ministers' meetings, and I stayed back to chat with Sir Abubakar, they would leave one of their men behind to watch their interest. With time, and with the friendship which I was cultivating among all members growing stronger and solid, confidence returned rapidly, and we were soon all at ease among ourselves. The Northern group soon developed the confidence to believe that all decisions we took jointly were meant to benefit Nigeria as an entity, not a section of it. That was how we succeeded in making them accept the idea of self-government for Nigeria, after the initial misconception had been removed.

Chapter 10

The Coalition Government Of The NCNC And NPC In 1954; The Position Of Lagos.

The coalition government of the NCNC and the NPC started in 1954. However, the incident in the House of Representatives between the Action Group and NCNC, and the embracing of Zik and Awolowo, lingered in the minds of the NPC with its attendant suspicion.

However, the coalition was not proclaimed with a bang. It developed gradually but firmly. As mentioned above the relationship between me, as the Parliamentary Leader of the NCNC, and Alhaji Abubakar Tafawa Balewa, as the NPC Parliamentary Leader, developed into great friendship. After that initial mistrust, all my colleagues in the Council of Ministers accepted self-government for all Nigeria.

Then there was the self-government of the Regions. The Leader of government business in each region became the Premier: late Sardauna of Sokoto, Sir Ahmadu Bello in the North; Dr. Nnamdi Azikiwe in the East; and Chief Obafemi Awolowo in the West. We now mounted a louder campaign in the papers and in the air for a meaningful, complete autonomy. We made a strong case in our speeches. Labour unions drummed it louder into everybody's ears. It was "Independence for Nigeria - no more, no less".

Having attuned their minds towards the inevitable fact that one day they would have to grant Nigeria independence, the British introduced their notorious divide-and-rule system into the national fabric and exploited the fears and prejudices of some sections of Nigeria. Three issues dominated their thinking, namely:

1. The Northern leadership had continuously been made to believe that their interests would suffer if they dared go with the rest of the nation into independence right then.

2. By the grant of seperate regional self-government to rigidly self-conscious regional administrations, the British believed that the tempo of our demand for central autonomy would be slowed. They encouraged Awoist rigid regionalism. They fostered the fear of domination by others in the Northerners.

3. That fact that the political party leaders found a secure haven in their Regions, and that no one would want to risk such security, added to the problem of building one strong voice for national independence.

Alhaji Tafawa Balewa was the Parliamentary Leader of the NPC and Alhaji Muhammadu Ribadu, his Deputy. They were all wonderful human beings. Balewa, I called "The Black Rock". "The Golden Voice"; Ribadu, I called "The Power of Powers". Balewa referred to me as "Speed and Magic". He said it took time to convince me on any line of action, but when I understood the issues thoroughly, I would jump with lightning speed to the accomplishment of those issues. We, the trio, rode on the crest of great wave of confidence and affection for one another.

We outlined the goals for the new coalition, what we wished to tackle immediately, after the "self-government motion". First on the list was what should be the position of Lagos. Were we to have Nigeria with no head, no capital and with its head buried under one of the Regions - the Western Region? The Macpherson Constitution divided the country into three regions and merged Lagos, which is the capital of Nigeria with the Western Region. In effect there was a Nigeria without a head, without a capital city.

And as the leader of a party that believed in the unity of Nigeria, as the corner-stone of its political credo, I felt that the first task before us was to fight the Macpherson Constitution, and by fighting the Macpherson Constitution, we were also fighting the political party that was in charge of the Western Region to which Lagos was merged. So that was one of the greatest tasks facing the coalition and it was a sad task which must be done.

After regionalisation, the British then stood by as umpire and spectator. I felt immediately that the British had a case to answer in the merging of Lagos to the West. The government must make a statement to the people of Nigeria whether it had renounced its treaty obligation with Lagos of 1861. There must be no equivocations. It must be definite. That was the stand I felt my party should take. The NPC might have a different view. But because of the confidence and interest their leader and other colleagues had in me, they were willing to go along.

We had also to watch Chief Awolowo. In his position as Minister of Local Government for the Western Region, he had started to introduce His Highness, Oba Adele, as a natural ruler to be the Chairman of the Lagos Town Council. The people of Lagos had twice rejected the Action Group in elections. By taking advantage of the Macpherson Constitution, which merged Lagos with the West, Awolowo was thus imposing leadership on the Lagos electorate.

De-Merging Lagos from the Western Region

There was only one answer - separation of Lagos from the West. That was the issue of the day. On that issue, Lagos must demonstrate its stand and all of us Nigerians must give a fight to redeem the harsh measures of the Macpherson Constitution to give Nigeria a place of honour.

This was the great issue that became the cornerstone of the fight. And my party the NCNC as the mover and spearheader of this fight gave me the fullest support. The Action Group opposed my motion vehemently.

Chief Awolowo as the Minister of Local Government, Western Region, was opposing it from Ibadan. His deputy, Chief Bode Thomas, the Minister in Lagos Central Legislature, was opposing it from Parliament.

However, I had no alternative than to file my motion.

It read:

Whereas it is the supreme desire of the peoples of this country to have one Nigeria, in place of a sectional and divided country, and whereas Lagos has for decades remained the seat of the government of this country and through this unique position has provided a meeting ground for various elements comprising this vast country, on the basis of equality and consciousness of oneness, regardless of regional or sectional interest or affiliation; And where Lagos, because of its independent status, has been built up into a vast prosperous metropolis with the combined resources, material and moral, from every section of Nigeria and the Camerouns, for common good and common objective of all;

And whereas the said Lagos has been merged with the Western Region, thus depriving it the status of capital city of Nigeria.

And whereas the said merger was accomplished against the popular wishes of the majority of citizens of Nigeria and the Camerouns as expressed by the Ibadan General Conference. And whereas the afore-said merger has deprived the majority of the citizens of this country their rights of a common concern; And whereas the people of this country view the said merger as a deliberate attempt to break up that foundation upon which the ultimate unity of Nigeria revolves and hinges;

And whereas the said merger has rendered Nigeria at present a country with no capital,

Now therefore be it resolved:

That in the interest of National Unity and fraternal fellowship among the Regions of Nigeria that Lagos, be separated from the Western Region and henceforth remain independent of any and all the Regions of Nigeria.

Signed: **(K. Ozuomba Mbadiwe).**

The motion was naturally opposed by the Action Group. And as the British formed and ordained the Macpherson Constitution, the motion was not to their liking. The first day it was announced that the motion would be debated, the precinct of the House of Representatives was besieged by thousands and thousands of people. Market women, labour leaders, people from all walks of life in their thousands came to hear that great debate. The motion automatically made me a hero of the nation. Of course outside Parliament were the supporters of the Action Group opposing the motion. When we came out from the House great shouts of 'K.O.! resumed with great intensity and enthusiasm. That ' was the picture. It was a motion that involved all aspects of life of Nigerians. It was the talk of the day throughout the length and breadth of the country.

On the first occasion, it was ruled out of order because it was like amending the Macpherson Constitution. The Constitution cannot be amended by such a motion, but I argued that either by amendment or by whatever name it was called, the motion was of imperative necessity, irrespective of whose ox was gored. A great debate inside and outside Parliament ensued. This was how the Nigerian press saw it then. The *Daily Times* of Wednesday March 12, 1952 under the heading: Oppose Separation of Lagos: Action Group men told" reported:

Before the Action Group mass meeting dispersed on Monday night at the Glover Memorial Hall, Lagos, the House unanimously agreed to a suggestion by Mr. M.A. Ogun, Propaganda Secretary of the Group, that all Action Group members in the House of Representative be empowered to oppose "vehemently" a motion by Hon. K.O. Mbadiwe seeking the separation of Lagos from the Western Region.

Sir Adeyemo Alakija who occupied the chair congratulated the Western Region on its achievements. Dr. Akinola Maja appealed to all to give more support for the Action Group which he said, stood for the people's welfare.

Hon. Obafemi Awolowo, leader of the Action Group paid glowing tributes to the loyalty of Lagos branch members. He told them that although they have no representative in the Western House of Assembly, yet they have one consolation in that it is their party which controlled the Western Region.

He also paid tributes to the interest and love shown them by all the Western Obas. There are no black sheep among them, he declared. He gave as an instance of their interest in them, the recent Budget meeting of the House of Chiefs which ratified all the laws passed in the House of Assembly.

He was impressed by the loyalty and discipline prevailing among Action Group members. Each Action Group Assembly man contributed ten percent of his salary to the Group's fund. Hon. Awolowo said they had adopted the "frigidaire" policy in the Western Region in order to hasten the Nigerianisation of the civil service.

He hinted the House of a motion scheduled to be heard in the present Budget session of the House of Representatives seeking the separation of Lagos from the Western Region. He said he was strongly against that motion and said that it must be fought tooth and nail. The

Action Group had started from the West, he said, it would soon extend to the East and North. He gave a vivid review of the achievements and plans made by the Group for the progress of the West, like the award of 200 scholarships, recreational facilities and the building of an up-to-date hospital in every province in the Region. Other speakers were Hon. A.M.A. Akinloye, Regional Minister of Agriculture, Hon. S.O. Awokoya, Regional Minister of Education, Chief the Hon. A. Prest, Minister of Communications, Hon. T.A. Odutola and Hon. Tony Enahoro.

In another page of the *Daily Times* the same day, there was the headline and report: "Awolowo Will Quit the Centre if Lagos is cut off from the West":

Addressing the supporters of the Action Group at a mass meeting held yesterday in the Glover Hall Lagos, Hon. Obafemi Awolowo declared that he would no longer remain in the House of Representatives if "Lagos is separated from the West".

The *West African Pilot*, in its Week-end Catechism had this to say on March 15:

Adolphus Obi, Lagos: A fortnight ago the Western Minister of Local Government said that the passage of Honourable Mbadiwe's motion to make Lagos enjoy independent political status would mean the end of the Macpherson Constitution.

Answer Not in progressive circles. It was boastfulness, a political bluff that must be called off sooner or later. For Action Group members of the House to resign in protest against the motion of sanity and unity for Nigeria, then there will be a new election in the West to fill their seats. That would be most useful for attaining political freedom for all Nigeria more quickly. History is clear on the status of every federal capital the world over. It is so in Canada where Ottawa is independent of state control; in USA where Washington D.C. enjoys political freedom from the state. In all these places the question of the owners of the site is not disputed for owners of land at Ibadan, Enugu or Kaduna have never been deprived of their lands without compensation. Surely, all lands in Lagos now held by Government are legally negotiated for.

And that is why a family can sue Government on land problems. Let Action Group trite writers deny this. Let them deny that where Port Harcourt is now located was bought or leased by Government from the rightful land owners.

For if the whims of the Action Group in regard to Lagos is to be approved, no region would be foolish to offer any land for our Federal

Capital on any other terms. And what is worse is that Nigerians are expected to sign away to Action Group ambition the city of Lagos which for three quarters of a century or more has been developed with Eastern, Western and Northern funds.

Even if the Action Group claims were to be granted, that party would

(1) refund to the East and the North what they paid towards the building of Lagos as a national capital.

(2) Give the nation time to locate and complete an alternative capital and move over before Action Group would rule and own Lagos.

This is not a matter of who owns Lagos because I know that non-Nigerians own more land in Lagos today than does either the Central Government or non-Action Group Lagosians. The Groupers have not raised a word of protest against these alien landlords of Lagos.

They just want to rule Lagos, from Ibadan in order to wipe off the tears being shed over their losses at the LTC elections of 1950 and 1951. I wish these braggarts knew what others, including a majority of progressive Yorubas and non-Nigerians, think of their Lagos merger ambition.

Will the East and North plus NCNC Western members of the House of Representatives permit the Action Group to dictate terms of the status and destiny of Lagos in which all Nigerians have equal stake?

Heroes and heroines of ONE NIGERIA how long must this confusion be tolerated on our road to freedom?"

On August 21, 1952, I petitioned His Excellency, Sir John Stuart Macpherson, Governor of Nigeria. I protested as follows:

Your Excellency,

I am addressing this letter to you in your capacity as the Governor and Commander-in-Chief of the Nigerian Armed Forces and I write in my capacity as a citizen and a Legislator of this country. I wish to call your attention to the fact that my two motions duly presented to the Clerk of the House have been suppressed, contrary to the provisions of the Standing Orders of the House, Section 18, Sub-section 5 and 6. The first Motion under reference deals with the separation of Lagos from the Western Region and the second Motion simply requests the Government to send congratulations to Dr. the Honourable Kwame Nkrumah, on behalf of the Nigerian people on his elevation to the high office of the Prime Minister of Gold Coast. The explanations of Mr.

Fellowes on the Nkrumah Motion are most unsatisfactory and I intend to press the matter further.

Although, you are not at the present time, the President of the House of Representatives, yet as the Governor of the country, you cannot, Sir escape the responsibility of seeing to the smooth working of this Constitution. As the Father of this New Constitution, your absence from the House is very much regretted, and I trust it will not continue hereafter.

It should be noted:

1. My motion urging the separation of Lagos from the Western Region was properly brought before the House, in that it was printed in the Order Book. I was called upon by the Chief Secretary to the Government to argue the motion just on the very day the House adjourned *sine die*. I contended that the Motion came up too late when most members were tired and several others left for their homes and therefore asked that it be deferred until this present meeting. That the same Motion in this meeting should be ruled out of order has created suspicion in the minds of the public, the explanations of Mr. E.A. Fellowes notwithstanding. I felt that our Government should be above suspicion.

2. I am happy that the President of the House has waived customary procedure and has made it possible for me to challenge his ruling on the matter. It is a democratic process.

3. I am happy that the Lagos Separation Motion has achieved its first objective, though not final objective - in the Chief Secretary's statement on Lagos issue as authorised by the Council of Ministers, admitting the dual nature of Lagos as a Capital and principal Port of this country, and making it clear that an expert will review the situation.

4. The Chief Secretary's statement has averted grave crisis in this, and the Council of Ministers must be congratulated for placing the welfare of this great country above regional or selfish considerations.

5. Under the present circumstances, I respectfully call upon your Excellency to exercise the Powers conferred upon you under the Nigerian Constitution Order in Council 1951, Section 96, Sub-section 2b to see that the administrative and financial arrangements of Lagos are not interferred with until the expert opinion on the subject is obtained.

6. I have again given Notice of a Motion on Lagos which has been accepted. It is not likely that this Motion will be debated before this House adjourns *sine die*, but if the issue of Lagos is resolved before

it is debated, I will gladly withdraw same to the glory of Nigerian Unity, but if not, I will press the matter to its final conclusion.

7. The NCNC believes in the unity of this country. It is my firm conviction that to deprive Nigeria of its Capital is to break up that foundation upon which the ultimate Unity of Nigeria revolves and hinges.

Your Excellency, I respectfully submit,

Yours truly,

Signed **(K.Ozuomba Mbadiwe).**

The question of Lagos became a hot debate both in the Council of Ministers, the Legislature, in the Regions and throughout the country. It continued that way until the country's delegation arrived in London for the 1953/54 Review of the Constitution. The matter was so sensitive that all concerned left it with His Majesty's Government to determine the final position of Lagos, after submissions by the delegations, Mr. Kola Balogun, our National Secretary, read the NCNC submission.

Sir Oliver Lyttleton, the British Colonial Secretary, asked the conference in session, representing all parties from all Regions whether he, as His Majesty's representative, could look into the issue, and whether all were ready to accept his verdict on the issue. The conference accepted that the matter be referred to him and that his decision would be accepted by all. The matter was adjourned that day till after a few days when Oliver Lyttleton was ready with his verdict.

He made a lengthy statement on the position of Lagos, as a seaport for Nigeria, the Capital of the Government and everything which is associated with it. He said, "Gentlemen, I have come with the enviable conclusion that Lagos should be separated from the West and remain a neutral and independent capital of the entire Nigeria". There was a burst of applause and within few hours, the matter re-echoed everywhere. I cabled immediately to Nigeria.

On the return of the delegation from London, our arrival was greeted by a great crowd. Market women composed songs in our praise. Shouts of "K.O". filled the air. Ours was a major victory against the Action Group. That was the first major event for which two parties had challenged each other, a challenge that was vehement and ruthless. Victory came to us.

It was a matter of honour and glory for the whole of Nigeria. I felt that this was a great day in my life, having regard to my contributions.

The Lagos Slum Clearance Scheme and The Surulere Housing Scheme

In 1954, I was appointed the Minister for Lands and Natural Resources. It placed upon my shoulders another task of changing the society, by the clearance of the slums of Lagos, and the rehabilitation of those who might be displaced, by housing them in a virgin area in the mainland of Surulere.

On my return from the United States, I was unhappy about the slum in which my own people were living, especially in Lagos. How can human beings live in such a surrounding? In one corner of their dwellings were the toilets and bathrooms, with no demarcation. At the other corner was the crowded living rooms. In front was a rubbish heap. It was ugly. The general atmosphere was gloomy. It was a fitting area for a plague that could wipe a whole people out. This constituted a great challenge.

I saw that plans had already been made several times over many years, but nobody was ready to implement them because of the enormous cost that was involved. Moreover it needed great courage. I decided that this would be my task in the Ministry.

I got my officials of the Ministry to work out the plans. Well, it is never an easy task to touch peoples' lands or houses. Therefore the first task was to reassure them that nobody was depriving them of their lands or their homes, that it was to their best interest. Whatever land was reclaimed remained their own. Nobody was going to acquire or sell it. It would still be in their names and they would be given an alternative place to settle, if need be. They were assured that the place would be well-planned with toilet facilities, running water, recreational facilities, schools, shopping centres and so on. That laudable scheme was again hailed. Again standing firm behind me were my friends in government, Balewa and Ribadu.

Opposition usually emerged from the Action Group which warned me that there would be no slum cleared in Lagos, that I should rather go to my own homeland in Orlu and clear the slums; that the slums of Lagos would only be cleared "over their dead bodies".

They were talking to a fighter by nature. The more I was threatened the firmer and stronger my resolutions became. I accepted their challenge and told them to wait and see; that the slums of Lagos must be cleared. The Action Group said, Never, and another fight ensued with the same ferocity as the de-merging of Lagos from the West.

On the historic day, November 17, 1954, when I was going to turn the first sod in Surulere, a virgin forest, with nothing like human habitation, I gave the following address:

Gentlemen,

It gives me great pleasure to come here today to perform the commencing ceremony of the new Surulere Re-Housing Scheme. The company here is small but it contains those persons who are most intimately connected with the development of Lagos; the development not only of its physical structure but also of its welfare.

Firstly, I should like to thank the Chairman of the Lagos Executive Development Board for his kind remarks and his welcome address. Today, we hope that we are seeing the start of a new era in the development of Lagos. Before us is a large piece of undeveloped land, behind us is the teeming population of Lagos, in many cases ill-housed, living in unsanitary conditions, in constant danger of diseases and suffering great discomfort. We hope, before long, to see in front of us, not waste land, but a modern estate where people can live in healthy conditions with modern amenities and everything which makes for better living.

The Chairman has just told us, that for several years attempts have been made to better the housing conditions in Lagos but for one reason or another, none of the plans has come to fruition. At long last we see the first attempt at making a better Lagos. In years to come, people can look upon this day as one of note in the history of Lagos. The housing which will grow on this land will have two purposes. On the one hand, it will assist in housing those persons who may in the future be displaced temporarily where various clearance schemes are in operation, and secondly when the slums of Lagos are no longer with us, it will become, we hope, a flourishing suburb for the Capital of Nigeria. Many months, I may say years, have been spent in drawing up the plans for this new scheme. Arrangements are being made so that the inhabitants of this new estate will have the usual amenities required, and I may say, expected by people in these times, namely, medical facilities, schools, community centres and all the benefits of what is called and known as social welfare. I wish to pay tribute to all those persons in the Lagos Executive Development Board who have worked to bring our plans to fruition. A word of thanks must also be given to the Government which has supplied the funds for this undertaking which will bring benefits to many people.

In almost every country in the world housing development has been progressing at a great rate. Here in Nigeria we have a great deal of leeway to make up. This country is on the verge of great development constitutionally, economically and socially. Let this commencement of the new housing estate be a good augury for the future. I am confident of the support of all right-thinking Nigerians in any endeavour which we may make to better the conditions of the people of Lagos.

In conclusion, I wish to thank all those who have come this morning to see this opening ceremony. I hope that before long you will be able to come to the same spot and look over a new housing estate and feel that you have played a part in improving the condition of Lagos and bringing welfare to its population. And finally, I wish to extend my appreciation to all those not present here who have made this development possible through their moral support".

Thirty years after these words, you take a look at Surulere and see that a mighty and formidable city has sprung up on the site where the turning of the sod took place on 17th November, 1954, and where there was no single building then. It is amazing! In it are many facilities, including schools, and the National Stadium. From the success of Surulere Rehousing Scheme have development towns like Festac and many other estates too many to enumerate sprung up. The slum of Lagos Island was cleared with vigour. Dredging and reclamation had since added more new space. When you look at Lagos, as the capital, you see springing up from the cleared slum, skyscrapers and modern buildings running into many floors. Citizens are better housed. They have lifted up their heads in pride.

Subsequently, Governments should borrow a leaf from what we did to succeed in slum clearance, in spite of opposition. The steps to be taken are simple and direct. First, give those concerned clear and long notices to quit the slum. Convince them it is in their own interest, because people are naturally reluctant to move away from their existing abodes, however filthy. Secondly, find an alternative residence for them. It may be far from the slum to be cleared, but they are aware there is an alternative housing, even though temporary. On the appointed day, be ready to assist in the evacuation. Thirdly, go ahead with the demolitions.

When the cleared area is re-developed, as far as possible, re-instate the inhabitants who meet the conditions for living in the new better planned estate or city.

Chapter 11

The Making Of The Nigerian Nation: The Quest For One Central Leadership; The Supreme Sacrifice; The London Conference.

In making Nigeria one nation, I want to state without fear or favour that my role stands out as one of the greatest contributions anybody could make to his political party and to the people of Nigeria.

So far efforts have been made in the right direction to strengthen the capital of Nigeria by the de-merging of Lagos from the West. It remained then to give Lagos, the capital, a leadership in government, and in place of the British Governor-General to have a Nigerian leader.

The first option under the current Constitution was to get one of the three leaders of the political parties who were all entrenched in the Regions to come to the centre. They had to contest elections which would not take place until 1959. If elections were contested and all three came to the centre, there was also the further problem of who would surrender to the other in the leadership of the Federation. Already there was an element of balkanisation and pakistanisation by the rigid regionalisation under the Macpherson Constitution. India once faced that dilemma: Pakistan for the Islamic section and India for the Hindu. The British knew all and cherished the situation.

The second option was to leave the situation to be sorted out by the two lieutenants in the Federal coalition government: Dr. Mbadiwe of the NCNC, lieutenant to Dr. Azikiwe, and Alhaji Abubakar, the lieutenant to Ahmadu Bello of the NPC.

102

Mr. Oliver Lyttleton , the Colonial Secretary, watched our dilemma. Based on what he observed, he said about the Independence of the people of Nigeria: "There must be a proof positive of the desire of the people of Nigeria for Independence, because unity has not been shown, hence no firm date for Independence can be given".

Analysing the situation, a U.K. paper, the *London Times*, wrote an editorial on August 28th, 1957 on the possibility of making a Northerner our leader. It said:-

The appointment of a Northerner as the Prime Minister *may seem strange*, since the NPC (The party with its base in the North) has only three seats in the Council of Ministers, whereas six are held by Dr. Azikiwe's NCNC having its support in the South (representing both the East and the West).

In a determination to thwart the colonial plans at sowing seeds of discord among us in the Federal Government thereby postponing our Independence date, I began assessing the situation. I deliberated over it within myself. I arrived at the conclusion that God has His way of dealing with His people. He acts through men to achieve what He wants for the people.

I said to myself, "Few years ago I returned to this country from the United States, bent on joining hands with other forces to free this country. I had convened the National Rebirth Committee which gave the NCNC the mandate to continue the struggle for Independence until it was achieved in 1956. But here we are, faced with the problem of one leader for Nigeria in order to secure that Independence. How do we solve it? Which is more important, being a leader or gaining independence?"

We were soon preparing to go to London for a Constitutional Conference for that independence. No party had taken a decision as to how a central leadership was to emerge. In the centre already there were two "I ams", as I always described it. Abubakar was an "I am", and I was another.

The former led three Ministers, the latter six. How much sense does it make for the one leading six Ministers to surrender such leadership to the one leading only three?

Voluntary Sacrifice for Nigerian Unity

I saw three options of roles left for me. First, to jettison the ambition for Prime Ministership. I had one good reason for that stand. I was not the leader of my party. It was Dr. Azikiwe. I was here in the centre, he was not, but I did not see it logical to lead him by becoming the nation's Prime Minister. Well, if that was the situation, I thought, then I had to allow God to arrange His system His own way.

One thing was clear in my mind, in order for Nigeria to have one central leadership, there was bound to be sacrifice with no pre-conditions, a sacrifice for the sake of Nigeria. This sacrifice will ensure two things. First, that there will be one united Nigeria and not a pakistanised or balkanised state. Already the danger is there. God may have arranged the Centre to put people that would make the sacrifice to bring a change. We were already involved in such a situation. But who will save us? Who will go for that sacrifice? These were the questions at issue, so that we would finish with the exercise and emerge with one leader and still have one country, not divided between religious groups. There is a reality of pakistanisation the Northern Moslem element had already made up a group in this country, the Christian South is another. The British will be satisfied that the population of each group would just be sufficient for any reasonably sized separated country.

Division was not the spirit which brought me back from the United States. I wanted a big country, bigger than the United Kingdom, and as big as the United States of America, secular and free. A price must be paid.

Secondly, since my party stood for the unity of the country, it was an eminent opportunity. It may not be easy for the party. If the involvement was between Azikiwe and another party leader, I do not think my party would agree for him to surrender to any other partisan leader to lead Nigeria in view of his seniority in Nigerian Politics. I said, perhaps that was the reason why I was involved in the exercise.

Thirdly, I also thought beyond ourselves. I thought about what my efforts and sacrifices would mean to the black Americans who look up to us. Our freedom would place them in a higher position of honour in their adopted home, in the United States. I saw them lifting up their heads in pride as we took our place in the world community of Independent states singing unto the high heavens:

"Swing low, sweet Chariot,
Come forth to carry me home".

What home? No longer a home under economic bondage, exploited and made impotent. Yes, I thought, we should welcome them inside a united and strongly fortified Africa. Only African countries that acted with one voice would inspire them to greater heights in the land which they had adopted, and give them a pride of place. So, I thought, they deserved that, and it was a challenge that we should offer them no less. That was the third reason for sacrifice. In the circumstance, therefore, we returned to a short-cut already tailored by God.

Since Dr. Nnamdi Azikiwe could not be the pre-independence Prime Minister, and I had no ambition of being Prime Minister over and above him, the next best thing was for me to make a sacrifice to achieve independence so that a new nation, Nigeria, would be born. Because, this done, the NPC would appoint a Prime Minister and a Resolution on Independence, as required by the British Government, would then be smoothly carried by the Federal Parliament.

I was in that spirit when I called on the National Secretary of my party, Chief Dr. Kola Balogun , and bared open my mind to him. As we were to go to London, I told him, we should not return home without a leader. And if no one was giving it a serious thought, I explained, I was prepared to sacrifice self ego in order to allow one Nigerian voice to emerge. It was a great sacrifice, but it was necessary that I make the sacrifice so that Nigeria could achieve a common voice, a single leader.

I pointed out to him that even though we had six Ministers and had the right to claim first place as Prime Minister at the

London Conference, we could be arousing fears and acrimony. Rather, let us buy independence for Nigeria with sweat and sacrifice. It was worth it. Then we would be a land of destiny with great heights prepared for new heights. We would have survived the British ways of thinking, and developed our own way of growth.

Chief Kola Balogun saw with me. He had been equally busy with the issue. He could not contain his happiness at the turn of events. He welcomed the decision I took. He confessed that he could not have had the courage to suggest such a stand to me. I left it to him to ask Sir Abubakar if he had given the issue any thought, and what formula he had for our London meeting. What plans had his party, the NPC?

My experience with Alhaji Abubakar had been exciting. God had put us together to work effectively for Nigeria. He always referred to me as "Speed and Magic" because he believed that whenever I understood a point I pounced on the issue with lightning speed. I also called him "The Black Rock", "the Golden Voice".

After making known my decision, it was left for Chief Kola Balogun to prepare the minds of our party men before we went to London. By the time the NCNC delegates assembled in Lagos for their journey to London, I had spoken to some members about my intention. Among them were Chief D. C. Osadebay, Dr. M.I. Okpara, and Alhaji Adegoke Adelabu. They had nothing but praises for me. At the meeting of the NEC, that momentous decision of mine was tabled as a resolution of the Party aimed at Nigerian unity and safeguarding Nigeria for posterity. We should sacrifice the Prime Ministership to the NPC and return from London as a united and indivisible Nigeria. The Party also decided that the post of Deputy Prime Minister be created.

It is true that we talked about Deputy Prime Ministership. No one made a very great issue about it. On a format of two parties in coalition, one side takes the Prime Ministership, the other, the Deputy. The sacrifice which we were called upon to make could in no way be equal to the idea of Deputy Prime Ministership. But at the London Conference most of us were greatly surprised. After the discussion on the creation of an office of the Prime Ministership, we were to move for a Deputy Prime Minister's office. But at the very moment the motion was expected, it was discovered that no one would present it. It had been withdrawn.

A report written by late Professor S.D. Onabamiro, who was appointed the Secretary of the NCNC delegation to London, summed up the situation. Extracts of the report dated March 4, 1958 read:

> When K.O. Mbadiwe arrived in London, I found that as the No. 2 man in our delegation, he was the person I had most to deal with apart from our leader. It was in these circumstances that I knew of his personal involvement in a particular memorandum that I was mandated by the delegation to send to the Conference Secretariat.
>
> The Memorandum was on the creation of the post of Deputy Prime Minister in the Federal Government. Careful lobby had ensured for our delegation the support of the powerful NPC delegation. We were therefore pretty confident that the Constitutional Conference would approve of the creation of the post, since the combined votes of the NPC and NCNC delegates at the Conference would neutralise the Action Group opposition if, indeed, they chose to oppose it.
>
> If the post was created, it would have to go to the NCNC. And since K.O. was the most senior NCNC Minister in the Federal coalition government, it goes without saying that this post was being tailor-made for him. K.O. was therefore understandably excited over the contents of the memorandum that I sent to the Conference Secretariat on my signature as Secretary to the delegation. As a personal friend of his, I too, was rather excited myself.
>
> Then the unforeseen happened. When we got to the Conference Hall we discovered that this all-important memorandum had been withdrawn. It was not on the agenda! To this day, the mystery of the disappearance of that memorandum has not been unravelled.
>
> Saddened by this episode and with the additional crises of the internal NCNC debacle on the issue of the creation of States, I left dejected, disappointed and disillusioned. I left the London Constitutional Conference before its close and returned to Ibadan to resume my research work on *Dracunculum Medinensis*, the Guinea worm.

But how did K.O. take the shock? Dr. Onabamiro then asked in his report. Let's hear him again for the answer:

This episode revealed the resilience of his (K.O.'s) character and indomitable spirit with which he is gifted. He continued to play his role as leader of the NCNC contigent in the Federal Cabinet and to discharge his party functions loyally and diligently with cheerfulness and friendship to one and all, the epitome of the man of timber and calibre.

It is indeed true that I took the issue calmly. I remained unruffled, though I realised that it was meant as a rebuff. What the others never realised was that in actual fact, I was not seeing myself in the role of a Deputy Prime Minister. I felt I would allow whoever the party appointed to take it.

We went to London, met the doubting Imperial Overseers, and won the day. We surprised them. They had predicted a schism in our rank, but we came out much sturdier. They had expected us to fight like jackals over those issues, but we told them we knew how to settle our quarrels without intervention. It was Nigeria's Golden Age, the base period from where Nigeria, as a nation took root. With that single successful resolve to create one voice, one image, one leader, the powers of the British officials in the Council of Ministers were reduced and the Prime Ministership became a reality.

The Decision and the Issue

Like Dr. Onabamiro stated, since the Constitutional Conference arose in London, Alhaji Abubakar and I had worked hard and harmoniously together. We succeeded in achieving rapport, not only of the two component parts in the coalition government, but also of minds with which we were able to agree on several national issues. Indeed, the artificial barrier between the North and the South once created by the colonial masters began to collapse, and the erstwhile British policy of separate development was put to rest.

Henceforth decisions were made and implemented in all Nigerian interest. We discussed memoranda and papers with only the interest of the nation at heart. No wonder we had a very peaceful transitional period from the London meeting until

Monday September 2, 1957 when the Prime Minister was officially inaugurated.

To achieve all these was a triumph for Nigeria, now united, indivisible and indissoluble. This is the greatest single legacy, passed on to generations yet unborn, namely, the destiny of one Nigeria which they could advance to further unprecedented heights.

The Historic Inauguration

That eventful morning will remain ever fresh in my mind. It was the day Nigeria made its first effective move towards achieving independence, for the British Government seemed set to measure our determination to remain united and peaceful, in our march towards independence.

There had been partial self-government in the South for some fourteen months, and so the nation's reaction to the appointment of a Prime Minister was being watched in London with great interest. Then in 1959, the U.K. government assured Nigeria that:-

> If a resolution was passed by the Federal Parliament early in 1960, asking for Independence, Her Majesty's Government would agree to that request, and would introduce a Bill in Parliament to enable Nigeria to become a fully Independent country on the 1st of October, 1960.

No doubt, after a year's practice, the new Nigerian Government had succeeded.

How did it happen that morning of September 2, 1957? On that day, one of the biggest crowds ever seen in Lagos, comprising all tribes, from North and South, East and West, lined up the sides of the over one-kilometre-long route from the Government House to the House of Representatives to greet the first Prime Minister of Nigeria, the late Sir Alhaji Abubakar Tafawa Balewa. As he drove round the Race Course in a new Rolls Royce, he received the tumultuous ovation of all the Nigerian peoples.

The Dawn Came

On the historic day September 2, 1957, the Governor-General of the Federation of Nigeria, Sir James Robertson, in a motion for the appointment of the Prime Minister of Nigeria, described the great Prime Minister as a man of great integrity, hardworking and blessed with abundant commonsense. The Governor-General said:

I have exercised the right given me by Section 81(1) of the Constitution to come and address the House this morning because I myself and my Ministers consider that today's meeting of the House is an important milestone in the history of Nigeria.

As a result of decisions taken at the recent Constitutional Conference in London, the Federation now has a Prime Minister whom I appointed three days ago as soon as the amendments to the Constitution enabling me to do so became Law. As you know, I am instructed in the new Royal Instructions, given me as a result of the Conference, to send for the person who appears to me to command a majority in this House. I therefore sent for Alhaji Abubakar Tafawa Balewa who leads the largest party and he has formed a Government.

Mr. Speaker, you and the honourable members of this House know Alhaji Abubakar as well as, and perhaps better than I do, and I am sure you will agree with me that in him the Federation has a Prime Minister who will command the respect and affection of all, he is a man of great integrity, hardworking and blessed with abundant commonsense. He has a heavy task ahead of him, much work lies before us all, and the problems of this country are many but the heaviest burden will fall upon him.

In congratulating him on his appointment therefore, I wish to give him my very best wishes for the future and for success in his work, and to assure him that I shall always be available if he wishes my advice and assistance. The second point I wish to make is that the Council of Ministers, over which I, or in my absence from Lagos the Deputy Governor-General will continue to preside until Independence, now contains no ex-officio members. Similarly in this House you will no longer have the benefit of their advice based on long experience of Government Service nor will some members of the House have the pleasure of heckling them and asking them awkward questions.

A Step Forward

With their departure from the Council and the House, another big step has been taken on the road to full self-government. I am sure that the work which these officers have done and the help which they have given in the past formative years have been of great assistance in the development of ministerial government in Nigeria, and for it they deserve great praise and thanks. The very fact that they can now safely be permitted to leave the Government Bench is in itself convincing evidence that they did their work well.

Now that they are no longer members of the Council, the burden of office with all its responsibilities must now be carried by Nigerian Ministers alone and I am confident that,"under the wise co-ordinating influence of the Prime Minister the new Council will prove to the world that they can do so successfully. The great majority of the new Council have already held office and are no strangers to these positions of responsibility. I feel sure their experience of affairs will be of great value in the days ahead.

It is not my duty today to make any statement of policy on behalf of my Council - the general programme of my Government for this financial year was announced last February and the new Council of Ministers has had no time to review it yet. I should like to point out that the changes which have taken place subsequent to the Constitutional Conference in the higher organisations of the Government, in full accord between Ministers and myself, have meant considerable reorganisation of the administrative machine, and the new machine may take some time to run itself in. I am sure that this will be realised and that should the engine not develop its full power immediately, you will understand the reason, and not blame the Council too severely.

It is not for me to give an opinion about the success or failure of the Constitutional Conference. Perhaps like most things in the world, its results were not absolutely perfect. But the Conference has left us all with a formidable programme of work to be done in the next two years. You will be glad to know that progress has been made in setting up the commissions which the Conference decided upon. Chairmen have been chosen for the three commissions dealing with minorities, fiscal matters and the delimitation of constituencies and three distinguished personages have accepted these appointments. I have every hope that the three main commissions will be formed and will be at work by November.

I have recently held a meeting in Lagos of the Electoral Committee of the Conference to continue work on electoral rules and regulations for Federal elections and I hope to hold a further meeting of this body before very long. I have also invited the Ministries concerned to study and submit for consideration by the Council of Ministers their views on other matters left over by the Conference, such as recommendations regarding the position of Lagos and the inquiry into the Central Marketing Board. It will be my earnest endeavour to do what I can in cooperation with the Prime Minister and Council of Ministers to ensure that all these inquiries are pressed on with expedition so that their conclusions are not delayed.

Progressing Fast

This country is progressing fast towards its national goal of independence within the Commonwealth, which has been accepted and agreed to by Her Majesty's Government in the United Kingdom. The date on which that goal will be reached does not depend solely on Her Majesty's Government, it depends equally upon the peoples and leaders of Nigeria. If they can maintain their unity of purpose, avoid disagreements and work in harmony and cooperation for that goal, its achievement will be early. The ball is at your feet and it is for you to shoot the goal.

Mr. Speaker, I believe that a great responsibility lies upon the Council of Ministers and upon this House to give a lead to the whole country. I should like to quote the recent remarks of the Under-Secretary of State for the Colonies in the House of Commons: He said: "We ought not to be mesmerised by an actual date for independence. Twenty years from now, neither the Nigerian nor we would argue whether Independence Day should have been on April 2, 1960 or on some other date close to that. All that will matter is that the country will have been well prepared for Independence when the day comes."

Mr. Speaker and Honourable Members - Let us press on with our preparations. I now wish to end on a personal note. When I came first to Nigeria in June, 1955 and took the oaths of office, I said in my address that I hoped to be able to identify myself with the aspirations of the Nigerian Peoples, and promised solemnly to do my best to serve this country.

I wish on this auspicious day to reaffirm these undertakings, and to assure you of my own personal determination to do all that lies in my power to carry out the policy agreed upon by Her Majesty's Government and the Nigerian parties at the Conference - namely that we should press on towards Independence as quickly and as surely as possible. I know that in this determination I can count upon the support of all those members in the Public Service, Nigerian and expatriate alike, who have worked and will continue to work loyally in the interests of Nigeria.

With this motion and its acceptance in the House of Representatives, the central figure we were looking for was created. By it a new spokesman and new leadership for one country and one destiny was achieved. The new Prime Minister, Alhaji, Hon. Abubakar Tafawa Balewa then addressed the House of Representatives. He said:

This is a great day for Nigeria. It marks the beginning of the last stage of our march towards independence and all of us who are here today should be thankful to Almighty God who has given us the opportunity to witness events of this most memorable time.

The next three years will see the culmination of a process which has been gathering momentum, year by year, ever since a part of what is now Nigeria first became a British Colony, 96 years ago. Many things have happened between 1861, the year of the annexation of Lagos, and 1957 the year in which two Regions in the Federation have been granted self-government, and in which the independence of the Federation itself looms large upon the horizon. We have travelled a long way and we can congratulate ourselves that after 34 years of being associated with what I may loosely call a form of Parliamentary Government, we, the people of Nigeria have reached the stage we have today. The old Nigerian Council which was established in 1923, and which survived up to 1951, though under the new name of Legislative Council could well be regarded as the foundation of this our House of Representatives. We should therefore express our thanks to those eminent Nigerians, dead and living who played so great a part in that council and who thereby made possible the important political advance which we are witnessing today.

It was in 1952 that Nigerians were appointed Ministers and so for the first time in history, Nigerian politicians became directly associated with the formulation of Government policy. Then in 1954 as a result of the constitutional discussions of 1953, Nigerian Ministers were charged with both collective and individual responsibilities over departments and other Government bodies. But to me the most important result of the Constitutional changes in 1954 was the introduction of a federal form of government for Nigeria - a system which I had advocated as far back as 1948 in the old Legislative Council.

I am pleased to see that we are now all agreed that the federal system is, under present conditions, the only sure basis on which Nigeria can remain united. We must recognise our diversity and the peculiar conditions under which the different tribal communities live in this country. To us in Nigeria, therefore, unity in diversity is a source of great strength, and we must do all in our power to see that this federal system of government is strengthened and maintained.

Today we have reached the beginning of the end of our country's political advance as a colony and protectorate. At a ceremony in this House in 1956, the leader of the United Kingdom Parliamentary Delegation, in presenting the generous gift of the mace to this House, from the United Kingdom branch of the Commonwealth Parliamentary Association, said that the mace symbolised the transfer of power. This statement is being truly fulfilled because now as a result of the 1957 Constitutional Conference which was recently held in London, Nigeria has to wait less than three years before that transfer of power is complete.

We have been given a great opportunity. What we shall make of this country after we finally assume complete control and how we shall be judged will depend upon the way we manage our affairs during this interim period. The biggest task before us today is, therefore, the work of preparing Nigeria for independence on the 2nd of April, 1960. I want everybody in the country to realise that this is by no means an easy task. It is a task that will fall, not only upon Ministers in the Federal Government and members of the House of Representatives, but also on all Ministers in the Regions and all Members of the Regional Houses of Assembly. In short it is a task for every Nigerian, because it is only by the personal effort of each individual that independence for the Federation can become a reality in 1960. It is our duty to demonstrate during this interim period that we have the capacity and the capability to rule ourselves.

Today I ask you all to give very serious thought to this most important goal of our ambition. Let us remember that we have irrevocably committed ourselves to the attainment of independence for the Federation on the 2nd of April, 1960 and if the world is to continue to take us seriously we must make every effort to see that this important aim is achieved. We must now show ourselves to be fully mature and above all we must show a sense of responsibility in whatever capacity each one of us is called upon to serve.

Nigeria has now reached a critical stage in her history and we must seize the opportunity which has been offered to us to show that we can really manage our own affairs. Every Nigerian of whatever tribe, of whatever status in life and of whatever religious belief, has his or her share to contribute in this most important and most difficult task. I appeal to all my countrymen and women to cooperate with us, the

Members of the Council of Ministers and the House of Representatives and of the Regional cabinets and the Houses of Assembly, to create a better understanding among our peoples, to establish mutual respect and trust among all our tribal groups and to unite in working together for the common cause, the cause for which no sacrifice can be too great. My colleagues and I pledge ourselves to the service of this cause and I want to assure the country of our determination to do everything in our power so that Nigeria can achieve independence in April, 1960.

Because of my firm belief in the need for national unity, I decided that the country ought to have a national government so that the major political parties, the NCNC, the Action Group, and the NPC could be closely associated with the making of policy and planning in preparation for 1960. I regard the period between now and 1960 as one of national emergency - a period in which we should bury our political differences and work together as a team so that our ambition to achieve independence may be realised.

In all this I must express my gratitude to Dr. Azikiwe, to Chief Awolowo, to Dr. Endeley and to the leader of my own party, the Sardauna of Sokoto, for their cooperation and support for my decision. It is not uncommon for parties in a country, no matter what political views they hold, to unite to work for a common cause. It was done at the time of a great national emergency by the British in 1940. It should be done by us today. Now is the time when cooperation is most essential. Let us all get together and try to forget our political differences and petty tribal jealousies and work together to create a strong and united country. I am confident that we can do so.

This then Mr. Speaker, is the first aim of the New Government's policy; to create an atmosphere of mutual trust and inter-party cooperation in which preparations for independence may go forward unhindered. But we must not remain content with this. The main object of Government whether it be government of ourselves by ourselves or government of ourselves by others is to ensure the welfare and prosperity of all sections of the population and to develop to the maximum the potential resources of the country. I assure the House that our preparations for independence will not divert the Government's attention from the necessity of carrying through to a successful conclusion the 5 - year plan of development which was approved by this House in 1955. Indeed, in my view our economic progress is part and parcel of our march towards independence. It is most important that our political independence should be backed by a really sound and stable economy. At first we shall still need financial and technical assistance and we trust that our friends abroad and in the Commonwealth will not fail us here, but in the future we ourselves must work to create a balanced and, as far as is humanly possible,   self-sufficient economy.

Mr. Speaker, I should like, on this historic occasion, to pay a warm tribute to the British statesmanship which has granted to Nigeria the opportunity which we are celebrating today. Our association with the people of the United Kingdom has been a happy one and there has always been tremendous goodwill on both sides. Their system of democratic Government has now become part of our own heritage and we should now make readjustments here and there to suit the peculiar circumstances of our country.

Nigeria's economy has been closely linked with that of the United Kingdom, and we intend to strengthen that link to the advantage of both countries. After independence, we shall continue to look first to Britian to supply those technical officers whose services we need so much. We are indeed grateful to the United Kingdom for many things and it is our desire that our association shall continue even closer than now. Truly, Sir, Nigeria speaks with one voice in the expression of its desire to remain in the British Common-wealth of Nations.

I now want to express our hearty thanks to all members of the Federal Public Service and our appreciation of the work they are doing. The stage the country has reached today has been brought about to a great extent by their sincere and loyal efforts, and no country in the world could expect to be served better than we have been. We all know that constant political changes must be a big strain on members of the civil service and that some officers may not find the new changes palatable, but I must emphasise that Nigeria has now taken this bold step forward and there is no question of going back so that now more than ever we must have the loyalty of all, be they local staff or expatriate, in helping us to make a success of this last stage before self-government is achieved. I should like to reassure all our overseas staff of our sincerity in the pledges we have given and to say to them that they need have no fears about their position under the new order.

Nigeria also owes a debt of gratitude to all those Non-Nigerian African Civil servants from what is now Ghana, from Sierra Leone and from the West Indies who have contributed so much to our success and progress.

Many other classes of people have served Nigeria well. I would particularly like to refer to the Christian Missionaries of all denominations who have done so much to encourage the development of our country. They have the distinction of being the first in the field in spreading Western education and providing our peoples with modern medical facilities. We greatly admire their efforts and we shall continue to be grateful to them for all that they are doing. Many of them are working in very remote places caring for the sick and the suffering and I want to assure them that Nigeria will never forget the work that they have done and are still doing.

Yet another group of people to whom Nigeria owes a great deal are the Commercial firms and those employed by them who have helped to build up our economy to what it is today. Many of them have sunk big sums of money in a variety of undertakings and they have thereby provided a large number of our people with employment and with the type of training which we so badly need for the future. We thank them for what they are doing and we ask them to continue to do more and if possible to increase the training facilities already provided both in technical and in managerial skills.

But, Mr. Speaker, having paid tribute to those who have helped us in the past and to those who are still assisting us today, I must return to my main theme. The future of this vast country of Nigeria depends in the main on the efforts of ourselves to help ourselves. This we cannot do if we are not working together in unity. Indeed, unity today is our greatest concern and it is the duty of everyone of us to work to strengthen it. Bitterness due to political differences will carry Nigeria nowhere and I appeal to all political leaders throughout the country to try to control their party extremists.

Nigeria is large enough to accommodate us all in spite of our political differences. It is my hope that this House will give a lead to the country. It would, I know, promote unity if members would refrain as much as possible from criticising on the floor of this House, the activities of the Regional Governments. Those Governments no doubt get ample criticism in their own Houses of Assembly and there is no need for us to add to it.

Mr. Speaker, the eyes of the world are now upon us. We have many friends and well-wishers but let us not forget that we have also enemies and that while our friends will delight in our success, our enemies would rejoice at our failure. Sometime ago I said in this House that Nigeria can exert a great influence on the affairs of the world if she is united, and none if she is not. This country has a great future and if we are careful to keep the goodwill of our friends and well-wishers, Nigeria will one day rank among the most powerful states in the world.

Mr. Speaker, God has willed that those of us who are here today are those to whom destiny has entrusted the work of seeing the country through the last stages before independence. This is an exciting time for all of us, and at a time like this we must all turn our minds to God Almighty and seek His guidance and assistance. We must be honest with ourselves and sincere in our actions. Let us not be selfish but let us try to do only what is right for the thirty three million inhabitants of this country who now expect us to guide them. I am certain that we can do so and by the grace of God we shall succeed.

Then, I made my speech to second the motion

Mr. Speaker, I deem it memorable and significant to-second this Motion so ably moved by the Prime Minister of Nigeria expressing our thanks to the Governor-General, Sir James Robertson, for his address.

Mr. Speaker, the importance of this day, September 2nd, 1957, is lost to none of us. I have seen many a day. I have witnessed and participated in many momentous occasions, but to them all this is a day of days. It is the close of an era of human degradation, intensified by colonialism and slavery. Today, this hour, we are laying the foundation stone for April 2, 1960, when the new nation now conceived emerges fully. Today, we celebrate the end of spiritual and psychological frustration. Today we have written "Finish" to periods of uncertainty as we move forward to accept the most difficult assignment of building a nation.

Today Alhaji Abubakar Tafawa Balewa emerges to accept this responsibility on our behalf. He accepts it with a ringing voice which resounded in this very chamber when he spoke during the motion demanding independence for this country. Alhaji Abubakar said: "We are the biggest African state in the world and we should regard it as a duty to bring prestige and recognition to the African wherever he may be in the world."

Challenge Accepted

Today this gallant son of Nigeria is given the opportunity to fulfil this task.

Today he is fortified and admirably recharged to accept this challenge. When he spoke on the independence motion in March of this year, there were two "I ams" in the Federal structure, there was the NCNC "I am" and the NPC "I am." Under such a climate people thought that the London Conference would not succeed in the one respect of evolving a unified leadership. People thought that tribal consideration, party advantages and ideological differences would make it impossible to accept one central spokesman.

Today we have faulted them and stultified their anticipations. There is no longer the NCNC "I am" or the NPC "I am." Today has emerged one unified leadership, one spokesman of the nation, one testing barometer of our national consciousness, the Nigerian "I am." This person is Alhaji Abubakar Tafawa Balewa, by the Grace of God, Prime Minister of Nigeria and the Cameroons.

We are determined to succeed. Who can predict the future with any accuracy? None. However, guided by the lamp-post of the past, we can examine the present and forecast the future. The activities of the last Government laid the foundation on which this present government now stands. For nearly three years that Government continued without a hitch, without a crisis but growing from strength to strength.

The NPC had three members in that Government, the NCNC six, but the NPC had a majority on the floor of the House. There were many in the NPC circle who thought that the NPC should not join' the Government under such circumstances. But the leaders of NPC with mature experience thought otherwise.

They had faith in Nigeria and in its people. The work began, and sincerity brought in sincerity. Nobleness enkindleth nobleness. Affection and devotion were generated. The two parties melted their ideologies for Nigeria's purposefulness. When the NCNC had six members in the last Government, heaven did not fall because NPC had three. Today, the NPC has supplied Nigeria its first Prime Minister. By the same calculations heaven will not fall, rather it will be strengthened.

Mr. Speaker, permit me to take this opportunity to pay tribute to our Regional Premiers and the Leader of the Southern Cameroons. Our Regional Premiers have displayed the highest of patriotic motives, in making this day possible. As leaders of the various political parties they could have thwarted our national effort, by postponing the creation of a leadership in the centre. They were great, and magnanimous enough to put the country in the forefront, before anything else.

I wish to assure them that by this act, they have earned an indelible niche in Nigerian history. No person can be truly great who has not shared in making others great or sharing in the hour of their triumph. Their presence today has given added foundation to this structure.

Idealism Shared

Dr. Azikiwe is not here today, but the weight of his Government is here. The Eastern Government is fully represented. But more than this Dr. Azikiwe shares in the idealism of the Prime Minister in the formation of this National Government. The Prime Minister in his speech has thanked Dr. Azikiwe for his support in this direction.

What is uppermost in Dr. Azikiwe's mind and in the minds of all of us is that no sacrifice will be too great for the realisation of our independence on April 2, 1960. The Prime Minister has made this objective the cardinal principle of his Government.

We are with you in the march towards our independence on April 2, 1960. We will not look back. We will not withold anything. We will all go into the field to prove to the world that Nigeria can accept and follow one leader.

Mr. Speaker, I pay tribute to our colleagues in the last Government. These stalwarts had shown that politics is a noble science in the affairs of mankind. Through their efforts, their tolerance, devotion, understanding, and passion for Nigeria, this day has been possible.

To you Alhaji Abubakar Tafawa Balewa, the Prime Minister, this is your day in the political history of this country. I share with you personally this your hour of triumph. When I styled you the "Black Rock" after one and a half years of working with you, I know the stuff you are made of.

Unpretentious, industrious and always equable, you are the leader whom we are all sure will fully justify the trust and confidence which not only this House, but the entire Nation, has placed in you.

The Prime Minister, later the same day in the evening, addressed the nation. The address was carried by the national dailies. The next day, the *Daily Times* of September 3, 1957, published what Dr. Nnamdi Azikiwe had to say under the headline: Zik says, Balewa has my support.

Dr. Nnamdi Azikiwe, Premier, Eastern Nigeria had promised the new Prime Minister, Alhaji Abubakar Tafawa Balewa his "whole hearted support" as long as he does not compromise fundamental issues affecting the independence of the country not later than April 2nd, 1960.

In a telegram to Alhaji Abubakar yesterday, Dr. Azikiwe congratulated him on the assumption of his "high office".

He said that all those who had faith in the capacity of the African to guide and control his destiny would appreciate "your very wise decision to form a National Government in which all major political parties were represented.

This course of action would minimise unnecessary friction usually caused by squabbles and bickering that were mainly political in nature, he added.

Dr. Azikiwe continued, "Having removed the potential obstacle to our unanimous struggle for complete independence in 1960, you have my unqualified support because the objective of all true patriots of Nigeria, is one united country, speaking with one voice through a strong centre.

Permit me to remind you that history has presented you with a glorious opportunity to salvage Nigeria from political degradation. No doubt your way will be strewn with man-made barriers, but God will give you strength to hurdle over them and you will pull through.

The Prime Minister takes over from the Governor-General

Following his appointment, all the white officials in the cabinet resigned. Nigerians were appointed to take over the Council of Minsiters. The Prime Minister had two years to work uninterruptedly, until the general election under the new Constitution drawn up at the London Conference. Proclamation of Independence was later set for October 1st 1960, instead of April.

In the 1959 general election all the three political parties contested. Each party wanted to appoint the next Prime Minister in succession to Sir Abubakar Tafawa Balewa. The NPC sponsored the incumbent Prime Minister to succeed himself. The NCNC put up Dr. Azikiwe as its own standard bearer for the office and the Action Group backed Chief Awolowo. The result was that each party won where it held away; the NPC won in the North, the NCNC won in the East and the A.G. won in the West and so there was no overall majority for the NPC to retain the incumbent Prime Minister.

The Action Group picked up the loophole and offered to go into coalition with the NCNC. If that was done, both the East and the West would hold the majority. The Action Group surrendered the Prime Ministership to Dr. Azikiwe. Here was another lesson I want the country to learn. Philosophy is very important in the life of any nation. Any nation without a guiding philosophy cannot succeed or have a prosperous future.

The NCNC and its leadership have been committed to one and indivisible nation, Nigeria, and it had been clear, how, as its Parliamentary Leader, I made the great sacrifice that brought the premiership to the NPC. On that, I was guided with the ideals of my Party which stood for the oneness of the country.

When the plan of the Action Group was thrown open, we discovered that it would not fit into the noble philosophy of the NCNC. The move was not implemented. However there were some selfish politicians who were in the House for selfish interest, who suggested, "let us go into a coalition with the AG." Dr. Azikiwe was above that. To the party he led, he applied the same principle of one nation which I applied as his deputy in the Federal Parliament. He turned the AG offer down.

During the row over the 1963 census figures which threatened the break up of the Federation, a Northern Nigerian Minister of Agriculture, Alhaji Ahman Galadima Pategi, veered away from the controversy and abused Dr. Nnamdi Azikiwe, then the President of the Federal Republic, by saying that he (Dr. Azikiwe) "the predecessor of the present Premier of Eastern Nigeria (i.e. Dr. M.I. Okpara) lost his seat in the Eastern House of Assembly in the attempt to become the Prime Minister of the Federation."

Zik took exception and hit back. In a telegram despatched to the Minister, he warned against "any attempt to bring chaos and disaster to the country." The Premier of the North, Sir Ahmadu-Bello, the Sardauna of Sokoto, apologised to Zik on behalf of the mouthy Galadima.

Dr. Azikiwe used the occasion to restate why he refused Awolowo's offer and preferred a coalition with the NPC. The *Daily Express* of 9th March, 1964 bannered a headline, and reported the content of Zik's telegram, part of which read:

Since I am the predecessor of the second Premier of Eastern Nigeria, and I have no tangible reason to question the accuracy of this world famous News Agency (Reuters) despatch, I am obliged to join issues with you .... What you are alleged to have said about me is false in two respects.

Firstly, I resigned my seat when I was elected to the House of Representatives and I had to resign this as well on my election to the Senate as its first President according to the coalition agreement.

Secondly, I declined the offer of the Action Group to become the first Prime Minister of an Independent Nigeria by forming a coalition between the NCNC and the Action Group, because I personally believed that a coalition between the NCNC and the NPC would bring in an element of stability in the country. It is not true as some misguided Nigerians and misinformed Anglo-American writers have deduced that I declined this offer under duress...

The NCNC rejected the overtures of the Action Group and the Alliance of the NCNC and the NPC continued which gave Abubakar another lease of office. This is the end of the first phase of the march towards the new Nation.

Chapter 12

The NCNC Crisis And Its Aftermath

We all in the NCNC had grown to admire the fervour of nationalism, the captivating oratory and the gallantry of Dr Nnamdi Azikiwe. For me, he was in addition, a close family friend, a mentor and a guardian. Under his inspiration, I went to the United States to study. His paper, *The West African Pilot* frequently and copiously reported favourably my activities while in the United States, the cause of the African Academy of Arts and Research and of the Greater Tomorrow ventures.

No third party qualifies to give a full view of the NCNC crisis of 1957/58 more than the principal actors themselves. The disagreements were on principle and never on personal relationships. As our teacher, mentor and hero, Zik would have been disappointed and irked if his lieutenants perceived what they considered wrong and failed to react.

The NCNC crisis of 15th June, 1957 was no personal quarrel between me and Azikiwe. In fact, the event was rather "Zik must not go" abroad which he planned for 17th June, 195? to stay for some four months, while a lot that could destroy the NCNC as a party remained unattended to at home. If Zik goes who comes? If Zik threatened: "I will go," Mbadiwe would be the first to reply, "Whither goeth thou, Rabbi?"

The genesis of the crisis can be traced to the report of the Fuster Commission of Inquiry set up by the Colonial Office to probe the affairs of the African Continental Bank (ACB) Although, the Commission agreed that the purpose of establishing the ACB was to "liberalise credit to Africa businessmen", it found Dr. Azikiwe's conduct in injecting publi funds into a private bank owned by him as wrong and "falling short of conduct expected of public officers." Dr Azikiwe, as Premier of Eastern Region was faced with resignation, as was the case when NCNC pressed for and obtained the resignation of Alhaji Adegoke Adelabu whom the Nicholson Commission indicted in his conduct as Chairman of Ibadan Municipal Council.

While reporting the verdict of the Fuster Sutton Commission at the Rex Cinema, Onitsha, Zik openly wept. I rose up and declared, "Wipe your tears. We are still alive. Mr. Lenox Boyd (the colonial Secretary) cannot rule this Region for us from London. The voice of the people will rule. We shall show you that you have loyal followers who will never see you disgraced."

With speed, I moved to the Eastern House. I discussed with the members and proposed a motion that the House be dissolved to allow for fresh elections to demonstrate our confidence in Zik. It was agreed that the Ministers who were returned would be given back portfolios, and that any member who suffered unduly because of the dissolution, having just a year before, contested elections, should be rehabilitated. NCNC members of the House contributed money both for the Fuster Sutton Tribunal and the fresh elections. It was also agreed that the ACB should be nationalised.

The elections came and went. The NCNC won, though with a reduced majority. Dr. Azikiwe was reinstated as the Premier of the Eastern Region. But not all the Ministers were reinstated, nor was the ACB nationalised. I did everything constitutionally possible to make Zik rescind his decision and call back the sacked Ministers. All to no avail.

Then the Ikpeazu Commission was set up in 1955 to look into allegations of corruption by public officers. Before submitting its report, the Chairman, Mr. Justice Chuba Ikpeazu, went ahead during the sittings, to pass judgement against Hon. Mazi Mbonu Ojike and Hon. M.C. Agwu. Humiliated and broken hearted, Ojike died in November 1957. And when the report was submitted to Government, it took two years (November 22nd, 1957) for Government to comment and indeed reject it. The editorial on this issue in the *Daily Times* of November, 25 1957 said it all;

> "A good many people will find the Eastern Nigeria handling of the Ikpeazu Report baffling ...
> To begin with the Ikpeazu Report should have been published as soon as it was received. One would have thought that a document of such importance, affecting as it apparently did, the fortunes of prominent people in the Region's public life, would have been treated with the urgency that it deserved. But the government right from the start only aroused unwanted misgivings by refusing to make any comment on the matter. Now, nearly two years after the report was submitted, the Government has turned round to say that the Commission failed "in several respects in their duty under the law" and that no useful purpose would be served by publishing it. No useful purpose to the Region? To Mr. Micheal Awgwu and Late Mbonu Ojike or to whom?"

The Premier, who was also the Minister for Local Government injected twenty three traditional Chiefs into the Onitsha Town Council, thereby sparking off a confrontation between the Onitsha and non-Onitsha Igbos. The other town Councils of Enugu, Aba and Port Harcourt did not have such provision.

In February 1958, the Eastern Region Universal Free Primary Education collapsed, while the Action Group-free education in the West flourished. As a result there were riots in parts of Eastern Nigeria for which the Governor-General declared a state of emergency on nine administrative divisions of the Eastern Nigeria.

As all these were going on, our rival political parties were not sleeping. The Northern Peoples Congress (NPC) was expanding and waxing stronger in the North. The Action Group was sweeping the West. The National Council of Nigeria and the Camerouns (NCNC) was grappling with many problems, while our National President became more and more aloof. The pre-independence elections of 1959 were around the corner.

In the heat of the preparations *vis-a-vis* what other political parties were doing, Zik was to embark on an overseas travel that would last up to four months. Most of us objected to that.

But none of us would think of toppling or unseating Zik. If anybody had such an ambition, the Fuster Sutton Report offered a chance. The Reform Committees resolution was merely to emphasise that bonds must be kept, party interest must be uppermost, and individual members must be protected. The method may not be perfect, but it was necessary that it should happen, so that history would be fulfilled. And God has His own way of shaping history.

The crossroads were arrived at on 15th June 1957. After touring the North, passing through Ibadan to see Adelabu's family, Zik arrived at Lagos to preside over a NEC meeting. His tone was most conciliatory. But Dr. O.N. Egesi, while thanking the National President for the appeal to close ranks, nevertheless said that, before any dirt could be swept under the carpet, it was necessary to read the proposals for NCNC reform. Zik flared up. The atmosphere was charged. Many, including myself walked out. Zik turned round, checked the quorum and continued the meeting.

Perhaps, it was God's design that we walked out. Had we stayed, Zik would have turned and threatened to resign. And I, as the Deputy, would immediately say, no. And perhaps the actual reforms and reinvigoration of the NCNC which followed could have been lost.

Thirty one leaders met separately and signed the NCNC reform document. But Zik had his trump card. He was a boxer who knew where to apply the knock-out blow. He sought and got extraordinary powers as President of the NCNC. He was incumbent Premier of Eastern Region Government where the NCNC held sway. He was owner of the African Continental Bank from which many signatories had taken loans. His party, the NCNC nominated the six Federal Ministers, two of whom, myself and Kola Balogun, signed the reform document.

I resigned from the cabinet on 26 July, 1958. The Prime Minister, Sir Abubakar must accept the resignation. His party the NPC, and NCNC ran the coalition government and, in spite of his personal relationship with me, he must heed to the NCNC as a party.

Zik postponed his overseas tour and mounted a counter offensive. People came to me and said, "Withdraw your signature. Apologise." My colleagues who understood me knew I would rather resign than give in to humiliation. I become stronger when I fight issues. I accepted the challenge. I pressed that I wanted the NCNC reformed and nothing more.

On July 31st, 1958 a delegation of seven members of the NCNC, led by Chief T. O. S. Benson and Mr. Jaja Wachukwu called on the Inspector-General of Police, Mr. C.S.K. Bovell, and made grave allegation that a plot existed to murder Dr. Azikiwe.

On August 9th, in the House of Representatives, the Prime Minister, Alhaji Tafawa Balewa, declared that "there was no substantial evidence of any plot to assassinate Zik. Nobody said he had personal knowledge, except rumours".

Life is mysterious, more so as we never know what the future holds. I had no plans. Soon after my resignation as a Minister, a position highly-priced then, my cousins, Chief L.N. Obioha and Chief C.N. Obioha came down to Lagos. They said, "Rise. We must clear away your belongings from the Government quarters before any one else could come to do so on orders." Chief J. Green Mbadiwe gave instructions for me to move into his mansion at 113 Hundred Foot Road, Aba. I occupied the whole compound. I was better housed than even when I was a Government Minister and occupied government quarters.

The turning point was at Onitsha. When I left Lagos for the East to go to settle in Aba, I arrived at the Onitsha ferry. I was surprised at the mammoth crowd that had assembled to receive me as a hero of a liberated conscience. I did not know that the disagreements in the NCNC and the cause I had championed caught people's interest and rapt attention. Spontaneously, the Iweka brothers (Dr. and Engineer Iweka) the Onitsha merchants led by Chiefs J. Nwafor, A.A. Nwizu, Augustine Umeh, S.I. Ajih and many others had arranged for my reception at Onitsha. The admirers carried me shoulder high from the ferry to an open car at the head of a motorcade which stretched two miles to the reception ground. Songs were composed and sung. It was amazing.

In their address, read by Engineer I.R. Iweka, now the Igwe of Obosi, they said,

> "We have come to welcome your bravery, in stating your mind, and agreed that you did well to resign. We shall fight for your independent greatness. You must not stop. We shall see you through. This will stop the crucifixion of any one who criticises the NCNC." The crowd chorused, "Aye!"

What started like a play, led to the organisation of a political party called, the Democratic Party of Nigeria and the Camerouns (D.P.N.C.). It was launched on August 4th, 1958. Its motto was "Forward ever, Backward never".

There is no doubt that the NCNC was a rock of Gibralter in Igboland. Orlu, my own constituency stood for NCNC, but they still regarded me first as their son and leader. Chief Gregory Agbasiere put it more succinctly. "K.O., our good son, you are our leader, but not outside NCNC." Yet many said "K.O. we will sail or sink with you."

But the tide immediately changed when I accepted the overtures of the Action Group (A G). Chief Obafemi Awolowo had come with all his might to support us. As soon as I aligned with Awo, many said, no; but Iweka and others stood firm.

How did the DPNC fare?, one would ask. It was a herculian task. People were aware that anyone who was against Zik, right or wrong, was easily rooted out. Therefore, the first challenge was, "who is your audience?" This became the primary task of the DPNC as a party. But it soon proved to be equal to that task.

First a revolutionary body was organised. Their members were called "Demo Guards". They were accoutred in brightly coloured uniforms with staff to match. Some served as outriders on motor cycles. Youths were drawn into it. Their rallies compelled audience. Secondly, songs composed told tales of the extravagance and other true sordid stories of the NCNC government of the East. The battle was between the cock and the elephant, symbols of the NCNC and the DPNC respectively, where the elephant reigned supreme. Thirdly, the merchants and well-to-do members provided their cars and other vehicles so that any movement appeared like a universal military campaign. With all these logistics, we proceeded to capture the four NCNC cities of Onitsha, Enugu, Aba and Port Harcourt. The long cars of DPNC excited these people and frightened the NCNC members. We grew in confidence to be able to give advance notice to the towns of our arrival. The traders and crowds of Onitsha and Aba joined us in the procession to any area where we addressed rallies.

To enter Enugu, it was necessary to plan in detail because it was the seat of the NCNC controlled government. Ministers, on hearing of our arrival deserted the city, obviously to avoid responsibility for the result of any fracas. The day arrived. We amassed our men and cars, stretching two miles from Ngwo down the Milikin Hill. I stood in an open car, waving my wide feather-fan to the crowd. The Demo Guards cleared the way and the field where I was to address the rally. Chief C.C. Onoh organised his NCNC men to distract us. We were unmoved. I spoke at length and the rally peacefully dispersed at the end.

In Port Harcourt the story was different. The Premier had complained to the police of our success and his discomfiture. The Police stopped us four miles to Port Harcourt. The Police said they had orders not to allow us in. We argued for many hours. The great issue was the uniform of the Demo Guards. The Demos disembarked and trooped out, downcast. They were not allowed to enter the place they had so well prepared to show our strength.

I addressed them, "Gentlemen, take away your uniforms. Behold your velvet, skins. What else do you need in life. You will move into "Pitakwa", without the uniforms. We must enter.

Songs were rendered. The youths pulled out their dresses. They all joined in their bare body and ebony skin and entered the rally ground. I gave the signal and they struck and cleared the field. I was heard in silence.

When the 1959 general elections came, the DNPC was barely one year old. The DPNC as a party contested several seats. We lost. But the audience we mustered won. The principle we stood for won. Democracy won.

Reconciliations

One may ask, were any moves towards reconciliation between the two erstwhile good friends and colleagues made to patch up their differences and become unified? Yes, there were various moves even before the general elections, but tempers had risen too high to heed those reconciliatory moves.

There was also the very fact that Chief J. Green Mbadiwe, my brother, and a great bosom friend of Dr. Azikiwe, was outside Nigeria when these battles of principles took place. He returned to find that things had gone out of hand, otherwise, there would have been an early strong move to resolve issues before they got escalated. There were other peace moves within each party hierarchy which indicated that time had come for the internal fight to stop, and all to face the future with optimism. The most striking peaceful move which caught the ear of both sides was that made by the President of Ghana, Late Dr. Kwame Nkrumah who made it clear to both sides that Africans needed the service of both of us. He said it was not the time for us to fight and separate the ranks. He made the approach through his Ambassador to Nigeria who contacted Dr. Azikiwe. Dr. Nkrumah made it clear that he was intervening personally in the matter. Though, he could not come to Nigeria, his Foreign Minister, Mr. Ako Adjei represented him with the Ghanian

Ambassador to Nigeria. Dr. Nnamdi Azikiwe of course, welcomed this move. So did I.

In all fairness, Dr. Azikiwe was not happy about what had happened; nor myself. One wondered how I, as the main peace maker of the NCNC, who was sent on all missions of peace and unity could be involved in a move that split the party. Many could not contemplate it. So, when I was notified of Nkrumah's move, I welcomed it. The meeting for this reconciliation was to be held at Dr. Nnamdi Azikiwe's office. As the President of the Nigerian Senate, his office was selected and no other person than himself, myself and the two leaders from Ghana were to be there. The Foreign Minister of Ghana flew in the evening before and the next morning the meeting started.

Even though there were party hierarchy within the Assembly grounds, they were not informed or allowed in. The thing went quietly. At 10 a.m that morning we all assembled. Of course, there was nothing than for both of us to embrace each other. Two good friends that were being separated over principles. Not one of us could point to a personal interest in what had turned into a disruptive force.

Zik opened. The Foreign Minister of Ghana brought his message from Dr. Kwame Nkrumah. Dr. Nkrumah had sent him to say that two of us should come to a complete understanding and move on as we used to. We had a duty to Nigeria and Africa. If we continued, we could have lost every gain which we made for Nigeria's freedom. In God's name, he urged us to reconcile and move on as before. Mr. Ako Adjei asked if any of us had anything to say. Dr. Azikiwe had nothing to say than praises for me, what I have been and what I have done. I had nothing to say about Dr. Azikiwe than praises for his leadership, for his quality, for his devotion and sense of commitment all along. We regarded what had happened as an act of God because there was a silver lining in that murky cloud of the past few months.

In thirty minutes, it was all over. We embraced again and parted. Zik prepared and left the next day for Ghana and I also

nt Nkrumah a message, through Zik, that reconciliation had
:en concluded. We wanted Nkrumah and his lieutenants also in
e same spirit to reconcile, so that the work started also in
hana could be completed without disruption.

irty Merger

ollowing the reconciliation between Dr. Azikiwe and myself,
e next issue was the reconciliation between the NCNC as a
rty and the DPNC. The Deputy Secretary General of the
CNC, Chief I.O. Dafe said of the peace that returned, "We are
t to look for the victor or the vanguished. We will treat all as
:onciled." The DPNC was dissolved and all its members
admitted into the NCNC.

There had been newspaper reports and publications of what
d happened and how all sides were reconciled. Nevertheless, I
)orted in detail personally to close aides like Engineer Iweka,
ief Awolowo who gave us support and to the Orlu people,
/ home base.

Engineer Isaac Iweka was not a soap-box politician. Rather
was a practical philosopher, besides being a construction
gineer. He had come out in full force to support the cause. He
w in the DPNC what he described as "democratic
lependence" for the first time in Nigeria.

Before the NCNC crisis, opposition was ruthlessly crushed
/ where. Iweka felt that with such a trend, all African nations
ght in time go one party state, a situation he saw as "perpetual
prisonment of the individual." An opposition was necessary,
only because it kept the ruling party on its toes, but because it
/e the people a hope of an alternative government. That was
at the DPNC had done *vis-a-vis* the NCNC in Eastern
;eria, and the country at large Iweka then said:

"No longer would any individual believe that every one else must be tied
to his apron strings".

when I told him of the complete reconciliations, he praised
magnanimity and sporting spirit of myself and Dr. Azikiwe,

blessed the peace that returned, and added: "The point has be
made"

When I reported to Chief Obafemi Awolowo, his reacti
was a disdain of the rapport. Perhaps, he would have wanted
schism to continue, so as to reap any political advantages fr
it. Later, he sued me in court as Dr. Mbadiwe for grant of mor
which he made to the DPNC. That case failed. It came up a
point when he was also quarrelling with his deputy and so
national officers of the Action Group, such as Chief Ayo Ro
the National Secretary. It also failed because it was a party
party affair, and not Mbadiwe versus Awolowo, as contained
his statement of claim.

Chief Awolowo admitted later in life that this financ
assistance was rendered to the DPNC as a party, and not to I
K.O. Mbadiwe as an individual. In his *Adventure in Pov
Book II* (*The travails of Democracy and the Rule of La*
published by Evans, 1987, at page 7 he stated:

> Dr. K.O. Mbadiwe sought alliance of his Party (DPNC) with the A.
> and wanted financial assistance well, we gave him both.

The Aftermath

After my reconciliation with Zik and a return to the Party
major social event took place. I invited Zik for the christen
ceremony of my youngest son, the now late Udokac
Mbadiwe. Zik, evidently having our past quarrel at the back
his mind, said in his short address before the naming of
child: "What keeps K.O. alive and going is "OBIOMA' (mean
"Clean Heart"). Because of his clean heart and clean spirit at
times, I give this son of his the name "OBIOMA"as a remin
of his father's nature. Hon. Ribadu, the then Minister
Defence, was also in that naming ceremony which took place
my residence at No. 9 Liverpool Road, Apapa. It was
occasion for socially ceiling a formal reconciliation.

Another major event was at the inaugural meeting and fu
raising dinner for the Ojike Memorial Medical Centre at
Federal Palace Hotel. On that occasion, Zik was the chairm

The Prime Minister, Alhaji Abubakar, was the speaker. All the Premiers attended. It was a reunion gathering, and Zik gave his massive support for the Medical Centre in honour of the memory of the late Mazi Mbonu Ojike. By that sheer attendance and support, all that passed between Zik and Ojike was written off as one of those sorry spots in history, which people come across, not out of bad intention, but out of the tides and fortunes of life.

On subsequent events later, Zik knew and understood why and how K.O. took his stand on issues. In spite of our great family and personal relationship, in spite of my worshipping Zik as my hero and mentor, if need be for me to disagree with him on principle, I did not hesitate to do so. That was why in London in August 1969, I spoke against his reneging our stand on the Nigeria/Biafra war. In the heat of political campaigns in 1983 (we were in different political parties) for the impending general elections, I spoke and reminded him of the dangers of hobnobbing with Awo in the PPA/PPP alliance. I was just being myself. It is not unusual for close friends to sometimes disagree.

Writing about the Great Mahtama Ghandi of India and his close aide, the towering Jawaharlal Nehru, Mrs Dorothy Norman (Nehru's biographer) said:

> Despite their profound attachment to each other, the relationship between these two remarkable men was by no means ever a simple one. Inevitable differences of opinion were bound to arise between personalities of such remarkably divergent temperaments. Yet, although, both Ghandi and Nehru wrote with candour and sadness about their periodic disagreements, each was to cherish the other with utmost devotion to the very end of Ghandi's life.
>
> It may even be that their dialogue was to be quite significant to each other, as was the love they have for each other, and that it was of equal moment in shaping the destiny of India.

This last comment recalls to my mind the remarks of the late Alhaji Abdul Aziz Attah, one time Permanent Secretary in the Federal Civil Service. He confronted me in 1970, soon after the end of the Nigerian civil war, saying, "Had you and Zik not quarrelled in 1957/58, the history of Nigeria would have been different from what it is today." I was flabbergasted and wondered what he meant. But he went on: "If you had not allowed your ranks to be broken into, inconsequential opportunists, mediocres and people who did not value your sacrifices in building one strong, united Nigeria, would not have dug in and taken positions of power and responsibility which they mismanaged." He promised to expatiate this theme in a book. Unfortunately, he did not live to publish the work.

On personal relationships, Zik has spanned my life from my departure to the U.S. in 1938, to my wedding in 1950, and to the naming ceremony in 1962. On the political level he had schooled us to carry the credo of one Nigeria, and sing the song of unity in diversity. For this I have always been disposed to offer sacrifices, even where other politicians would say, let me taste that power for one day, whether Nigeria remains one or not. Take the question of the pre-independence Prime Ministership, considered earlier. Under the influence of the learning and lessons from Zik, my party was pleased, for the sole purpose of achieving independence and oneness of Nigeria, to surrender to the NPC, even though my party had the majority (six out of nine) in the Council of Ministers. The question of the Deputy Prime Minister was to come up at the London Constitutional Conference. I expected my party leader to champion it. But it was withdrawn. I knew Zik's style. Perhaps he was irked that I did not discuss that earlier with him. Nor have I done so ever since. My belief is that the Deputy Prime Ministership is of inferior and minor consequence to the big sacrifice already made.

Zik offers similar sacrifices for the preservation of the entity called Nigeria, like when Chief Awolowo surrendered the Prime Ministership to him following the 1959 elections. He would have readily accepted. But he calculated that the alliance would have amounted to South versus North. The confrontation could have led to a postponement of independence. That we abhored.

The foregoing explains why the reconciliations after the NCNC schism was very smooth and easy. As the *Headlines* of 10th January, 1974, put it, "Politics is one exciting game, in

which the player may be friends one day and "enemies" the next
... like the confrontation between Herbert Macaulay and Henry
Carr; Ernest Ikoli and Samuel Akisanya; Zik and H.M. Foot
(Chief Secretary to Government in the Legislative Council). But
as a rule the duellists buried their hatchet shortly after the fight."
For me and Zik it was no duel, it was a brotherly controversy.

Part III

The First Republic

Sharing pleasantries with a long-time friend of Nigeria and Africa, Chief A. G. Leventis. Also in the picture are (L to R). Mrs. Ashamu (Standing), Mrs. C.N. Mbadiwe (Sitting) Chief E.O. Ashamu and Dr. K.O. Mbadiwe.

At the launching, in 1962, of a monument for the "Boycott King," Ojike Memorial Medical Centre. Dr. Nnamdi Azikiwe addresses the audience. Sitting (L to R) are Rt. Hon. Dr. M.I. Okpara, Mrs Flora Azikiwe, Sir Abubakar Tafawa Balewa and Dr. K.O. Mbadiwe.

Mr David Flemming, former Managing Director, Shell BP, inspecting the grounds of Ojike Memorial Medical Centre built by contributions from Shell and other organisations, individuals and governments in and outside Nigeria.

With Alhaji Ado Bayero and Igwe D. Nwandu on the occasion of the opening of the Palace of the People, Arondizuogu, 1965.

The soap box. At a typical campaign rally.

Arriving at the International Trade Fair in Vienna, Austria, as Minister of Trade and Leader of the Nigerian contingent.

Celebrating the creation of Mid-western Region in 1964.(L to R) Chief D.C. Osadebay (First Premier) Dr. K.O. Mbadiwe, Sir Francis Akanu Ibiam (Governor Eastern Nigeria) and Dr. M. I Okpara (National President of NCNC and Premier Eastern Nigeria).

Chapter 13

Independence For Nigeria, 1960, Adviser on African Affairs.

On October 1st, 1960, Nigeria attained her Independence, a glorious culmination of nationalists' struggles. The day was celebrated with pomp and pageantry, the nation was full of merited jubilation. For me it was an event of personal satisfaction.

Nigeria watched the lowering of the Union Jack (the British Flag) and the hoisting of the Green-White-Green (the Nigerian Flag). As Sir James Robertson was stepping out as the last of the British Governor-Generals. Dr. Nnamdi Azikiwe rose to that position as the first and only Nigerian Governor-General of the Independent State of Nigeria.

At this juncture, it is just and timely to mention one of the private sector leaders in the economic life of Nigeria who steadily shared our aspirations for self-government and who was prepared to offer his own share of sacrifice for Nigeria's greatness. I have in mind Mr. A.G. Leventis, founder of the Leventis Group, operating in West Africa, including Nigeria. He died in 1978. I have briefly mentioned him earlier.

The late Chief Leventis was a Greek but he was more of a Nigerian, because he spent the glorious part of his life in the service of our country, Nigeria, and its people. It is therefore an irony of fate or birth that Leventis should be born a Greek. Probably, he should have been born a Nigerian but, when nature could not make this possible, he was sent as an economic ambassador to the people of this country and Africa in general.

141

Although, he started trading in Nigeria in 1937, my first contact with him was made in Ghana in 1948. The meeting was a memorable occasion indeed, as it was equally historical in the life of Ghana. It was on my way back from the United States, when I stopped to see my former classmate, the late Dr. Kwame Nkrumah of Ghana who introduced him to me for the first time.

It was a period when Ghana (formerly Gold Coast) was bedevilled with widespread confusion and rioting as a result of which several departmental stores were either looted or locked-up, and the whole country looked desolate. But one shop remained open, looking like a surviving hut in a city ravaged by war.

I could not refrain from asking the late Dr. Kwame Nkrumah whom the owner of the shop was and why it was not affected by the widespread rioting. It was then that I gathered from Dr. Kwame Nkrumah that Chief Leventis' shop was allowed to open because of his immense contribution to the Ghanaian economy and the great love he had shown to the Ghanaian people.

It was from this point that my esteem for the man began to rise. I soon discovered that his strength was rooted in his desire to share in the aspirations of the people with whom he must live to work. That is the sum total of A.G. Leventis, the man.

The Late Chief A.G. Leventis therefore became the pioneer of trade and general economic prosperity of both Ghana and Nigeria. Thus Chief Leventis was not only interested in trade but also loved Nigeria and the Nigerian people. In fact, the truth must be told that in those days when most other merchants still had their merchandise on wooden sheds, he had already started to build concrete buildings as stores. The sum total of these pioneering trading activities in Nigeria has given rise to the chain of companies established by this great son of Greece which now make up the "Leventis Group" today. The fruits of his noble labour have contributed in no mean degree in providing employment opportunities to thousands of Nigerians.

When I was a Federal Minister charged with the responsibilities of providing accommodation for all the guests attending the Nigerian Independence Celebrations in October 1, 1960, hotel accommodation was particularly more acute than it is today, and Chief Leventis again played another worthy role. All contractors of repute in the country were invited to undertake the building of the Premier Hotel at its chosen site at the Victoria Island. Most declined to take it up because time was running out as the Independence Celebration was already knocking at the door. Irrespective of the limited time, I appealed to Chief Leventis personally to come to our rescue. As usual, he saved us from this national predicament and embarrassment. Before long, he flew in both men and materials from abroad and completed what is known today as the Federal Palace Hotel before schedule, fully furnished with all necessary equipment.

It must be mentioned that at the time the hotel was taken over by the Federal Government, Chief Leventis did not fail to express his dissatisfaction about the colossal financial loss he suffered. Yet in his usual spirit of love for Nigeria and her people, he displayed a rare spirit of magnanimity and maturity of mind, with bitterness towards none. He got over the rude shock quickly with manly courage and went into new ventures with remarkable successes.

As a true mark of honour and appreciation for his selfless services for this country, His Highness, the Alake of Egbaland in Abeokuta, conferred on him a Chieftaincy title of Babalaje of Egbaland. This is a pointer to the fact that Chief Leventis' greatness and good deeds did not start and end with Lagos alone but cuts across the length and breadth of Nigeria.

Adviser On African Affairs

Soon after independence, the Prime Minister, the Rt. Hon. Sir Abubakar Tafawa Balewa appointed me his Adviser on African Affairs. It was a challenge which brought the reminiscence of my activities in the African Academy and of my dream of independent, free and united Africa. I quickly swung into action.

Meanwhile, there had grown two groups of Pan-African Organisations. They were referred to as the Monrovia Group, led by Nigeria and the Casablanca Group, led by Nkrumah's Ghana. My first major outing was to accompany the Prime Minster to the Monrovia Group meeting in Monrovia, Liberia, in May 1961. I drew an analogy of the then African situation with what happened in Nigeria in the days of the Nigerian Youth Movement, the NCNC and other nationalist groups, for which I had to organise the Committee on National Rebirth, in order to channel the efforts of the leaders to face one common foe. Every speaker in Monrovia agreed that it was wrong for Africa to break into two. It became uppermost in their minds to build one strong central African Organisation. On return home I met the press and commented as follows:

> First of all the Monrovia Conference was a triumph in ceremonial pomp and pageantry reminiscent of Africa in the ancient days. It was even more than this. Conscious of the past degradation of Africa by European powers through partition for and among themselves, the delegates armed with their newly won political power came determined not only to make history but to rewrite history. And that was accomplished. What happened in Monrovia was a revival and rebirth of New Africa. Sir Abubakar, in a mood of great inspiration, told his cheering delegates that they were converting the misfortunes of history into the greatest advantage for Africa. He reminded them that Europeans divided Africa into sections under their domination, but today these sections have fallen back into the hands of Africans. Such a large continent that would have been most difficult for one man to rule effectively and efficiently is now ruled by several brothers gathered at Monrovia. By each leader bringing wisdom, vision, and experience for the good of our people, a formidable and invincible Africa was in sight. The language barrier between the French speaking and English speaking Africans was overcome by common ideal and common destiny.
>
> Geographical separatism over the years got its biggest massive assault on history. For the first time in more than a century of European domination in Africa, the Moslem world and the Christian world defied artificial barriers and met on identical realism for existence. Here isolationsim was dethroned and inter-relationship was established.
>
> There were other things which touched the heart because of their genuineness and sincerity. The Monrovia Conference was not meant as a platform for acrimony and rehearsal for past wounds and bitterness. It was dedicated to explore those things which divide the States, and to overcome them, and to give strength to those things which unite.

The President of Liberia, His Excellency Tubman was an ideal host. His warmth, his hospitality and his keynote address to the Conference contributed to give the Conference an affectionate start and direction. Sir Abubakar gave the Conference its tone and pitch, when for fifty minutes he enunciated the *Abubakar Principles* for unity among African States. The Golden voice rang and one could hear a pin drop at its pause. His doctrine centred on the equality of all states, whether great or small. The sincerity and determination by which he propounded this theory brought confidence to the Conference. He said the Conference must guarantee the sovereignty of all states, and this without prejudice to the states who wish voluntarily to unite. He drew applause when he called for no interference in the internal affairs of other states, nor should any state underwrite subversive activities against another state. It was Abubakar's day when the Monrovia Conference adopted these principles as its rules for unity among African States.

His Excellency Philibert Tsirinana of Malagasy brought cheer and humour to the Conference. He said that for centuries Malagasy remained in complete isolation from the rest of Africa. In fact he said that Malagasy is half Africa and half Asia, but he announced amidst cheers his country's decision to cast her lot wholly with Africa. The Conference, in order to show its appreciation, instead of calling itself "Conference of Heads of African States added "and of Malagasy". His Excellency Felix Houphoet-Boigny, President of Ivory Coast emerged as a powerful orator in French language. He paid tribute to Abubakar for his wisdom and foresight. His political weight in the Conference was clear.

His Excellency Leopold Sedar Senghor emerged as the velvet voice of the French-speaking group. He sat next to Sir Abubakar, and when there was a thorny question, both conferred quickly. Senghor is a great scholar and renowned poet. His Excellency Ahmadu Ahidjo had great wit. His Excellency Sylvanus Olympio, President of Togo was a linguist. He was one person in the Conference who did not need an ear phone for translations. He addressed the Conference in English, but he was equally at home with French and German. His Excellency Sir Milton A. S. Margai stayed with the Nigerian Prime Minister in Government Ducor Guest House. He and Sir Abubakar established a reputation for being very punctual. Both made it a duty to arrive ten minutes before any meeting or party. Each of the Prime Ministers was provided with one car, but these two preferred to travel in one car. His Excellency Maurice Yameogo, President of Upper Volta, had a religious approach to many of his statements. Each leader of delegation played a most commendable role throughout the Conference".

The Monrovia Conference will remain one of the greatest achievements of African statesmen. Its maturity is clear from the way it treated the non-attendance of the Casablanca powers, even though two States from that group sponsored the Monrovia Conference. The Conference realised that only by united efforts can Africans command the respect of the world, and whoever by his own efforts could bring that about would have done the greatest good to the cause of Africa. These same sentiments, expressed in Monrovia, were passed to the Casablanca Group. A neutral ground, Addis Ababa, Ethiopia, was arranged for the two sides to meet. After series of talks, extremities of right and left were shed off the two groups, and the O.A.U. (Organisation of African Unity) was eventually born in May, 1963.

Fruit of Visit to U.S.A.

Meanwhile, in July 1961, the Prime Minister was invited by President John F. Kennedy to visit the United States of America. Nigeria and Africa were high on the agenda of the bilateral talks. I was on hand to accompany and advise. That visit yielded the fruit we harvested in the service of the American Peace Corps personnel. The Peace Corps solved a lot of manpower shortage which featured soon after independence, and it made the U.S. more familiar with the life in Nigeria, and aware of the nation's potentialities.

All-Nigeria People's Conference

As the Adviser to the Prime Minister on African Affairs, I organised the All-Nigeria People's Conference on Africa in August, 1961. This was to bring Nigerians to articulate their views on the African scene, particularly with regard to the urge for a central union for Africans on the background of the Casablanca and Monrovia groups of Associations. My keynote address hinted on the following among others.

> This All-Nigeria People's Conference is significant for two reasons. First it is in keeping with the Prime Minister's declaration made to this country, that we must follow the truth. Secondly, it is a fulfilment of a pledge which I made to this country on my appointment as the Personal

Adviser to the Prime Minister on African Affairs that I will seek the views of all shades of opinion in this country on Nigeria's role on African Affairs....

Our record as a nation since the attainment of Independence can withstand the most critical examination, and may I say, will pass with the mark of gold. It is less than a year since we assumed the status of independence. Many things have happened which should give satisfaction even to the most pessimistic among us.

On the question of South Africa we were adamant that South Africa should change her apartheid policy or be kicked out of the Commonwealth. In this vital issue the Prime Minister let it be known that there can be no half measures, or marriage of convenience. It is either South Africa remains and we quit. We won.

On the explosion of atomic bomb in the Sahara we took the sternest measures yet on record. We broke diplomatic relations with France. French ships and planes were banned from our seaports and airports. We took this step not because we hated France but because our duty and responsibility to Africa was more urgent and paramount than any other consideration. When we received pledges from France through the concerted action of African Heads of States at Monrovia that there will be no further explosions in the Sahara, our task was done and we restored normal relationship.

On the question of Angola our representative in the United Nation along with other Afro-Asian groups served notice to the world in no mistakable terms that Angola belongs to Africa and can never be an intergral part of Portugal.

Looking at the African question as a whole or what we call Pan Africanism, there seems to be some confusion among Africans themselves. Some say it will be political union now, and others say that at the present time that we must achieve the prerequisites which will make easier the attainment of the ideal. From critical analysis the final objective is not in conflict but the method is. It is my conviction that Nigeria can do a lot through her past experience. The political struggle in this country is still very vivid. All Nigerians agreed that the attainment of Independence is a political creed. Some wanted Unitary Government and some wanted Federal Government. After conferences, discussions and compromises the federal form of government prevailed. Our supreme duty today is therefore, to create an atmosphere for discussions and contacts, and to proceed from the simple to the complex. Once we can do these, there can be no doubt of our reaching ultimately, to the goal of our ambition. It is obvious that we cannot tackle all the problems of Africa from one spot. We must create zones within it, in order to achieve efficiency and administrative ease. We may have to take regional machineries already working efficiently in several parts of Africa as instruments of further progress.

During the British Colonial period, Nigeria, Ghana, Sierra-Leone and Gambia had one currency under the West African Currency Board; it had a unified Defence system under the West African Frontier Force; it had a unified Air Transport system, under the West African Airways; it had a unified Judicial system under the West African Court of Appeal; it had several research institutions. Now that these countries have become independent these machineries have broken down. It is a great challenge to all these countries. This is not the time to apportion blame as to who was responsible for the breakdown, but to accept the challenge of reconstruction.

All I have done is to set the tune for this Conference. It is not my duty to give solutions to the many problems facing us because that is the task which belongs to the Conference.

Central Labour Force

I later organised and initiated a labour reconciliation meeting at Ibadan on September 22, 1961. This was to forge a central labour union which in time grew into the formidable Nigerian Labour Congress. Excerpts from my opening address are of interest:

This Committee which is now about to engage in a great national task was established by the unanimous consent of the All-Nigeria People's Conference which was opened by the Prime Minister on the 19th August, 1961.

The establishment of the Committee was further motivated by the pledge which the leaders of the two Labour Groups made to the Conference that they would abide by the decisions of the Committee so established. This pledge should be honoured...

The very fact that the Speaker of the Nigerian Parliament is presiding over this important meeting is significant. It shows in bold relief that the Government of the Federation is not unmindful of its responsibilities to the working classes of this country. A Government that has selfish interest, a Government that does not derive its being from the people would have exploited divisions among its labour ranks and would have done everything to make it remain so. But this Government has confidence in itself, its people, and in keeping with its motto of "Justice and Faith" it has resolved to march with its people.

We firmly believe that the workers of this country contributed in no small measure to the attainment of independence, which we now enjoy. The presence of the leaders of the two Labour Groups today by their own free will and choice, and in response to the directives of the All-Nigeria People's Conference, clearly shows their obedience to the will of the people. In all your deliberations, I pray that you put Nigeria first and Nigeria last all the time and you cannot go wrong.

Before I undertook other schemes in my programme as Adviser on African Affairs, a bye - election in my constituency, Orlu North East, took me back to Parliament in November, 1961. After me, the post of Adviser on African Affairs was abolished.

Chapter 14

Back To Parliament, To Cabinet, To Party Post

As I concluded in the last chapter, a bye-election was held in the Federal Constituency of Orlu North-East in 1961. This was sequel to the resignation of Hon. Victor Eze who had won that seat from me in 1959. Pressure had mounted from many quarters, after the reconciliation, following the crisis in the NCNC narrated earlier that K. O. the erstwhile Parliamentary Leader of the NCNC at the Federal Parliament and the former First Vice-President of the NCNC would not stay at the periphery of events in the nation's Parliament. Hon. Victor Eze, MP. thereupon magnanimously resigned his seat in Parliament so that I could contest a bye-election and fill the vacancy. Hon. Victor Eze, a lawyer, is from Urualla and I owe him, his relations and advisers eternal gratitude for that wonderful gesture.

The bye-election was held and I was returned unopposed to the House of Representatives. On return to the House, I regained the Parliamentary Leadership of the NCNC from Chief Festus S. Okotie-Eboh, and soon after was appointed the Federal Minister of Aviation. The Prime Minister having been satisfied that I have returned to the frontline of political affairs, abolished the post of the Adviser on African Affairs which he especially created for me.

In my Party, the NCNC, I won as the Vice-President in a hotly contested election held during the 1964 Kano Convention. That completed my re-establishment in the frontline scheme of things.

Each of the three events is a story worthy of a separate book; but this summary is sketched to show the quick succession and speed at which things moved then, and the phase of what made

150

politics at that time exciting and worthwhile. Man cannot ever claim perfection, but I have always cultivated and retained good friendly relations, ever after, with those of the *dramatis personae* with whom I had debated, struggled and contested for any position in that noble game of politics.

Chapter 15

The Action Group Crisis;
State Of Emergency In The West;
The Treasonable Felony Trials

Had the resilience and accommodating spirit of the members of the NCNC pervaded the Action Group, perhaps the cracks in the monolith of that party would not have gone deep and the intransigence not led to chains of event that forced the event of 15th January, 1966. At the General Elections of 1959 the leaders of the A.G. and the NCNC, Chief Awolowo and Dr. Azikiwe respectively, left their regional bases and contested for the Federal seats for the House of Representatives. As Dr. Nnamdi Azikiwe left the running of the East to Dr. M. I. Okpara; so did Chief Awolowo leave the Western Region to his Deputy, Chief S. L. Akintola. Both aimed at being the next Prime Minister of the Federation, if their party won. Both failed to achieve that objective.

The Leader of the NPC, Sir Ahmadu Bello stayed back in the North and his Deputy, Sir Abubakar Tafawa Balewa, led the NPC team to the centre. None of the three major political parties won an overall majority to form a government. Schemes of alliances started. Eventually the NCNC and the NPC went into Coalition Government, under the Prime Minister, Abubakar Tafawa Balewa, which ushered in Independence in 1960. The Leader of the Action Group, Chief Awolowo, became the Leader of Opposition in the Federal Parliament.

In the Western region a quarrel soon arose as to who was really in charge, the Premier and Deputy Leader of the Action

Group Party or the National President of the Party and the
Leader of the Opposition in the Federal Parliament. One
memorable day in May, 1962, we woke up to the reality that all
had not been well with the leadership of the opposition party.
The two topmost leaders were not at peace with each other. Chief
Awolowo, the National Leader, wanted his deputy, who was
then the Premier of Western Nigeria, sacked. Chief Akintola was
not loyal to the AG, the party leader charged. He explained that
the Premier deserved 'trial' in accordance with the Constitution.
Chief Akintola ordered for the summoning of the Regional
House of Assembly to discuss any possible vote of confidence.
His party refused him this opportunity and went ahead to gather
some sixty signatures of legislators who allegedly demanded for
his removal.

The situation was confusing. Why did AG leaders refuse to
go to the floor of the House to test Akintola's popularity? Why
did they have to gather purported signatures of AG members of
the House in order to remove a Premier of a government elected
by all the people? We now realise there was much more to it than
met the eye. We spoke against this new development. A meeting
of the House was summoned. The meeting ended in uproar. But
then the wheel of crisis had been set in motion. There were
several charges and counter-charges from both camps.

From Chief Awolowo's camp we heard how disloyal Chief
Akintola was. He was going to sell Yoruba people to the Hausas
like Prince Afonja of old Oyo Empire allegedly sold the Ilorin
people to the Fulani mallams. Their evidence: Chief Akintola
belonged to that school of thought which believed that for peace
and unity of Nigeria all should join hands together in running the
country's administration in a national government comprising the
Hausa, the Ibo, the Yoruba and other nationalities. We all belong
to a common heritage, and we have a common stake in the
development of Nigeria. It was, therefore, incumbent on the
Yoruba leadership to accept this reality and join the NPC-NCNC
Coalition Government. According to Akintola, that alone would

remove bitterness and suspicion, create much-needed confidence and thereby speed up the rate of development.

But the accuser, Chief Awolowo, belonged to a different school of thought. To him, Chief Akintola was wrong to have approached leaders of the NPC, on an assignment given him by West Regional Obas and elders of his party, to seek NPC's support for AG's admission into the Federal Coalition Government, after the 1959 General Election.

On his own, Chief Awolowo had contacted Dr. Azikiwe for an NCNC-AG Coalition conceding the Prime Ministership to Dr. Azikiwe. Had we accepted that offer dangled before us by Awolowo, my leader would have ruled Nigeria as Prime Minister; but God knows where such a South-South coalition would have led the whole nation. So Awo and Akintola were on different missions, pursuing different objectives.

Zik showed that his determination for one indivisible Nigeria was as strong as ever, and if need be, he was ready to pay the supreme sacrifice necessary to preserve Nigeria as one nation, rather than accept the highest political office of the Prime Minister at the expense of one Nigeria. It was, therefore, not acceptable, to the NCNC, we told Awolowo. My party could not suddenly drop a policy for Nigeria's growth as a strong, united country where mutual trust and confidence is entrenched, for any material gain.

From the time of those two conflicting approaches by the AG Leaders, Chief Awolowo had not spared any opportunity to have it back on Chief Akintola. But Chief Akintola weathered the initial storm and became the Region's second Premier. It was a hot seat on which he sat. The whole thing exploded in a crisis at the AG Annual Convention held at Jos in 1962. At a stage, the Premier went to court to establish his right to continue in office as Premier. However, following the violent disturbances in the House, convened to affirm support for a rival Premier, to Akintola, the Federal Government decided to intervene and restore peace and order. We sought and received from the House of Representatives the power to apply emergency regulations on the Western Region. The Prime Minister suspended the Western House and Government, and appointed an Administrator who ruled for six months. He was Dr. M.A. Majekudunmi.

During those turbulent days, the Federal Government ordered that all the Region's statutory bodies should be probed in view of allegations of misappropriation of funds. This led to the Coker Commission of Inquiry. Chief Awolowo and several men in his previous administration were put to task answering some of the charges put against them. Meanwhile, the Police were also unwrapping a heinous crime of conspiracy by top AG party functionaries to topple the Federal Government. This was followed by the Treasonable Felony Trials. In the end, Chief Awolowo and some of his aides were found wanting in their handling of several millions of pounds which purportedly went to the National Investment and Properties Company. All known NIPC properties were, as a result, confiscated. As to the treasonable felony trial, Chief Awolowo and several of his party supporters went to long terms of imprisonment. Chief Awolowo got ten years. That seemed to have sealed a chapter in our history of bitterness in politics at least for a while.

It is under this background that the party realignments that preceded the next general elections in 1964 could be assessed. It was no longer a matter for the Action Group of the Western Region. It became a concern of all Nigeria. All other parties fished for gains in the West. The arms-attempt, with violence at take-over of government, was a new dimension in the quest for power in Nigerian politics. It unfortunately encouraged soldiers who had guns to try their hands on it in 1966. Since then Nigeria has ever sat on top of a fear of army take-over of government, an idea given to the soldiers by the event of the "treasonable felony trials".

Chapter 16

The 1964 Elections; New Alliances; National Government

On October 1st, 1963, Nigeria became a Republic and the Governor-General, Dr. Nnamdi Azikiwe, became Head of State as Nigeria's President. A general election was due for 1964. New political alliances emerged.

Chief S. L. Akintola had returned to power in the West and formed a United People's Party-NCNC Coalition government in the beginning of 1963. His Deputy was Chief R.A. Fani-Kayode of the NCNC. Shortly after, the Igbo people and the NCNC became the object of wild allegations made by the Akintola Government. Pamphlets, the "Government Papers," flew around all over the place, accusing Igbos of dominating of the public service. No one could easily understand Chief Akintola. My colleagues and I at the centre kept watching. At last the cat was out of the bag.

A new political party was being hatched by Chief Akintola to absorb virtually all NCNC members of the coalition government and of the Western House. Why not ? Chief Awolowo tried it in 1951 and succeeded, why not Chief Akintola in 1963? Who denies that the West was the tribal bloc which Chief Awolowo had created and Akintola nurtured?

Eventually, the NCNC lost all its key members to the new party, the Nigerian National Democratic Party. Domination was the main pawn in this new game of chess introduced into the politics of the sixties. The NNDP promised the Yorubas the tribe's share of the "national cake." For the 1964 Federal general

156

elections, therefore, the NNDP and the NPC formed the Nigerian National Alliance (NNA) while what was left of the Action Group, the NCNC and the Progressive Parties of the North formed the United Progressive Grand Alliance (UPGA).

With the spate of atrocities and gangsterism unleashed on people and property in the West, the UPGA unilaterally announced a boycott of the elections. The boycott was a disaster. Akintola took advantage of it for the broad-day robbery of democracy for which the 1964 elections in the West were notorious. People at the polling stations stuffed their *agbada's* with ballot papers and, walking like pregnant women, "delivered" them into ballot boxes. In some others, thugs would carry away the ballot boxes and declare an NNDP candidate, who definitely lost, as winner. And in any case, the UPGA supporters generally obeyed the boycott. No one heeded them. This was how Akintola, in that "alliance of chaos" which followed, brought MPs to the Federal Parliament and to share in the formation of the next Federal National Government.

The NNDP saw the office of the Vice-Chancellor of the University of Lagos as the first hefty cake they would want to grab and carry home for a Yoruba man, at all costs.

In a short while the competition for the office of Vice Chancellor became hot and bitter. It evolved from an ordinary two-man struggle into a national struggle, with most of the students of the young university taking sides. Some of us in the Council of Ministers saw the unhealthy inter-tribal competition as an evil cankerworm rearing its ugly head in an institution of higher learning. It should be killed early. A quick, sharp decision was, therefore, needed if peace was to return to the university. Students were now being used in the bitter rivalry.

But a clear decision was not forthcoming. The Federal Education Minister, Chief R.O.A. Akinjide, was the NNDP National Secretary. That confirmed the weight of the rivalry and the enormity of the issue. He was bent on having Dr. Saburi Biobaku, instead of Professor Eni Njoku, on the saddle in Lagos. It was his party's avowed policy. The Prime Minister was left in a quandary. He found it difficult to intervene. This was a man who believed strongly in the devolution of power. It was absolutely clear to fair-minded people that Professor Eni Njoku's case for retention as Vice-Chancellor was unassailable, but to the NNDP, it was the turn of the Yoruba man, at all costs.

Several university workers were persecuted for holding contrary opinion. In June 1964, I wrote the Prime Minister urging him to intervene to save the situation. I had just received a copy of a letter written to him by the staff of the University of Lagos complaining against the alleged dismissal of the university's Deans. The signatories to the letter threatened mass resignation of all senior staff if no solution was found. I reminded the Prime Minister of his preference for an "internal solution". I thought it should not be interpreted to mean "an open rupture that will involve us in an unpleasant relation with international bodies".

I advised that a small ministerial committee be set up to advise as to how to solve the problem in the interest of Nigeria as as whole. I made the Prime Minister know the feelings of my colleagues and I. We were "very much agitated over this new development (the dismissal of the deans)", and we wished for a clear decision to be taken in the settlement of the crisis.

Much as we prayed for a just solution to be made, and much as we worked hard on all concerned to allow peace and justice to reign, the issue went as far as to claim innocent blood. There was an attack on the person of Professor Biobaku on the day he assumed duty in the campus. Police came in and made arrests. In short, peace was disturbed by what appeared simply a scholarly rivalry.

Earlier on, I had approached the Prime Minister to press for a just settlement which was none other than the retention of Professor Njoku. I had never failed in my just demands on the late Alhaji Abubakar Tafawa Balewa. But this time, I was in for a shock. While with one hand he was trying to stop tears from his eyes, with the other the Prime Minister offered me a seat. He said, "Dear Speed and Magic, I'm under extreme pressure," and paused. And I believed him. I know that but for such strong pressures, justice would have been done and the appointment of a Vice-Chancellor would have gone to the right man, with no tribal consideration attached.

In brief, that signalled the evolution of suspicion between the NCNC and the NPC in the House of Representatives. With another party, the NNDP, in-between us, working hard at capturing influence through attendant patronages, it became very difficult for the NCNC partner to continue carrying the whole nation's troubles on its shoulders, as if we had more at stake in the Federation than any other people. The sad effect of this new development was clear to every observer.

The NNDP joined the race and brought in gangsterism into it. The UPGA had its own weakness. At one point, the Minister of Defence, Mohammadu Ribadu, met me and Dr. Okpara campaigning at Akure and called me aside. Here was a man who never travelled. He came all the way from Lagos to see me. He said to me; "Dr. Mbadiwe, what has the NPC done to the NCNC that this your imminent change should occur?" He shook his head. Before I could gather where I was or pinned together an answer, he had left.

I had discouraged this alliance at the time that Dr. Okpara consulted me until at one time when I was induced to attend one of the rallies of Action Group/NCNC in Ibadan. I saw nothing but a sea of heads, a massive crowd. It was staggering. I said, "if there was a new consciousness, it is the people's wish; so let it happen". When I was travelling back from Ibadan to Lagos, Okpara asked me what was my thinking. I said, well I can no longer resist or object. That gave Okpara the signal and I have lived to regret it.

The NNDP in alliance with the NPC, and the NCNC in alliance with the Action Group, divided the Federation, balkanised it, and made nonsense of the gradual and decent growth which we had achieved. From the golden age of the Federation and from the direction of one destiny of a people, we now turned to a journey without a radar and without a compass.

Because of the UPGA alliance, it became difficult for the Governor-General to give assent to a quick decision of who would be the Prime Minister after the disputed elections. The delay was geting too much. While consultations were going on in many quarters, some were saying that UPGA and the NCNC stalwarts were dissuading the Governor-General from reappointing Sir Abubakar. However, in all this confusion, I called to see Sir Abubakar Tafawa Balewa. When I arrived, he was lying on the floor. He got up, looked at me, and said: "For days I have not seen you". I laughed and said, "Don't you know that we are now in different camps?"

Sir Abubakar shook his head. He said, "If everything fails, and it is you, "Speed and Magic" who will become the next Prime Minister of the Federation, I will go home quietly and say that Nigeria is in safe hands, that it will emerge united". I turned to him and said, "Don't say that. I have no such intention. It is far away from my mind. You will become the Prime Minster". So I left him. The next call was to see Dr. Nnamdi Azikiwe, the Governor-General. He breathed a sigh of relief just for the mere fact that he saw me.

Naturally, we have always thought alike on major issues regarding the politics of this country. We met for a few minutes and our thoughts were going the same direction. After I left him, few hours later, he announced Abubakar's appointment as Prime Minister.

When the President reappointed Sir Abubakar Tafawa Balewa as the Prime Minister, a national government was again formed. I joined the National Government which was formed early, because I was returned unopposed the second time, in my Orlu North East Constituency, and was sworn in as Minister, while many of my party men were yet to contest the "boycotted" elections. The NNA Alliance weakened the structure of the National Government as was seen in the Lagos University episode. But I used my position as the Leader during the earlier NPC/NCNC government to hold the balance and try to keep the fabric from tearing apart.

There were other issues which would not have normally caused a stir, but which shook the nation because of latent and in-built suspicions, prejudices and intrigues. They included the Oba of Lagos tussle, the Ijora Causeway land, the 1963 Census, the creation of the Mid-Western Region and the Operation Fantastic. They merit separate accounts.

Chapter 17

Main Events Of The First Republic

Let us in this chapter examine some of the highlights and hotly debated issues of this epoch of our history. They include:

(i) The National Population Census

Among other issues worthy of mention under the Prime Ministership of Sir Abubakar Tafawa Balewa was the National Population Census conducted by the Minister of Economic Development, Alhaji Waziri Ibrahim, which ended in a huge drama and controversy. In the House of Representatives, the statement by the Minister occasioned a walkout by the NCNC contingent. It created a mild crisis but where men of goodwill were around, a major catastrophe and tragedy had always been minimised. That was what happened between the Prime Minister, Mohammadu Ribadu, the Defence Minister, and I. To find a solution, another statement was prepared for the Prime Minister which regretted the statement of the Minister of Economic Development and also regretted the walking out of the NCNC members. The two balancing statements made the NCNC members to troop back into the House of Representatives, thereby regaining the cordial relationship between the NPC and the NCNC. Other population counts since 1963 were failures. We pray for the success of the one projected for 1991.

(ii) The Creation of Mid-West Region

It was during this period that the creation of Mid-West Region was accomplished. It is most interesting to rehearse the incident which led to the appointment of the first Premier of Mid-West. This is to show the oncoming generation what service means in a thoroughly organised party. Chief Dennis Osadebay was the first

162

Premier of Mid-West Region. It is very inspiring how he came by it.

Between 1955 and 1956, late Alhaji Adegoke Adelabu, the "Lion of the West", was a Minister of Lands and Social Services in the Federal Government of Nigeria. But circumstances compelled him to resign that appointment. So his resignation and remaining in Lagos became a very great worry for the NCNC. Will he return to the Western Region just as an ordinary floor member?. A man through whom the NCNC had won and kept the West. A special meeting for his return to the West had to be called. Chief Osadebay was then the Leader of the Opposition in the West. He was quite a capable man who had no bitterness in his politics. He was a friend of all. People loved him as he loved them.

When he saw that this party was pondering what to do with Adelabu, Chief Osadebay volunteered his office as the Leader of Opposition for Adegoke Adelabu. The party took note of that great gesture on his part. The meeting took place at No. 2, Alexander Avenue, Ikoyi, (my residence as the Minister of Commerce and Industry). Zik presided. All I did was to speak to Chief Osadebay that the party was taking note of what he has done for it, and that his honour and sacrifice can never be forgotten.

So when Mid-West was created, the issue of the first Premier came up. Right there in the residence of T.O.S. Benson in Ikoyi, members of the NEC gathered under me, as the Parliamentary Leader, to consider this subject and advise the Party. Chief Omo Osagie was from Benin, the man that I often referred to as the "Duke with the Golden Sword", who brought his "Etu Edo" members to effect the success at any elections which the NCNC held. You can always be sure that any election which Chief Omo Osagie led would be victorious. So by any stretch of the imagination, he was properly qualified. Power is determined by the number of votes one delivered. So he was in the forefront of running, heavily supported by Chief Festus Okotie Eboh.

I got up and addressed the meeting, I said, "Well, you know one thing, we did not invite Osadebay to be present because we know Osadebay very well. If he is present, he would rather say that instead of a heated debate over him, he would rather surrender and decline any offer." So it was better he kept off from the meeting. But in the overall interest of the party, I presented his case.

I reminded my colleagues of the man who belled the cat during the days of Adelabu, when we were stuck in a dilemma. "Who could do what Osadebay did? Was it not with tears in his eyes that he resigned? This is the time he should be supported and compensated. It is a lesson for all members of this party that it is not by lobbying or constant struggling that people get offices in the party. People can be somewhere else, far away, and yet be remembered and nominated for an office".

After every consideration and debate, I clinched the day for Osadebay. Chief Omo Osagie left in silence. He was a great debater. If not satisfied over anything, he would shout and pound the table. But he left in silence, because he was convinced that the party was doing the right thing. He blessed the decision. I conferred with Dr. M.I. Okpara, Premier and National President, over what took place. That was how we reached the conclusion that Chief Osadebay should get the first premiership of the Mid-West Region.

So when finally the NEC met, Chief Osadebay was announced, and he was elected to the post of Premier by acclamation.

(iii) Code of Conduct: The Ijora Land Affair

Following independence, many knotty issues came up one after the other before the coalition government and they were tackled, free from emotion, quietly, and solved. We are rehearsing this mostly for the younger generations who have their eyes on politics. **Politics** is a very unsteady game; the unexpected often happens. **You** might get up one morning and what you have never planned for would happen to you, even in the midst of your great popularity, on the crest of your power, at the height of your fame. You should always realise that not everyone admires you. You still have enemies. Once you have that clearly at the back of your mind and constantly examine yourself critically, you hardly go wrong. So it is with me. At the height of my fame in Nigerian politics, everywhere I was driving through, even in crowded Lagos streets, it was 'K.O.', 'K.O'. If I was in Kano or Calabar or Ibadan, it was the same thunderous ovation of 'K.O.', 'K.O.'. That was how the rank and file of my party chose to honour and acclaim me.

But one morning, I woke up and got my morning newspapers. All of them carried banner headlines: "Prime Minister, sack this man." I wondered: What man? As if it was a big conspiracy one paper after another carried the same thing. "Sack K.O.", the editors must have conspired? If it were in one paper, it would have been different. But all the major newspapers carried this great banner headline. I could not believe it. In fact, I was trembling. I checked myself but I could not recall anything that I had done wrong.

Few months ago I was published to be one of the most effective Ministers. I got this commendation and honour year in and year out. But what can this be now?. Reading right through, I checked that the papers called for my sack. In their opinion I had violated one of the moral codes of being a Minister: that I got a piece of land, plot 7A Ijora Causeway, at a time I was a Minister, and that I went and sold this land to a government-sponsored concern, and that the operative thing was that "the said Dr. Mbadiwe, when this transaction took place, was a Cabinet Minister at all material times of the transaction." I was taken aback. I had forgotten about the land. I did not know where to look for the file. It had escaped my memory.

There used to be a strong cabinet like a safe that was given to all Ministers. It was not there. As I was getting confused, my nephew, Barrister P.C. Mbadiwe entered my house. I could not talk to him. I just showed him the papers. He also became confused.

Barrister P.C. Mbadiwe searched all over the place. Suddenly he came upon a document. He was reading it with rapt attention. Then he gave it to me. I looked at it, It read:

> Sir, I would refer to your letter No. UNPLI of the 6th of May, 1961, and a subsequent meeting held in the office of my Permanent Secretary, and confirm that you are hereby given an option to take up a Lease of Plot No.7A in the Ijora Industrial Area, subject to the normal terms and conditions appertaining to Government Leases of industrial land in that area.
>
> This option is open for a period of three months with effect from the 1st of June, 1961.

sgd. (Ag. Chief Federal Land Officer).

It was addressed to:
The Managing Director
United Nigeria Press Ltd.
Agege Motor Road
Yaba
Lagos

It turned out that I was not a Minister when I got the land referred to. Naturally, I rejoiced at the find. In 1958, when I was involved in the NCNC crisis, I was out of the government. I was not due to be in the government again as a Minister, until about 1964/65 after the general elections, if I succeeded. But Honourable Victor Eze shortened that period by resigning his seat at the House of Representatives. As stated earlier, I contested and I was returned unopposed in 1962. And that shows that I had already gotten this land one and half years before becoming a Minister.

I met my colleagues in the government, including the Prime Minister. Telephone calls were pouring in - Chief Osadebay was calling. He was worried, Dr. M.I. Okpara was worried. So what I did was to be in my fighting mood immediately. I gave a short press release that Dr. Mbadiwe has a total answer to the conspiratorial writing of the press. He will break his silence within 24 hours. Everybody should be on the alert.

So what I did was a write-up entitled "Why I Have Decided to Reply." The full text of that Press Statement is as follows:-

First: some sections of the press in this country have helped to portray to the outside world that the standard of public life of our country is low. People come to us with that fixed notion. I could have ignored these antics, but for the people who love Nigeria. However, these antics have provided an opportunity to reassure the people of Nigeria that there are people in public life who could lay claim to unimpeachable record of public conduct.

Secondly: To use this opportunity to expose the flagrant abuse of the Press to distort, lie and assassinate character. Before analysing the various gossips that have been made, there are some fundamental facts which the public must know as a prelude to the whole examination:-

(1) From July, 1958 until October, 1, 1962 I was a private citizen of this country.

(2) That but for the magnanimity of Hon. Victor Eze vacating his seat in Parliament, I would not have come back to the Parliament of Nigeria until 1965, if elected.

(3) That prior to my ever joining the politics of Nigeria in the early 50's, I had been a Company Director and engaged in other business enterprises.

(4) My first appointment as a Minister in this country was in 1954, as a Federal Minister of Lands and Natural Resources. That was the era of slum clearance. As a matter of principle, I never acquired a single plot; yet men with lesser opportunity could today boast of many Federal Government plots.

The sudden outburst, solidly and shamefully organised, was intended to cause alarm and create a situation that does not exist, just to confuse the ignorant and uninformed, and thereby create an atmosphere of distrust in the minds of the public and the nation.

What is their case specifically? It is in a nutshell according to them that: "Dr. K.O. Mbadiwe or a Company belonging to him got a piece of land from the Federal Government and subleased this piece of land to a Government-sponsored concern and that the said Dr. Mbadiwe was a Cabinet Minister *at all material times of the transactions."*

The operative key words in this case are that at all material times of this transaction, I was a Cabinet Minister.

I want to say quite categorically that the 7A Ijora Causeway was offered to me by the Federal Government when I was not a Minister of State, but was an ordinary citizen and Managing Director of the United Nigerian Press Limited. The Government's offer was made to me in May, 1961. This means to say that nearly one and a half years had elapsed between the period of my being offered the land and the time I became a Minister.

I tender in evidence the photostat of the Ministry's offer showing the exact date of the offer, and even indicating the purpose for which the land is intended. In the light of the evidence now adduced, the key on which their case turns has been demolished, and therefore the accusation cannot stand and must fail.

To go further, and for the benefit or information to the public, the land at the material time was acquired for a specialised printing factory which was estimated to cost nearly half a milion pound. Technical partners from Overseas were invited to the venture of which Nigerian holding was to be 51%. The Technical partners were actually flown from the United Kingdom to inspect the said site. All along, the development of the scheme was in progress until my sudden return to Parliament in early 1962 and my subsequent appointment as a Minister. With my appointment as a Minister two problems emerged: To continue with the scheme or to abandon it. It is in keeping with Cabinet Practice that when a person is appointed a Minister for him to determine how many of his business he can divest himself from so that it will not conflict with his public duties. Naturally, to carry on with half a million pound scheme would have interferred with my work as a Minister. Giving out 3 acres of land in a Premier Industrial Site to a company for a chicken fee rental in place of an elephantine income is a great sacrifice. The large income which would have accrued, if I had built on it, would no longer be possible.

Experience has shown that if that site was developed, the income accruing from it would be more than 10 times what has been offered to me for it. Any landlord in Lagos with experience in Industrial and Residential Areas of a similar magnitude knows exactly what I am talking about. In so far as the rentals charged the Nigerpools are concerned, I am happy that it is to them that the land finally passed. I know that I could get much higher rentals for this acreage if I were not dealing with Nigerpools on the basis of goodwill. Having invited me to serve them on the Board at the early stage of their development, I felt happy that I have been able to reciprocate in some measure to their goodwill and for their continued development.

All allusions to this land should be dismissed as prejudiced and unwarranted. In any case, it will be crazy and the height of folly for anyone to suggest that I should not do anything with a plot allocated to me because I subsequently became a Minister.

In a subsequent Press Release by the National Convention of Nigerian Citizens (NCNC) dated 2nd March, 1965, and entitled Closing the Chapter, it said:-

Both those who were after Dr. Mbadiwe's blood over the so-called Ijora land deal and the sections of the press that wanted Dr. Mbadiwe destroyed, because his company leased a piece of land, lawfully allocated to him by the Federal Government, to the Nigerpools Limited, have congratulated the Prime Minister on the resolution of the issue. We ourselves commend the Prime Minister's step as worthy of his nationalist leadership.

The principle involved in this Ijora land controversy however, is more fundamental than as it now appears. It involves the question of the Ministerial code of conduct which the Prime Minister may use his good offices to lay down for general guidance. Despite the antics of Dr. Mbadiwe's prejudiced critics, it is still our view that Dr. Mbadiwe by his magnanimity of placing the overall interest of the nation above his personal legitimate right has set a ministerial code of conduct which is a challenge to his kindly colleagues and foes alike.

On 23rd April, 1963, during a debate in parliament which turned out to deal with "Ministers' Code of Conduct", the Prime Minister stated inter alia as follows:

Nigeria is a young country. There are many Nigerians in business, some of them have also entered politics, but it does not mean that after they have come into politics and are lucky to be appointed Ministers, they should throw away all their former business interests.

That Dr. Mbadiwe has thrown away his former business interest is a precedent which keeps him in line with history. The Prime Minister, after referring to the fact that "Ministers are doing temporary job", continued in this vein; "We in the Council of Ministers have got what we call 'Ministers' Code of Conduct'"

Concluding his debate, Sir Abubakar averred:

I want to approach this matter with all sense of responsibility. I also want to tell the House straight away that I, as Prime Minister, cannot accept that whenever a man is appointed a Minister, such a man has to severe his connections with all private interests. I will not accept it (applause). If I am satisfied that this is not going to interfere with the Minister's duty as a Minister, then I will ask him to continue. But if I am sure that it is going to interfere with his duty, it is also my duty to tell him to severe his connections.

That is the existing code of Conduct as enunciated by the Prime Minister. It becomes quite clear therefore, that in view of the above statement of the Prime Minister, Dr. Mbadiwe has acted within the "Minister Code of Conduct" in his position as a Minister. This he has done and nothing more.

(iv) Operation Fantastic

In 1964, as Federal Minister of Aviation, I was responsible for bringing the Nigerian Airways and the Pan American World Airlines to establish the first direct commercial air service between the two countries - Nigeria and America.

In order to mark this great occasion of the inaugural flight between the two countries, I organised Operation Fantastic. On occasions like that, it was usual to invite eminent people to witness the inaugural flight of such importance. But I decided that I would rather take a representative culture of Nigeria, with young men and women who would never have dreamt of going to America, to take them as a team to exhibit the African arts, music and dances in that country. These were the exotic Atilogwu Dancers. They were accompanied by two long trumpeters from Kano. It was all a majestic affair.

I believe I was doing a great service to my country and to the young people. The scheme was very much widely discussed and appreciated in the country. However, there was controversy within the Cabinet. Some said that I took more dancers than was necessary. This brought about a lot of argument.

The Minister of Information, Broadcasting and Culture, Chief T.O.S. Benson, thought it was a slight against him. He argued that I was scooping his job. But the mission was not merely a cultural show, but an advertisement for the Nigerian Airways which was within my portfolio. T.O.S. wrote a very long letter; to which I in turn replied. But we must make progress. The misunderstanding was soon settled with laughter. That is how it should be. That was the spirit of ministerial cooperation in those days.

Later during Gowon's regime, after Abubakar had left the scene, there was an inquiry into the Nigerian Airways. What number I was authorised to take, and what number I did take came up. It was said that any excess was to be paid back by me. Nobody knew what was happening until I returned after the civil war. I did not attend the inquiry. The matter was concluded behind me. I had been surcharged to pay thousands of pounds for taking excess people on the inaugural flight.

I wrote a protest letter to General Gowon in which I insisted that I should be commended, rather than surcharged for excesses. I argued that the troupe I took stormed the United States, the International World Fair, and performed at various universities, colleges and at the auditorium of the State Department, sponsored by the Secretary of State, Dean Rusk. Chief Adebo was then the permanent Representative of Nigeria at the U N. He met this colourful team of dancers at the Kennedy International Airport. The Commissioner of Washington welcomed me with a key to the City of Washington. The Mayor of San Francisco presented me with a key. So did the Mayor of the City of Chicago. My strong case was accepted.

On October 6, 1972, the Federal Military Government reconsidered the whole issue and absolved me from payment of any money whatsoever in connection with "Operation Fantastic", by way of any surcharge.

It is not unusual that in the course of the tenure of his office, a public officer, an administrator, a politician or a statesman, may, with genuine and honest intention, pursue his assignment with extra vigour and overt exuberance which are born out of sheer patriotism. The success may invoke petty jealousy or genuine criticism. That was my position *vis-a-vis* "Operation Fantastic". If the Government was not convinced of my genuine motive, it would not have approved the cost of the "Operation Fantastic" in the first instance. Men in the public relations world know that publicity (external for that matter) is always a very expensive exercise. Indeed good external publicity which achieves the objective of helping to improve the image and the economy of any country is worth more than its value in gold. I presume that this consideration must have been the determining factor when the Federal Military Government decided in 1972 to absolve me from paying any surcharge. The conclusion to this event is nothing but a triumph for Nigerian external publicity and economic cooperation.

(v) Selection of the Oba of Lagos

My early return unopposed to Parliament in a general election which was generally boycotted by the UPGA did some wonders. While my other colleagues were to wait till the rescheduled time-table for a "bye-election", I was already in Lagos, and with the permission of my party, was admitted into the Government. The first task presented was the selection of the next Oba of Lagos, at that time a job for the Federal Government. I was briefed on the history and tradition of the selection. I took a fancy for Oba Oyekan and projected his case from among other candidates.

In fact when Ribadu saw how I felt he announced that, of the contestants, the NPC had no special preference. I thanked God and I could not make pretences. Right away I was supporting Oba Oyekans candidacy.

In fact some people who were supporting other candidates, on suddenly seeing me there, and the stand I took, withheld announcing their candidates. Well, the presiding Chairman, the Prime Minister, put it to the House. It sailed through. That was how Oba Oyekan got the Obaship of Lagos.

(iv) Palace of the People Opened

The relationship between the Prime Minister, Sir Abubakar Tafawa Balewa and the Premier of Eastern Nigeria and President of the NCNC, Dr. Hon. M.I. Okpara, since the formation of the UPGA was deteriorating. UPGA and NNA appeared to be tearing the nation asunder. I wrote a long letter to the Prime Minister on 22nd January, 1965. Though as a result, I got two new ministerial appointments for Hon. R.B.K. Okafor and Hon. F.E. Offor, I thought the official opening of my country residence at Arondizuogu would provide an informal forum for a full *tete-a-tete*, and complete reconciliation for all parties concerned, so that a National Government will have meaning and we can join hands to nuture this new Republic.

At Arondizuogu, I completed a house. I decided to call it the "Palace of the People", as a mark of my bond and alliance with the grassroots population. I arranged for an official opening of this country home. I would invite my good friend the Prime Minister, Sir Abubakar Tafawa Balewa, and the Premiers.

After it has been opened, and everybody dispersed, and the Prime Minister stayed overnight at Arondizuogu with the Premiers, the Governors and so on, we could then have a quiet time and I would introduce the subject of peace and reconciliation. That was the whole intention behind the opening of the People's Palace. It was not a show or demonstration of any wealth or fanfare or luxury or opulence.

The "Palace of the People" was built one step after the other. I had the blocks made for eight years and allowed rains to fall on them. I was working silently until it was completed. I said that this would be my gift to the country if I could assemble those leaders there and get the country going again .

So invitations were sent. It was a very elaborate arrangement. I had to speak to those concerned individually. My dear friend, Sir Abubakar Tafawa Balewa was the first person I spoke to. He agreed to attend. Dr. Okpara, Chief Osadebay, Sir Francis Ibiam also agreed to attend.

Then I turned to the Western leadership. I spoke to Akintola, and he agreed to come. Well, if the Prime Minister could attend, I felt that Sir Ahmadu Bello would. So I invited him, and he also agreed. The stage was set. Announcements were made. Each of the arriving personalities was allocated time of arrival at the junction-road between Akokwa and Arondizuogu where a motorcade took them to the centre of the activity.

Chief Osadebay was the first to arrive, followed by the Governor of the then Eastern Region, Sir Francis Ibiam. Then Dr. M.I. Okpara arrived and I was still expecting Tafawa Balewa. But the tension between Abubakar's and Dr. M.I. Okpara's government was mounting. Hostility was getting out of hand. Naturally the Prime Minister, arriving in another Region, would expect a universal welcome. He would not like to arrive at a place where he was not sure of a kind reception. The great event took place as planned, but it was NCNC Governors and Premiers who were in attendance.

My brother Chief J. Green Mbadiwe felt very much worried and concerned that Sir Abubakar did not come as expected. We got him on the telephone the evening of the party and both of them debated the issue in Hausa. The persuasive tongue of J. Green Mbadiwe in the Hausa language told Abubakar: "Look, it will be better for Dr. Mbadiwe to leave Arondizuogu and come over to meet you in Port Harcourt and both of you fly by helicopter and come to the spot. If they are to kill, let them kill both of you." The appeal of Green was most touching. At that stage Abubakar said that, in spite of everything, he must come. The next day, he would fly an eleven-man squad to Port Harcourt.

A helicopter was waiting at 10 a.m. to take them. I was there when Abubakar's plane arrived. The crowd at the airport cheered. Both of us flew by helicopter. We came down at the Akokwa School field from where the massive motorcade started winding down the road to the Palace of the People. Thousands of people who waited, cheered. Shouts of K.O., K.O., rent the air. We entered Arondizuogu and the "Palace of the People" with great pomp and pageantry.

There was a plaque which Abubakar unveiled at the main building. The main function had taken place the day before, but his arrival made it seem as if the function had just started. He received many gifts from the Mbadiwe family. Chief J. Green Mbadiwe blessed him. The head of the family Chief David

Mbadiwe gave him gifts. These gifts were packed and sent to Bauchi, from where Abubakar wrote me his appreciation letter.

From the "Palace of the People", Sir Abubakar had earlier gone to the Stone Palace - the palace of my father where the traditional kola was broken by the head of Mbadiwe family, who offered libations, making Abubakar and Dr. Mbadiwe and brothers, members of the same family. After that, prayers were said which fortified the friendship that was indeed deep rooted.

(vii) Headquarters of the United Nations Conference on Trade and Development (UNCTAD)

On the international level, I made a marathon effort to move the United Nations Trade and Development Headquarters to Nigeria in 1965. Shortly after assuming office, I led a delegation to the United Nations Conference on Trade and Development in Geneva. The Conference was one of the new bodies set up in the sixties by the United Nations Organisation. The objective was to tackle the problem of the imbalance in the trade between the 'Developed' and the 'Developing' countries of the world. At an earlier meeting, the issue of the location of the headquarters of the Conference was debated. The city of Geneva was selected as most suitable and a resolution, passed to that effect, was to be confirmed at the meeting of 1965.

But the city of Geneva itself had demurred to host yet another United Nations Organisations Conference. Geneva, they argued, had become a 'No man's city' without character of its own and dominated by foreigners who more or less outnumbered the citizens. The issue of location appeared on the agenda of the 1965 meeting under matters arising from the minutes.

I spotted immediately the opportunity to launch Nigeria internationally by reopening the whole issue of location. Why should the headquarters of an organ for remedying the disequilibrium between the under-developed and developed countries be located in a developed country?

With gigantic effort, I moved the General Committee to reopen the matter afresh, on the grounds that the original decision to locate the headquarters in Geneva was ill-advised. I was joined by other so called "developing countries" - Ethiopia, India, Ghana, Mexico among others.

A matter that earlier appeared to be of little importance when first debated was thus given a new importance and significance. As the Minister from Nigeria, I held the audience spellbound as I argued the case for relocation of the headquarters in a developing country. I won the acclamation of the meeting, and the matter became a tussle at that conference between the developed and the developing countries. Canada, France and even Britain joined. The meeting eventually decided to refer the matter back to the General Assembly in New York where the aroused 'developed countries' ultimately outmanoeuvred me and defeated the motion. Geneva, which had earlier demurred, quickly assented to play host to the UNCTAD.

In Nigeria, especially among the officials, nobody took me seriously at first. But as the debate progressed, however, I infected everybody with the enthusiasm. I moved the Federal Government of Nigeria to offer Lagos, as undeveloped as it was, to be the seat of the great UNCTAD. I painted to the Nigerian Government and the people glowing pictures of the advantages to Nigeria, should Lagos be selected. I set out to mobilise not only Lagos but the whole country to appreciate what opportunities it would open. To that end, I set up committees to tackle aspects of the problems which might arise. I tried to make the country to envisage what "greater tomorrow" the siting of the UNCTAD in Nigeria would bring. It would boost the tourist trade in Nigeria, enhance the avenues of business and improve the inflow of foreign exchange - among other advantages.

I ordered a census of available accommodation and made a projection of what was likely to be required and made available for UNCTAD headquarters in Lagos. Telephone, telegraphic and other forms of communication must be improved and modernised to meet the requirements of the world body. If Government were to achieve all those, I contended, government would create job opportunities for the people.

Though the bid for the UNCTAD headquarters failed in the end, I had stimulated much interest, and aroused an awareness which did not exist originally. In the process also, I endeavoured to boost the image of Nigeria in New York by throwing a dinner party for distinguished members of the world body at the Waldorf Astoria during the sitting of the United Nations Assembly. That was how to achieve greatness.

My years in the Ministry of Trade saw many changes. The Ministry of Trade was carved out of the former Ministry of Commerce and Industry. In an age when a new emphasis was being given to industrial development in the economy, I succeeded in making the Ministry of Trade one of the most pulsating in the Government. For instance, the Federal Loans Board for Small Scale Industries had become more or less moribund with little to show for its years of existence. I saw the need for reactivating it in the interest of the economy and the Nigerianisation of business in general. I contrived to have the Loans Board brought under my portfolio and similarly, I revamped the Import Licensing Section of the Ministry of Trade which had been practically dormant.

As the Minister of Trade, I had initiated an international trade policy which was meant to curb the excess of certain foreign countries. The policy was approved by the Executive Council and I gave directives to my officials to work out the modalities for its implementation.

It was at this point that the Minister of Finance, the Late Chief Festus Okotie Eboh, for reasons best known to him, and without consultation, came out with a new tariff which palpably cut across the policy of the Ministry of Trade.

I resented the action of the Finance Minister, Chief Okotie Eboh. But instead of taking up the issue with my Ministerial colleague, I decided to report the matter to the Prime Minister for a ruling. I surmised that the action of my colleague was deliberate and calculated to undermine my position and prestige in the eyes of the people and of the world, if not to frustrate the policy I had enunciated. As the Parliamentary Leader of his party, I took precedence over Chief Festus Okotie Eboh. The Prime Minister was away on vacation in his home town of Bauchi. When therefore, I could not reach the Prime Minister by telephone, I decided to go there by a chartered plane - just myself and three officials.

The news got to the Minister of Finance, Chief Okotie Eboh, who did not desire to be out-done. He ordered his own plane to take him to see the Prime Minister, if possible before I could get there, so that he would face Mbadiwe with a *fait accompli*. The question was whose action or policy should be implemented in the Ministry of Trade.

Two planes were therefore ordered from the Nigerian Airways for the same day, time and destination. The Nigerian Airways Operations Manager used his discretion and contrived to arrange only one plane instead of two for both parties.

I had done my homework, mapped out my line of attack and defence. Before setting out I had sent a telegram in advance to appraise Alhaji Tafawa Balewa, the Prime Minister, of my visit. But though I did not give details, at least the Prime Minister knew I was on my way.

My colleague on the other hand was less prepared and therefore had a less welcome reception from the host. The Prime Minister was unhappy about the visit, as it intruded on his peace and rest, moreso as the matter could have been resolved between us. In any case, he observed: "the heaven would not fall if you had to wait for my return". The Minister of Finance argued that he was defending his right under the Constitution as he had the power to pronounce on tariffs which the Minister of Trade should accept. The Prime Minister retorted, "If we all in our various works of life exercised the powers we have over others arbitrarily, it would be a disastrous world".

He then advised us to return to Lagos till he came back from vacation. Even though no clear ruling had emerged, I was satisfied that I had made my point. I went across to my colleague, shook hands with him and the two of us returned to Lagos, in amity.

In 1965, I staged the first ever Nigerian Trade Exhibition at the Victoria Island, Lagos. It was an international affair modelled on what I had seen in other parts of the world, with emphasis on the Nigerian contribution to industry and trade. Trade fairs have ever since featured in Nigeria as a means of rousing the awareness of the international community to our industrial potentialities.

There were more highlights of achievements made during the NPC-NCNC alliance led by Alhaji Abubakar Tafawa Balewa, the great Muhamadu Ribadu and my humble self.

First Nigerian GOC

When the British left the scene, they were also to hand over the leadership of the army to Nigerians. There was need to appoint a Nigerian General Officer Commanding (GOC) for the new Nigerian Army. Major. General J.T.U. Aguiyi-Ironsi visited me to tell me his position in the Army as the most senior, and to solicit my support because he was entitled and qualified. But he feared that the Sardauna of Sokoto was going to influence the appointment of someone else. It was the first time I met General Ironsi. He convinced me he was the most senior officer then.

I took up the issue with Ribadu because I knew that if I approached the Prime Minister, Alhaji Balewa, my bosom friend, "Oh", he would tell me, "talk it over with your other friend". So knowing that, I went straight to Ribadu and related what I know of the matter and all I wanted him was to verify who was the most senior. If Ironsi was not the most senior, I would not in the life of me, ask that the most senior be by-passed for Ironsi. I convinced him about Ironsi's right to the office, but that I understood that Sardauna had made up his mind for another person. We later heared that Sardauna had expressed the fear of insecurity with Ironsi as the GOC.

Ribadu went to Kaduna to speak face to face with Sardauna, because Ribadu was a person whose heart was clear and clean. I understood he let it be known to Sardauna, in order to allay his fears, that if it was destined by Allah that they would come to harm from Ironsi's hand, who were they not to submit to Allah's dictates?

And what Sardauna cannot concede to Ribadu, no other person in the world can get it. That fact I knew. Ribadu returned, having convinced Sardauna that the right person should get the chance. The right course should prevail. It was after that event that I christened Ribadu "The Power behind Powers, Constitutional or Natural" I explained it. Even if you took away that constitutional power which he wielded as the Defence Minister, Ribadu still retained some sort of in-born power which radiated around him, and made you do his bidding. He was an achiever any day.

Other Issues

There were other issues which progressed and were perfected during that peaceful period. Industries were built. As Minister of Commerce and Industries, I established the Nkalagu Cement Factory near Enugu. The mines at the Plateau were more efficiently equipped and run. As Minister of Communications, it was my duty to tackle another major job. That is to reorganise the entire Post and Telegraphs system in 1955. I said to myself: "The P & T has been known as the department of "Palaver and Trouble", but I will, turn it into a department of Peace and Tranquility." I infused a new sense of mission into its labour force and brought them out to be "Technicians". The postal system was reorganised. You got your mail within 24 hours of posting. Telegrams were received on time.

I also introduced good housing plan so that our citizens might benefit from improved standard of living. That motion was introduced in the House of Representatives and approved.

I said:

BE IT RESOLVED;

That the time has come for the Government to undertake a vast Housing project for low income groups of the workers of this country, as a first step in the field of Social Securities".

It was carried. Its first fruit was Surulere Housing Scheme discussed earlier. On 3rd April, 1952, the *Daily Times* carried the headlines:

Hon. Mbadiwe's Provide House for Nigerian Workers MOTION ADOPTED.

A motion by Hon. K.O. Mbadiwe asking for a Housing Project for Nigerian Workers was passed in the House of Representatives yesterday after an amendment by the Chief Secretary to the Government had been accepted by the mover.

On economic measures, I introduced a motion for the Central Bank and was supported by the Alake of Abeokuta. The Motion was moved in 1952 when I was not a member of the Federal Cabinet. I came later on as a member of the Federal Government to see that my motion on the Central Bank was implemented. This is how the *Daily Times* of April 10, 1952 reported it:

Central Bank Motion by Mbadiwe Passed

A motion in the name of Hon. Ozuomba Mbadiwe, seconded by the Alake of Abeokuta, which was later modified was carried. The motion in its final form, urges the Government to examine the possibilities of establishing a Central Bank as practical means of marshalling the financial resources of the country for aiding economic development in all its phases. The Government will examine the possibilities of establishing such a bank or any other central institution as well as strengthening the existing African banks, and make a report to the House as soon as possible.

Hon. Mbadiwe said that the finance of the country was decentralised and its productive economic power and marshalling force, low. Thirty-five million pounds investments were scattered abroad which could be recalled for the purpose of such a bank. Such a bank would serve as a nerve centre for the promotion of industrialisation projects. The Alake speaking in support, said that money was needed locally for industrialisation and that if investments were recalled for such a purpose, it would be easier to borrow locally than abroad.

The Central Bank of Nigeria is a practical means of consolidating and controlling the nation's financial resources, including regulations of gold and currency of this country, for the purpose of rapid economic development in all its phases. It was seen as a means of strengthening and guiding existing African Banks. Within three years of the passing of this motion, the present Central Bank of Nigeria was built and commissioned.

Under my Aviation Ministry, the International Airport of Kano was built and opened, and I set up a Committee of experts and talented businessmen to advise on the International Airport of Lagos which has since also been built and commissioned. The opening of Kano Airport was a vast event of great magnitude. The Emir of Kano got me a white horse.

I was seated on the white horse from the centre of the city to the airport site to open it. The late Sardaura magnified the whole occasion by sewing a special gown for me, which I have to this day, treasured and preserved. The commissioning ceremony of Kano Airport was turned into a mini dubarfeaturing traditional troops from other areas of Nigeria.

We achieved much with little or no resources - just conserving with prudence whatever resources that came into our hands. We were able to conserve funds in order to do the magnificent and enormous work of extending the railway to Bornu. At the same time that the railway work was going on, we were busy building the bridge across the River Niger at Onitsha which was commissioned by Sir Abubakar Tafawa Balewa. The first toll gate in this country was mounted at the Niger Bridge.

Many more of the achievements of the NCNC-NPC coalition government in the First Republic, would be recorded by future historians.

Chapter 18

End Of The First Republic
January, 1966 Coup
'The Handover'

As every school boy knows January 15th, 1966 marked the first Military *coup d'etat* and the end of the First Republic in the history of Nigeria. Watchers of contemporary events in Nigeria had then felt that a cloud was gathering. How it would rain was anybody's guess. The 1964 elections, boycotted by many and massively rigged by others; the unjust and unashamed grab for the national cake; the total loss of trust in the National Government which was finally formed; all these were rolling the nation into a precipice of chaos.

Nobody, except Major Nzeogwu, ever thought that a military *coup d'etat* was possible in Nigeria. I was, perhaps, the last person, after a day, to realise what was happening. In the evening of 14th January, there was a party caucus in my residence. Those present included NCNC Ministers; Chief Adeniran Ogunsanya, Dr. Jaja Wachukwu and Mr. R. Amanze Njoku. Mr. R.B.K. Okafor who was to be sworn in the next day as a Junior Minister was also there. We discussed the situation in the country and I was to meet the Prime Minister, Sir Abubakar Tafawa Balewa. I took with me Chief Ogunsanya and we met and discussed with the Prime Minister. The topic was the Western Region Crisis and an equitable solution for it. We were soon back and continued the meeting in my house. I was to send a letter as a reminder to the Prime Minister in the morning, before Parliament resumed sitting.

This is the text of that letter:

My Dear Rock,

As you go to Parliament today, to speak on the West, and find a
solution to the Western problem, I wish you the guidance of Almighty
God. I pray that we succeed to restore into the 55 million of our country
men that confidence and pride in their country. I have an unshakable
faith in this great country. It must survive. You go to Parliament as a
great father, as a soldier for Nigeria - not for any group or party. Your
words today can pave the way for final sanity, not only in the West,
but in the other parts of the Federation, as it can intensify and worsen
the situation or pacify it.

I came to you with a Minister on a genuine mission to assist and
help you. I was deeply touched by what you said, that even if you gave
everyone police or soldier in the West, this cannot restore peace, unless
peace is from the soul of men.

In view of the delicate task you are to perform, I suggest that you
may consider writing it out as you did in the census, and if it is your
pleasure, I will only be too happy to offer any advice.

Please note that many years of your parliamentary life have shown
you as the greatest master among Nigerian politicians and statesmen, of
a balanced statement, except when you are annoyed, and this happens
once in several years.

I am at your service. Here I am, Rock. Use me in any way you can
in the interest of our country. I pledge you the support of the highest
authorities of my party.

Sgd: Speed & Magic.

On that fateful 15th January, early, I handed this letter to the
Information Officer, Mr. Cyprain Ekwensi, to deliver to the
Prime Minister. Mr. Ekwensi came back and told me that on his
arrival, there was no Prime Minister for him to give the letter.
Rather, the family was thrown into confusion. People were
weeping. Sir Abubakar was nowhere to be found. It was
reported that some army officers came and took him away to an
unknown destination.

I could not understand the report. I never had an idea of what
a coup looked like. I dressed up as usual and drove to the
Parliament. On arrival, I noticed people waving me back, some
saying, "a coup, go back". I ignored them. Then I saw some
soldiers, with stern looking faces, standing still at some

ocations. In fact, I gave them instructions. I said, "should anybody want to see Dr. Mbadiwe, tell him I have gone over to the Senate Building to see the Acting President, Dr. Nwafor Orizu". Before walking further to the direction of the Senate Building, I felt an unusual loneliness at a place that bustled with life in the morning hours. I felt like a truant who went to school on a holiday and looked around in vain to see his playmates. I did not see Dr. Orizu and so I turned back.

Chief R.B.K. Okafor had known what was happening. But he quietly came to see if it was possible for Parliament to meet for his swearing in that morning. The soldiers told him, "Mbadiwe passed here. He has gone to the Acting President". Chief R.B.K. Okafor frantically rushed to my house and warned my wife that, evidently, I was ignorant of what a coup was. He lamented: "Here is a person who is one of the targets of the coup, telling the soldiers where he was, and freely offering himself to them". He insisted they should find me and recall me. I soon returned to my house. When the whole situation started to dawn on me, I shivered. Soon however, I recollected myself and started to meditate on the events. Unknown to us, there had been shooting the previous night, while we were at the meeting in my house, planning how to draw back Nigeria from a precipice. Unknown to us, the soldiers were on a bid to take-over Government by force, but were not unanimous about their operations. Unknown to us the first Republic was coming to an abrupt end.

The next morning, 16th January, 1966, martial music, a familiar feature of "a gun-change" of government in Nigeria ever since, supplanted the programmes of the radio stations in Nigeria.

The Prime Minister, Sir Abubakar Tafawa Balewa, the Premier of the North, Sir Ahmadu Bello, that of the West, Chief S.L. Akintola, and the Finance Minister, Chief Festus S. Okotie-Eboh were major civilian casualties of that first army intervention. The phenomenon of this change was most unexpected because the Federal Government had just ended the hosting of the Commonwealth Prime Minister's Conference, and ArchBishop Makarrios of Cyprus was still a guest of the Premier of Eastern Nigeria, Dr. M.I. Okpara , in Enugu.

The news of the Prime Minister's demise virtually clotted my blood. At first it was reported that he was "kidnapped". The remnants of the Cabinet held a hush-hush meeting and mandated me as NCNC Parliamentary Leader and Hon. Zana Buka Dipcharima, Ag. Leader of the NPC, to sign and hand over peacefully to the army a document of transfer of power of government, if only to prevent more bloodshed. That document of handover is reproduced here:

Transfer of Power

The Council of Ministers meeting on 16th January, 1966, have asked us to convey to you their unanimous decision to transfer voluntarily the government to the Armed Forces of the Republic and wish the Armed Forces success to bring about peace and stability in Nigeria, and that the welfare of our people shall be their paramount task".

Signed: Dr. K.O. Mbadiwe   Signed: Z.B. Dipcharima

Coup planners usually strike and take over the Government at gun-point. Not so in this case. In Lagos, the Federal Government did not fall, though the Prime Minister was kidnapped". The General Officer Commanding the Armed Forces was loyal to Abubakar's Government. A successor to Abubakar, myself as the NCNC Parliamentary Leader, or Alhaji Dipcharima, Acting Parliamentary Leader of the NPC, could have stepped in. Any such successor could have easily rallied General Ironsi and the loyal Nigerian Armed Forces to fight back and crush the rebellion in the Army in order to restore democracy. We would also, as an extreme measure, invite the British or any other world power to assist us. We did neither of the two in order to avoid further bloodshed.

We had to handover, with a pledge of assurances from the Army, represented by General Ironsi. But subsequent events within the Nigerian Army itself and the military regimes ever since, showed that they were no better than the civilians. This raises the question whether we could have trusted the army to save the corporate existence of Nigeria, give it good government, and lead it to prosperity. This question has been clearly answered in the negative by the civil war that was fought, our present economic woes, instability and the unending coups that we have since witnessed.

This is all the reason why I vehemently urge that the next Republic must reject any further military intervention. I shall dwell more on this later in this memoir.

The then General Officer Commanding the Armed Forces of Nigeria, Major General J.T.U. Aguiyi-Ironsi took over as the Head of the Federal Military Government. He set up groups of provinces in place of the strong Regions and placed loyal military governors to head them. He aimed at achieving one strong nation, rather than three strong almost autonomous regions. But his fellow soldiers had not been contented with the execution of the coup. His reign was short-lived.

On July 29th, 1966, another coup took place.

Ironsi was killed while on a tour of Ibadan, together with his host, Lt.Col. Francis Adekunle Fajuyi. Lt. Col. Yakubu Gowon announced himself as the new Head of State. Following the second coup, an unprecendented massacre of non-Northerners followed in that part of the country. The main target was the Igbos, forcing the survivors to troop down to their homes in the East. Tribal fears, exploited by unscrupulous politicians as shown in many instances elsewhere in this memoir, became once more rife and unimaginable, even with the Military rulers. Federal Military Government policies and actions appeared to be directed only against the people of Eastern Group of Provinces, specially the Igbos. Lt. Col. Chukwuemeka Odumegwu Ojukwu questioned whether the East was no longer a part of Nigeria.

Some Nigerians had jubiliated at the announcement of the Military debut on January 15th 1966, if only as a "corrective" government, and one "to teach" the politicians, considering what happened in Western Nigeria, that there was a limit to which power seeking could go. It turned out, unfortunately, that the soldiers were more tribalistic, more blood-thirsty and more callous to the suffering of the citizens than the thugs of the political days. From then until now, I have held the view that however benevolent a military regime can be, it is still worse than an inept civilian administration. The latter can, in time, be changed by the ballot, the former cannot. We grapple to achieve in one swoop, as a new nation, what Britain took several centuries to evolve, and what America spent several decades to experiment. It would have therefore been unnatural if civilians did not make mistakes. Since January 15, 1966, the threat of a coup always hangs like the dagger of Damocles over any government in Nigeria, whatever assurances by the soldiers to the contrary.

Chapter 19

The Immortals Of The Nigerian Nation

In the history of every nation, there are persons whose contributions are so permanent that even when they die, those deeds of theirs will never die. Those are of history immortals. They are found in every field of human endeavour - education, the economy, sports, the sciences, arts, the professions, administration, and politics. God plants them here and there, sparingly, once in a while, and scattered through the terrain of human history.

In Nigeria, they are many, but all cannot be the subject of mention in this memoir. First I cannot claim to know everyone who should be remembered in his field of excellence. Secondly, in a personal recollection of this nature I can only remember and comment on people with whom I worked closely in politics, or who, for my topic, helped in the birth and the making of the Nigerian nation. I cannot have a definite order or chronology either, and space will allow the mention of only a few names just to illustrate my point.

On the page of *Dead But Living* we have the following: Herbert Macaulay, Mazi Mbonu Ojike, Sir Ahmadu Bello, Chief Obafemi Awolowo, Alhaji Sir Abubakar Tafawa Balewa, Dr. M.I. Okpara, Chief S.L. Akintola, Mallam Aminu Kano, Mr. J.S. Tarka, Dr. Alvan Ikoku, General J.T.U. Aguiyi-Ironsi, General Murtala Mohammed, Sir Adesoyi Aderemi, Dr. Kenneth Onwuka Dike, Alhaji Adegoke Adelabu, Sir Kashim Ibrahim, Chief F.S. Okotie-Eboh, Professor Eyo Eta, Chief Omo Osagie, Sir Louis Mbanefo etc.

On the chapter of the *Living Legend* we have: Rt. Hon. Dr. Nnamdi Azikiwe, Alhaji Shehu Shagari, Dr. Akanu Ibiam, Chief

Dr. D.C.Osadebay, General Olusegun Obasanjo, General Dr. Yakubu Gowon, Prof. Chinua Achebe, Professor Wole Soyinka, Chief Michael Imoudu, Chief Emeka Odumegwu Ojukwu, Sir Mobolaji Bank-Anthony* , Chief Jerome Udoji, General Ibrahim Babangida, Chief Dr. Kolawole Balogun, Chief Anthony Enahoro, Chief M.K.O. Abiola, Chief Emmanuel Iwuanyanwu, Chief Gabriel Igbinedion, Dr. A.A. Nwafor Orizu, Dr. T.O. Elias, Chief T.O.S. Benson, Chief S.O. Adebo, Chief A. Ogunsanya, Alhaji Ibrahim Dasuki, Alhaji Dantata. And many more. Permit me to now comment on one or two.

A. Herbert Macaulay:

Variously described as the doyen of Nigerian nationalism, and Wizard of Kirsten Hall, Herbert Samuel Heels Macaulay was born at Broad Street, Lagos, on November, 14th 1864. He was the son of Rev. Thomas Babington Macaulay, and his mother Abigail, was the daughter of Bishop Ajayi Crowther, the first African C.M.S. Bishop. Herbert Macaulay was trained in England, on Government Scholarship as a surveyor. On return, he was the surveyor of Crown Lands for seventeen years. In 1897, he went into private practice.

From his family background, education and employment, he had all it took then to live comfortably. But that upbringing, and a christian conscience, made him care for his fellow men. His politics started when Southern Nigeria was to be alienated by Britain. In 1920, he went to England to fight and win the Apapa land case and took the opportunity to meet the British Monarch, King George V. He pleaded with him for fairness in Nigeria.

Herbert Macaulay was the first Nigerian to found a political party, the Nigerian National Democratic Party, in 1922. The NNDP dominated Lagos Politics till 1937 when the Nigerian Youth Movement (NYM) stole the show from it.

When the National Council of Nigeria and the Camerouns (NCNC) was formed on August 26th, 1944, Herbert Macaulay

---

* **Died before Publication**

became its first President. It was during the country wide tour of the NCNC that he took ill and died on May 7th, 1946 at the age of 82.

Patriotic, humane, philanthropic, Macaulay was a foremost nationalist of his time. He loved freedom but did not live to see Nigeria free from serfdom.

B. Mbonu Ojike (The Boycott King)

In a preview to the 33rd remembrance ceremonies of the death of Mazi Mbonu Ojike, one Mr. Dons Eze in the *Daily Champion*, of November, 25, 1989 said of Ojike:

> He was born a dove, trained as a teacher to impart discipline to the younger ones, but later ended up to become a rebel. He went to a foreign land to learn every thing about the white man, but came back home to reject everything foreign. He stood for financial prudence and accountability, but later lost his ministerial job on account of blackmail on financial misappropriation. He led the struggle for national independence, but never reached the promised land. If after 33 years of his death, Mbonu Ojike's ideas are still found relevant in contemporary Nigeria, and are now being popularised by the Federal Government in the form of MAMSER with its gospel of self-reliance, it then means that Mbonu Ojike was a politician of the future.

With the above summary and epitaph, need one say more? Yes. Why not.

(i) *The Man, Ojike*

Publisher, author, parliamentarian, statesman, nationalist, Ojike was born at Arondizuogu, Imo State in 1914. He trained as a teacher. He taught last at the Dennis Memorial Grammar School, Onitsha, before sailing to the U.S. as the leader of the eight Argonauts in 1938. In the United States, he was a brilliant student and the author of *My Africa* and *I Have Two Countries*. He was a keen Pan-Africanist activist, who together with me presented a memorandum to the first meeting of the United Nations Assembly in San-Francisco in 1946.

After Ojike returned to Nigeria in 1947 he served first as General Manager of the *West African Pilot* newspaper, and then as Deputy Mayor of Lagos, before he became a member of the

Eastern House of Assembly and Minister of Works, and later Minister of Finance in the then Eastern Region. He initiated and successfully led a campaign against the Colonial policies which discriminated against our traditional culture, dress, music, food and other heritage that gave us our unique African personality and identity. He campaigned against everything that was foreign and dysfunctional to our culture and way of life. His familiar appeal to Nigerians to "boycott the boycottables" earned him the nick-name "Boycott King".

Ojike died in 1958, at the age of 42, but not before he had cut for himself an image as a foremost Nigerian nationalist and one of the greatest Africans that ever lived.

(ii)   *Ojike Memorial Medical Centre (OMMC)*

A few years after the death of Ojike an idea was nursed by me, then member of Parliament and Federal Minister of Trade, to perpetuate the ideals and principles for which Ojike lived and died, by the establishment of Ojike Memorial Medical Centre at Arondizuogu. In October, 1962 the scheme was launched at the Federal Palace Hotel, Victoria Island, Lagos.

On that occasion the former President of the Federal Republic, Dr. Nnamdi Azikiwe said of the proposal:

> This gesture will immortalise the memory of a great freedom fighter, it will become a source of pride and an inspiration to posterity, and it will prove that we the living neither broke faith with our compatriot, nor did we allow his good to be interred with his bones. Our act will proclaim the virtue of service and philanthropy and also vindicate patriotism, industry and public recognition ...

The Prime Minister, the Hon, Alhaji Sir Abubakar Tafawa Balewa asserted that:

> The decision to build a hospital in his (Ojike's) memory is the appreciation of his friends and country men. I call on all nationalists and friends of Nigeria to come forward to give generously to this humanitarian venture.

Friends far and near indeed contributed to the building of OMMC. When the outpatients department was completed and opened in 1974 it sparked off great enthusiasm.

On that occasion I said:

Today marks the first step of a long and tedious journey which we have embarked upon. Like everything mortal, great accomplishments are not easy to attain. Ours is no exception to this general rule ... Never in the history of philanthropy in our country has so much been done in erecting a memorabilia of a great statesman and patriot of our land".

C.   Chief Obafemi Awolowo, SAN, GCON

I have mentioned Chief Awolowo elsewhere on some specific issues - where I agree and where I differ with him. His biography is well known. My assessment of Awo as a Nigerian statesman and politician is summed up in the tribute which I paid to his memory when he died. It is hereby reproduced.

15th May, 1987

My dear Chief Mrs. Awolowo,

The news of the transition of our dear Chief Obafemi Awolowo, your loving husband, reached me during my sojourn in my home town Arondizuogu, Imo State, like a thunderbolt. The shock and grief left me dumb-founded for a while.

It is a mystery of life that death should come calling with its kleptomanic claws at a time it is least expected, having regard to all the activities your dear husband was able to undertake during these last few months of his life on earth.

However, you and indeed Nigeria as a whole should take consolation in the fact that the late Chief's life was an exemplary one. The chief was an indomitable and indefatigable fighter, who once set on a particular course, will not stop until the set objective has been achieved. Chief Awolowo in his life time carved out a place for himself in Nigeria's Hall of Fame. It is beyond dispute that any history book about modern Nigerian politics which seeks to omit mention of Chief Awolowo is incomplete. It is equally true that the course and direction of policy in this country which purports to omit Chief Awolowo's opinion is incomplete, be those opinions accepted or not.

It is therefore a monumental loss for Nigerian politics. It is hard to imagine politics without Awolowo in Nigeria. Nonetheless, we should be deeply grateful to God for **having** granted him enough time to make his numerous achievements for his motherland, both economically, socially and indeed on the whole body politic of this nation.

I recall my contacts with Chief Awolowo. The first was in the year 1951, at a meeting held in Glover Hall, Lagos. Present at that meeting were the length and breadth of who is who in Nigerian politics: Chief Dr. Nnamdi Azikiwe, Chief H.O.D. Davies, Dr. Maja to mention a few. The meeting was titled "National Rebirth." Chief Awolowo's contributions were impressive.

The second contact was during the Independence motion by Chief Anthony Enahoro in 1953, before a packed House of Parliament. I was able to arrange the historic coming together in a warm embrace between Dr. Azikiwe and Chief Awolowo, the first since they both parted ways. Both were leaders of their respective parties, the NCNC and the AG. From that period on, the planning and consolidation towards Independence caught its momentum.

In 1958, our contact became closer. During the political crisis of that year, he gave me massive support, and flew in his helicopter to Arondizuogu and constituted a friend in time of need. He was dependable, a man of his words, and above all, a person of unconquerable spirit.

For these and many other reasons, the death of the irrepressible Chief is a personal loss, a physical loss to the nation and Africa as a whole. Because of his monumental achievements, Chief Awolowo has joined the corps of Nigerian immortals; for as long as there is Nigeria, there will always be Chief Awolowo.

And for you, Chief (Mrs) Awolowo, who have been all and all to your husband, the entire Mbadiwe family, myself, my wife and children pray that God will give you and your children the courage and strength to bear this irreparable loss.

D. The Rt.Hon. Sir Abubakar Tafawa Balewa KBE, LLD.

Sir Abubakar was the first Prime Minister of the Federal Republic of Nigeria. He was popularly called the "Golden Voice of Nigeria," but I chose to call him also "The Rock". That means rock of Nigerian oneness. A teacher, humanist and great leader, he placed Nigeria on the world map of fame, hence when he was killed in the first *coup d'etat* of Nigerian history in 1966 the world was indeed shocked.

At 48, Sir Abubakar successfully led Nigeria from colonial status to freedom. His sense of honesty, unity and brotherhood stood him above the common herd of men. As a wonderful link between the North and the South, Sir Abubakar enjoyed the confidence of all, because of his practical approach to thorny problems in Nigerian and world affairs. He was a beacon of Nigeria and world peace, love and concord. His addresses to Nigeria, to the Organisation of African Unity (OAU), to the United Kingdom Parliament, to the U.S. Congress and to the United Nations Organisation (UNO) fully demonstrate his great leadership qualities.

Born in December 1912, Sir Abubakar was educated at Tafawa Balewa School, Bauchi Provincial School, Katsina Higher College, and the University of London. On his return he became an Education Officer and was appointed a member of the Old Legislative Council.

In 1951, he was returned as first member for Bauchi in the Northern House of Assembly, and re-elected to the House of Representatives. He became Federal Minister of Works in January, 1952, and was Federal Minster of Transport from 1954 to 1957 when he was appointed Nigeria's first Prime Minister. As Prime Minister, Sir Abubakar believed that democracy in Nigeria needed to be nurtured with care, patience and single mindedness. So he made haste slowly. But when the Military first struck on January, 15th 1966, Sir Abubakar Tafawa Balewa was one of its casualties. But his memory lingers and his works stay.

E. Alhaji Shehu Usman Aliyu Shagari, LLD (ABU)

Much like Sir Abubakar, Shagari's obsession for oneness and greatness of Nigeria made him supercede all conspiracy and insult against his person and his office from political opponents as the first Executive President of the Federal Republic of Nigeria. And also like Sir Abubakar, the soldiers did not allow him time to heal the cracks in the national edifice caused by the hotly contested 1983 elections.

Born May 1924 in Shagari village, Yabo, Sokoto State, Alhaji Shehu was trained as a teacher and in 1954 was elected Member for Sokoto West in the House of Representatives. From 1954 till 1983 he was almost continuously in Government: Parliamentary Secretary to the Prime Minister (1954-1958). Minister of Economic Development (1959-1960), Minister of Pensions and Establishment (1960-1962), Minister of Internal Affairs (1962 - 1965) and Minister of Works (1965-1966), Commissioner for Establishments North Western State (1967-1969), Federal Commissioner for Economic Development, Rehabilitation and Reconstruction (1970-1971), Federal Commissioner for Finance (1971-1975), Chairman Peugeot Automobile (Nigeria) Limited, (1975-1978), Member Constituent Assembly (1977-1978), First Executive President of Nigeria (1979-1983).

F. **Dr. Akanu Ibiam MB, CH.B, D. LITT, (U.I), DSC (OAU)**

Traditional Ruler, Educationist, Physician, Politician and Humanist, Dr. Francis Akanu Ibiam was born in Uwana*, Imo State, 1906. He was the first Easterner to enter Kings' College, Lagos, and probably the first Igbo man to qualify as a medical doctor.

Dr. Ibiam is imbued with those qualities which raise a man above the ordinary and make him appear as though he were of a different clay. Those who have come in contact with him are compelled to be influenced by his dominating and lovable christian personality. He admonishes us to shed off fear in order to speak the truth, and to cast off hatred in order to love our fellow men. He abhores injustice. In protest against the British attitude towards Biafra during the civil war, he dropped his British title of Knighthood.

Educated at Uwana, Hope Waddel Training Institute, Calabar, Kings' College, Lagos, University of St. Andrew's,

---

* Uwana now in Abia State

cotland, Dr. Ibiam worked as a medical officer in the Church of Scotland Mission Hospitals at Calabar, Uburu and other places. He was a long time member of the Board of Hope Waddel Institute, Calabar of which he became Principal in 1957-1960.

For many years he was a member of the Eastern House of Assembly, and of the Old Legislative Council. A great religious leader, Dr. Ibiam also was Chairman, Council of the University College Ibadan (1958-1961) and Governor of the Eastern Region, 1960-1966.

Currently Dr. Akanu Ibiam is the Chairman of the Imo State Council of *Ndi-Eze* (Traditional Rulers) and Chairman Board of Governors, Ojike Memorial Medical Centre, a role which brings me in regular contact with him.

Dr. Ibiam is never silent on any national issue bordering on discrimination, injustice, corruption, and godlessness. Whenever Ibiam speaks, the nation listens.

G. Chief Dennis Chukwude Osadebay LLB, BL, GCON, D.LITT, LLD.

Osadennis, as he is fondly called in literary circles, is a lawyer, poet and politician, and one of the great builders of what is today called the Nigerian nation. Born in Asaba, Bendel State, in 1911, he was educated at the Hope Waddel Training Institute, Calabar, and the University of London.

The pride he brings to this country started in 1929, when he led twenty-four Boys Scouts who represented Nigeria to the first World Scout Jamboree in England. When a student in London, 1947, he was elected the Director of Information for the newly formed West African Students Union.

On return to Nigeria, after qualifying as a lawyer he took active part in the nationalist struggles that eventually brought Independence in 1960. He was elected to the Western House of Assembly in 1951 and from then till 1966, at various times became leader of Opposition Western Region, Deputy Speaker Western House of Assembly, President of the Nigerian Senate, Acting Governor-General of Nigeria, Administrator of Mid-

Western Nigeria, and Premier Mid-Western Nigeria (now Bendel State) 1964 - 1966.

The poet - politician, Osadennis, published *Africa Sings* in 1952. This book gave him instant fame in the literary world. He had other publications to his credit. Chief Osadebay believes in truth, loyalty and service, qualities which made him an automatic choice to lead the newly created Mid-Western Nigeria in 1964.

This simple, kind and frank christian is a great leader of thought whose eternal youthful appearance continues to shine as he grows older!

Part IV
The Nigerian Civil War

General Yakubu Gowon. He ordered "police action" on Biafra and later declared a total war

Lt Col C. Odumegwu-Ojukwu who led the Biafran cause.

Stopping the war and restoring peace. (L to R) Professor Eyo B.E.Ndem, Dr. K. O. Mbadiwe and Dr Nwoye Otue, at a press conference in Toronto, Canada, March 7, 1968.

Delivering gifts, including the unnumbered Mercedes Benz lorry and food items at Enugu for the war affected areas. Watching are members of Mbadiwe family.

At home in Ideato, his Local Government Area. Sharing a joke with (L to R) Chief (Councillor) A.C. Umeh, Dr. Rowland A. Anyanwu, Chief (Councillor)S.I. Anyikwa, Mazi Luke Agusiegbe (first Chairman of Ideato Local Government) and Mr I.O.G. Okereke. The occasion was the reception for the Mayor of Campdem, Mr. Angello Erichettli.

As Presidential Adviser, presenting a Bill from the National Assembly to Mr President for signature into Law. (L to R) front President Shehu Usman Shagari, Chief R.A.O. Akinjide, the Federal Attorney General and Minister of Justice, and Dr. Joseph Wayas President of the Nigerian Senate.

Ambassador Extra-Ordinary and Plenipotentiary. Sharing a joke on the swearing-in-ceremony with from (LtoR) (Chief J.O.Udoji, Sir Mobolaji Bank-Anthony, Chief M.N. Ugochukwu, Chief D.C. Osadebay, Chief Bayo Kuku and Sir Chief M.O.Kanu)..

A Reception for the Vice-President. (L to R) Dr. K.O. Mbadiwe, Chief J.O. Okoroafor, Chief Dr. Alex Ekwueme, (Vice President), President Shehu Shagari and Chief J. Green Mbadiwe.

Arranging for the visit to Nigeria of His Holiness Pope John Paul II, in 1982. In the picture (L to R) are Mr President, Shehu Shagari, Dr K.O. Mbadiwe, a Monsignor of the Catholic Secretariate Lagos, Cardinal Francis Arinze, then Archbishop of Onitsha and President of the Catholic Bishops Conference of Nigeria, and Archbishop A. Olubunmi Okogie of Lagos.

Chapter 20

The Gowon Era: The Coup And Counter-Coup

As stated earlier, Hon. Dipcharima and I signed the handover note to the Army on 16th January 1966. In March, Chief T. O. S. Benson, Chief M. N. Ugochukwu, other NCNC members and I were detained in Ikoyi Prison. It was a an unique experience in itself.

We adjusted to prison life with calmness. Our friendly greeting was, "Man No Die" to which the other responded "Man No Rotten". From prison, I wrote Gen. Ironsi. There was no reply. On August 2nd 1966, after the second coup of 29th July, 1966, I was released from prison. In fact the gate of the prison was opened. We just walked out. I hurried back to rejoin my family at Arondizuogu, East of the Niger. An open air thanksgiving service presided over by Bishop J. B. Whelan, of Owerri Diocese, was conducted in my honour at the Orlu stadium.

With the mass return of Igbo people, stories of atrocities committed on them, descriptions of the mass graves for those killed in the North, filled the air. People who had not visited or returned home for a long time had to beg for shelter and food from both close and distant relatives. Homes were packed with returnees, and compounds littered, in the sun and the rain, with belongings of those refugees. Day after day, the position worsened.

On the other side of Nigeria, Chief Awolowo was released from prison. He later joined the Gowon Government and was made the Federal Commissioner for Finance and Vice-Chairman of the Executive Council.

The Consultative Assembly

In the Eastern Region, Colonel Ojukwu rallied the leaders and set up a Consulative Assembly. I contested the seat there for Orlu and won. In the Consulative Assembly, I was consistent in opposing secession and urged for a peaceful settlement. My views in this were identical with those of Dr. Azikiwe. Other elders in the East who were foresighted urged for a negotiated settlement, in spite of the mass killings that occurred, following Nigeria's second coup.

Within two months of his assumption of office as the Head of State, Gowon, who had in his maiden speech said that "the basis of unity is not there", convened an ad-hoc Constitutional Conference of September 12, 1966. In his opening address he said

> It is very clear to me that it will be economically and politically suicidal to harbour any idea of a complete break-up of the Federation. Therefore we seem to be left with the alternative of (a) Federation with a strong central government, (b) a Federation with a weak central government, (c) a Confederation.

Hopes were raised in Eastern Nigeria. However, that all important Conference failed.

Meanwhile, the quarrel between Ojukwu and Gowon continued, and culminated in a peace-meeting in Aburi, Ghana. Col. Ojukwu returned and reported this to our joy. We heaved another great sigh of relief and a hope of Nigerian peace and unity, was rekindled. The body of the dead General Ironsi was brought back to his home and re-buried at Umuahia, in a gesture of reconciliation.

The War Sets In

But on Gowon's return to Lagos from Ghana, the agreements the two sides had reached at Aburi in January 1967 received a different interpretation. Ojukwu in the East held to the terms of their accord namely, a confederal arrangement for a true unity. When those agreements were not implemented, tempers began rising again. Events started moving dangerously fast. On May

27th, 1967 Gowon announced the creation of twelve States in the Federation. It was a bomb shell. Three days later, on the 30th of May, 1967, Ojukwu declared the independent State of Biafra. It was a 'cannon ball'. The fall-out from both actions was the trauma of thirty months, now called the "Nigerian Civil War".

On July 6, 1967, the Nigeria/Biafra war started with first shots at Gakem near Obudu, in what Gowon described as a mere 'police action". It raged for two and half years. My opposition to secession led to my house-arrest and other harsh treatments meted to me by the government of Biafra. I was silenced for peddling Nigerian unity. The Orlu People's Assembly which I had founded was banned. When I was released from house arrest, I was surprised to be sent out in September 1967 as a special Envoy of Biafra to the United Kingdom and the United States. In the same way, Dr. Nnamdi Azikiwe was sent to East Africa. Mr. C. C. Mojekwu was sent to Europe. I was faithful in seeking support abroad for the starving people. It was also an opportunity to seek for a peaceful settlement of the war and to re-unite Nigeria. I believed that a people had been wronged. It hurt me deeply. I also regretted to see that the Nigeria we had toiled and sacrificed for, was being allowed to disintegrate. I was equally sad.

My activities abroad are better summarised in the following sketch. On 30th September 1967, I landed in Paris from where I sent a cablegram to Prime Minister Leslie Pearson of Australia, asking for permission to come and discuss of the situation in Nigeria and the role I think the Commonwealth Prime Ministers would play. I also wrote Lt. Col. Juxon-Smith, Chairman of the National Revolutionary Council of Sierra Leone on the same topic.

On October 6th, 1967 I arrived London and shortly after, addressed a press conference. I blamed the British press for their lack of sufficient concern and accuracy in their reports. I expressed alarm at the interventional policy of the British Government, and asked the press to play a role as moulders of public opinion for peace. I addressed a letter to Prime Minister

Harold Wilson and sent telegrams to Emperor Haile Selassie and President Tubman, two of Organisation of African Unity's appointed mediators in the war, urging them to use their good offices to ensure a successful peaceful settlement of the dispute.

To Prime Minister Wilson, I protested his apparent opposition to peaceful settlement and his supply of arms and other weapons to Nigeria. I urged him to press for a peaceful settlement.

November 20th, 1967, I arrived U.S.A. On meeting with Mr. Melbourne, Deputy to Joseph Palmer II, Assistant Secretary for African Affairs at the State Department, Washington D. C. he (Melbourne) protested my involvement and activities for Biafra as a foreign envoy, thereby contravening the terms of my visa. I spiritedly defended myself against this charge. Then the dialogue turned on the subject of approaches to negotiations in the conflict and the denial of American visas to Biafrans. On December 4, 1967; I delivered a lecture on the topic "REFLECTIONS ON NIGERIA-BIAFRA CRISIS", at Northwestern University, Evaston, Illinois. My theme was the effectiveness of negotiations as an avenue to peace. My aim was "to stimulate discussion... and provide a guideline for peace and stability". That lecture was under the auspices of the African Studies Programme of the University. Professor Mabogunje and his wife presented the Nigerian perspective of the crisis.

Soon, after visiting the Chicago Chapter of Biafran Students Association, I wrote a long report of the first phase of my mission to Ojukwu. I made recommendations on the subject of Biafra's diplomatic offensive in the U.S., Great Britain, the Commonwealth and the O.A.U. I also forwarded all money aid obtained for the medical supplies and relief to victims of the conflict. On January 11th, 1968 Ojukwu wrote Bishop Swanstrom of the Catholic Relief Services expressing gratitude for the sympathetic co-operation of late Cardinal Francis Spellman, of himself, and the CRS., and especially for the gift of $15,000 for drugs and other reliefs. The same date also he, Ojukwu, wrote to Mr. H. E. Schueller of the African Concerns

Committee, N. Y., thanking him for their generosity in donating $10,000 worth of medical equipment by his organisation.

On January 13th 1968, Mr. G. A. Onyegbule, Permanent Secretary, Ministry of External Affairs of Biafra, prepared a document, "Programme of action for K. O. Mbadiwe as approved by His Excellency, the Military Governor and Head of the Republic of Biafra". That document specified the nature of my assignment in London, Africa and the U.S. I was to be accompanied by Dr. N. Otue and a student in the U. S. to serve as Secretary. An approved allowance was specified. Copies of the document were given to Biafran Representatives in Lisbon, London and New York. From then I went about for the rest of the engagements with Dr. Otue.

On February 17th 1968, I established Club 250 in London as a means of generating more funds for Biafra. Each member was to contribute £100.00 towards the war effort. In the inaugural meeting I recounted the background of the struggle. Many Biafrans rushed to join and contribute. The proceeds were recorded and sent to Biafra.

On March 14th, 1968 I gave a press conference at the National Press Club, Washington D.C. on the nature of the war and obstacles to peace. I condemned the attitude of complete "indifference" by America which contrasted with U.S. policy over Cyprus. I urged America to use its moral weight to see that the bloodshed of the Biafra-Nigeria war was stopped.

By March 16th, 1968, in a letter of that date, Lt. Col. Ojukwu wrote me in New York, thanking me for my "magnificent efforts" in America. He requested that I raised $100,000 before the end of March.

On April 20th, 1968, I wrote to Ojukwu, telling him that my partners and I had raised $110,000 out of which $102,000 had been sent to meet the March 30th deadline. I informed him of the phase two of the fund raising, aimed at Biafran Refugees. I reported our meeting with Senator Brooks, Bishop Swanstrom and listed unfinished tasks, in view of the order that the delegation should return. Up to date records of account of collections were kept. In August, I was back to Biafra.

On September 17th, 1968, I initiated a move to persuade Ojukwu to end the war, by "accepting the realities of the situation". A delegation of seven, led by the late Dr. Alvan Ikoku, including four prominent traditional rulers in Igboland met him. I had moved outside and come back home recently to face the position inside Biafra, therefore, I was in better position to advise.

At the Biafran Consultative Assembly meeting, the next day, during which the recent abortive peace negotiations with Nigeria at Kampala, Uganda, was reviewed, I addressed the Assembly and urged members to pass a resolution in support of peace and to give implicit vote of confidence to Justice Louis Mbanefo who led the Biafran delegation to Kampala.

By September 24th, 1968, after obtaining permission to travel abroad on health reasons, on an application made to Ojukwu on 17th, September, 1968 I left Biafra for a London clinic. Even with my poor health, I did not relax working in the best interest of my people, and was in constant contact with Ojukwu.

On October 6th, 1968, a meeting of Biafrans held in Conway Hall, London agreed to set up a Biafra National Loans Account. The Committee set up to manage its funds was headed by the Biafran Special Representative, Dr. Kooffrey. The target was £50,000.00. Three teams were despatched to tour zones in Great Britain, and within a short time that target was met.

On January 4th, 1969, I wrote Prime Minister Harold Wilson, again expressing disappointment at his role in fuelling the war, by giving diplomatic and military support to one side. I also wrote other Commonwealth Heads of State who were to attend the Commonwealth Conference in London, namely Mrs Indira Ghandi, Mr. P. E. Trudeau, Archbishop Makarios, Kenneth Kaunda and Julius Nyerere. I urged all to take the initiative to promote a peaceful settlement.

On January 16th, 1969, Chief Obafemi Awolowo called me by telephone in London offering to meet me any where I preferred. The meeting could not hold because Chief Awolowo made his invitation public through the press. I wrote him back.

Because of poor health my activities were minimised. But I attended rallies in London. By 30th January 1969, I was able to write Ojukwu announcing my departure to the U.S., after a long contested battle for passport and travel documents. I got a passport waiver. I reported that £50,000 had been collected in London, and despatched. I also despatched 800 bicycle tyres for the Biafran Government to distribute.

The role of the press is relevant here to be mentioned. The Biafran propaganda machine was a very effective vehicle of sustaining the war. Its foreign office based at 136 Route de Chene, 1224 Geneva, Paris, issued powerful daily releases. But the U.S. Press was biased in favour of Nigeria till I made a tour of North America and addressed press conferences with Dr. E. B. Ndem and Dr. N. Otue in my company. Then balanced assessment of the situation started to emerge.

The *Time Weekly News Magazine* of April 4th, 1969 carried a detailed report by Winston Spencer Churchill II who toured both sides of the war front. His series of reports compelled Prime Minister Harold Wilson to visit Nigeria as the British public's discontent over his handling of the situation increased.

Churchill described *kwashiokor* children and the scene of an air raid in Biafra. Hear him;

> Their bellies were as large as a pregnant woman's; their limbs like match sticks, and some had testicles swollen to the size of a large grape fruit. One approached a Priest at a refugee camp and asked, "Father, what is happening to my body?"
> After a Nigerian plane bombed a civilian market place Churchill saw, there were so many unattached feet, hands, legs, and arms that it was impossible to tell to which body they belonged.

On April 26th, 1969, black American leaders, A. Philip Randolp, Congress woman Shirely Chisholm, Roy Wilkins, etc. cabled a plea to Ethiopian Emperor Haile Selassie at the OAU meeting in Monrovia, urging the OAU to find a solution to the Biafran-Nigerian War. The plea from the National Association for the Advancement of Coloured People's (NAACP) office in New York was indicative of the softening of their antagonism towards Biafra. This followed my lobbying and balanced press report. Earlier I had met U.S. officials like Mr. John Volpe, the Transport Secretary, Hon. Elliot Richardson, and Senator Edward Kennedy. His Eminence, Cardinal Cushing of Boston was instrumental in linking me up with some of them.

Individuals who helped to organise aid or who took risks of travel need be mentioned. They included Dr. Rowland Anyanwu and Mr. Eguzoikpe Wachukwu of the Biafran Relief Fund Inc., U.S.A.; Mr. Levi Unam and others of Club 250, and more importantly, the late Bishop G.M.P. Okoye of Missio Catholica, Sao Tome. Others are Mrs. M.M. Agbor, Dr. Osita Agbim, Rev. E.C.O. Ilogu, Dr. U.U. Uche and others of the Biafran Relief and Rehabilitation Organisation based in London.

The End of the War

On January 15th, 1970, the civil war ended. As I was active in war, so was I in peace. I held discussions in New York with senior Biafran colleagues on our new role. We first sent a fact finding mission to Nigeria in February. Because of my health, I could not return till July. When the green light was given, I flew in company of Chief M.N. Ugochukwu from London. I bought relief materials and assisted in the relief and rehabilitation of the war-torn area, and of the Government of the East Central State.

My next mission would be to fully assist in the reintegration of the East Central State people to the rest of one great Nigeria. A letter I addressed to General Yakubu Gowon, dated July 24th, 1970, says it all.

Your Excellency,

Chief M. N. Ugochukwu and I thank you once more for the audience you have given us today in the interest of our country.

I like to take this opportunity to give my personal response to your call for a programme of national reconciliation and reconstruction. By this call, you have given opportunity to every citizen of this country to rise to the great occasion of being his brother's keeper; of serving other causes greater than himself.

By reconciliation, we attempt to join together hearts which otherwise were disappointed and dislocated. By this we come to realise that we cannot do without each other, that the sorrow of one automatically becomes the sorrow of the other and that our happiness is fulfilled in the happiness of others. By reconstruction, we normalise the abnormal.

Your call is a challenge to all of us to make the supreme sacrifice in building a great country which is only possible when its citizen begins to think of the welfare of others as he does for himself and his relations. Any organised society which cannot provide succour for its needy millions cannot offer security to the few who are rich. I am convinced that this country is richly endowed and has the capacity, the capability and world-wide goodwill to rescue all its citizens from want, hunger and insecurity.

It is because of my earnest belief and conviction in this noble cause that I hereby present, to Your Excellency, for the war-torn areas:-

(1) One new six-ton Mercedes Lorry
(2) Ten bales of clothing, bill of lading attached.
(3) Ten tons of rice to be distributed to the orphans in the badly affected areas. In order to facilitate purchases from the closest areas, I attach a cheque of £1,000 to cover this tonnage.

I have made these gifts to you, not because I have the material resources to do so, but because to forge the nation, all of us need make sacrifices by donating our widow's mite, in order to reassure the widows and the orphans of the wounded and the dead that they will never starve or remain unclothed or unsheltered in the midst of plenty. I like to see our churches and mosques flooded with yams, beans, loaves of bread and whatever we can lay our hands on every Sunday and Friday, for distribution to the destitutes and the disabled. I like to see our students in schools and colleges deposit any extra thing they have for the comfort of those who have nothing. That is total commitment for building national solidarity and rehabilitation.

Your Excellency, since the war-torn areas will take time to reconstruct, it is only your personal leadership, backed up with all the man-power and resources this country can muster, that will bring it to a quicker realization. I pray to the Almighty God to give you the strength to cope with this immense and gigantic task. Your leadership in this respect is in the absolute interest of this country.

It is my fervent hope and wish that never again, as a people, should we give opportunity for any war situation to reappear in our midst.

Your being in the forefront will also be an inspiration to those who are now immediately presiding over the destiny of those in the war affected areas, when they know that you and the nation are behind their efforts. By the very nature of things, we cannot normalise a situation which has become desperate until the abnormality is wiped out.

Your Excellency, the part which I know you played to bring the bloodshed to an end has endeared you to my heart. That single act was responsible for our return to answer your call.

Yours truly,
K. O. Mbadiwe

I have always been a firm believer in the concept that if Nigeria has to remain a united and strong country, one must of necessity cultivate a sense of determination and realism and make all the necessary concessions required to handle the precarious balances associated with complex and multi-ethnic societies.

Consequently, my political philosophy which is a basic factor in my role during the civil war of 1967-1970 emphasized mutual understanding as a pre-condition for tolerance and cooperation in a strong united Nigeria. When these two crucial factors were missing from the Nigerian society in 1967, and there was no indication that attempts were being made to understand ourselves or the issues involved in the tragedies of 1966 and 1967, I sought solace in my next most fundamental philosophy- namely human rights, enunciated in terms of dignity of the human person.

I was for peace, but not for peace by the death of a people, no matter their ethnic origin. Peace for me any time is synonymous with justice. As a realistic politician, I know that peace without justice is a mission impossible. What therefore is important for all to understand is that from 1952 to 1966, I was a well integrated political figure and a political office holder, not a disgruntled, complaining Nigerian. During that period, I served as Federal Minister in the Ministeries of Land and Natural Resources, Communication and Aviation, Trade and Industry.

Therefore throughout the war, my role concentrated on alleviating the suffering of the victims of the war, and appealing to the two young leaders of the combatant forces to make peace, based on a durable future for all concerned. It is between these two rather conflicting feelings that my dilemma lay throughout the war years, love for my kinsmen and love for my country.

My Motivations

In summary, I wish to restate, even at the expense of any repetition, that the two motivations which propelled my action through out the civil war period were: "Humanitarian" and "Peace effort".

(i) *Humanitarian*

In spite of detention and house-arrest, (I was told it was for my security), I agreed to work for Biafra, in order to help reduce human suffering attendant on the war. I had made my stand clear that the first approach for ending the sufferings was to stop the cause of it, by ending the war and negotiating for peace. When it failed, I set out abroad.

In Britain my first task was to insist on a balanced report, because the press, the government and the British public were one in their bias against Biafra. I reversed the situation. The British Prime Minister had to visit Nigeria to assess the situation personally. Philanthropists rallied to assist. The church came in through the World Council of Churches. Oxfarm started sending relief. The blanket of press bias was lifted and British journalists went on both sides of the war front and on return home reported the realities of the war situation and the untold human sufferings.

In the U.S., I started through the church. Cardinal Spellman was wonderful in his understanding of the sorry situation in Biafra. But he died before action really began. His successors took over. The U.S. Government was initially indifferent. So were Negro Organisations. But due to my activities and approaches both the Government and the Negro groups were so aroused that they started to send relief materials.

In both Britain and the U.S., Biafrans breasted up to what happened at home with great concern. They formed committees and associations which they managed. They raised the funds which were sent to the Biafran government for their suffering parents, brothers, sisters, and relations at home.

On return home, I met General Yakubu Gowon and offered to help in response to his appeal on the three R's:-reconstruction, rehabilitation and reconciliation. I made the donations to that cause, not because I had a surplus or had adjusted personally but because I wanted to identify with whatever brought relief and succour to my people of the war-torn area.

(ii) *Peace Effort*

Since my return from the U.S. in 1948, I had preached and practised and worked for one nation. I firmly believed that Nigeria, with multi-ethnic groups, could still forge unity in diversity in order to be as great as the United States of America whose populations represent all races of the world. Every American is proud of the U.S., whatever his or her race.

It is the same overriding spirit of one united country which informed our peaceful and voluntary handover of government to the military in 1966 thought to be the only institution better placed, than any political party then, to continue the objective of one nation. As a national army it was better placed to continue. Sir Abubakar's great task of binding together the country which was being torn apart by over emphasis on regionalism and ethnic groupings. Therefore all my efforts between 1966 and 1970 were geared towards peace.

My addresses at the Biafran Consultative Assembly were directed to peaceful settlement of the grave conflict. Inside and outside the Assembly I advocated for peace. Letters, interviews and delegations to Col. Ojukwu were on peace.

In Britain, I confronted Mr. Wilson, British Prime Minister, to bring the two sides together. I urged the Commonwealth leaders attending the biannual conference in London to address themselves to the situation in a sister Commonwealth country. From Britain also I addressed messages to the leaders of the

Organisation of African Unity (OAU) to intervene on the part of peace, and step up the peace effort.

I roused America and moved them from sitting on the fence. I urged them to bring the two sides together. I pointed out their inconsistency of policy by collaborating with the Soviet Union to supply arms and ammunition to one side instead of arranging for both sides to sit and talk.

Apart from contacts with world leaders, I also arranged and contacted Nigerian leaders. I condemned Chief Awolowo's philosophy of "hunger as a legitimate instrument of warfare" and arranged to talk to him. He made it a press debate and the effort failed. I asked Gowon to appoint another person. He appointed Dr. Dikko. I met Ahmed Joda and we had useful discussions which would lead to peace. As I was in contact with Gowon on the Nigerian side, on the Biafra side, I was also in contact with Ojukwu.

When I was away, either in Britain or in the United States the quest for peace and the situation at home was a great subject of discussion with Biafran leaders - Dr. Kooffrey Mr, C. C. Mojekwu, Dr. Otue, Dr. Ndem, the Biafran elders and group leaders.

I doubled my efforts in reconciliation at the end of the war, as I did for the search for peace, meeting persons in authority and addressing press conferences. If there were "no victors and no vanquished", I said, then what used to be Biafra must be re-integrated into the Nigerian community, money made to circulate there, their work positions secured, and their property returned. Only by the good management of peace can the many hearts broken and homes disorganised be mended.

Harsh Effects of Government Policies

Despite the amnesty declared by General Yakubu Gowon at the end of the war, the declaration of no victor no vanquished status for both sides, and the launching of his three R's (rehabilitation, reconciliation and reconstruction), some of the fiscal policies of the Federal Commissioner of Finance and Vice-Chairman of the

Federal Executive Council, Chief Obafemi Awolowo impoverished and demoralised people of Eastern Nigeria.

First was the currency exchange. People in the war affected areas were asked to deposit all the money they had into banks or government sub-treasuries for exchange with the Nigerian currency. To everybody's surprise, and several months after the lodgements, the Federal Government directed that for whatever value or amount of money any one deposited, he would be paid only £20.00 (N40.00) in exchange. And again if any account, opened anywhere before the war for any amount, had been tampered with, at the end of the war, such an account was to be frozen and the proceeds exchanged with £20.00.

As if that was not punishment and reprisal enough, the Nigerian Enterprises Promotion Decree and the indigenisation policy were announced early in the 1970's. By these, Nigerians were to buy up foreign businesses; and for certain other conglomerates, Nigerian participation was to be sixty percent. One cannot but interprete all these as aimed at the people just from the war zone, who were being paid N20 each. The war of the bullet failed to crush a people. The battle of the naira was launched to cripple them. But providence, industry and determination triumphed over the war of the pound and later the naira for the discriminated people of the war affected areas.

The war years coincided with the years of the oil boom. It boiled to its peak during the rule of General Gowon to 1975. To assuage the hardship associated with the war years, workers had demanded for a review of their salaries. The Udoji Award of 1974 brought in an avalanche of money into the market with its inflationary characteristics. But the general standard of living had improved. Then came the change of government by yet another *coup d'etat* along side the ebb of the oil boom in 1975/76.

On my return to Nigeria after the war in 1970, I bent down to reorganise myself and my businesses. I relaunched the African Insurance Company Limited, founded in 1950. I resuscitated the Afro World Merchants, and later founded the Afro Motors. Less of public life helped me to revive the work on the Ojike Memorial

Medical Centre. I was able to care for my family and look after the less privileged in the society through the Dr. K. O. Mbadiwe Foundation.

Part V
The Second Republic

217

Lecturing at University of Nigeria, Nsukka in 1974 on "The Visions for the Republic after the Military."

With Japanese Trade & Technology Mission to Nigeria.

Chapter 21

The Murtala/Obasanjo Regime

Between 1966 and 1976, I watched the scene in Africa and military regimes with disgust and helplessness. Most African Nations which recently attained Independence caught the infection of the *coup d' etat* in Nigeria in 1966. Dr. Kwame Nkrumah's government was toppled, so was Abubakar's in Nigeria. Later the same year, General Mobutu Sesseseko of Congo strengthened his hold on that country as ever before. Togo, Dahomey, Central African Republic, Chad and Mali came under military rules within the period.

When I was dreaming of independent Africa twenty years earlier, it was not to replace the imposed colonial rule with another imposed rule, by the force of arms, by our own soldiers. Yet these coups were often greeted with initial applause by the citizens who took to the streets in support. Coups were further encouraged by the admission of these new military regimes into world and regional bodies like the United Nations, the Commonwealth and the Organisation of African Unity. If these bodies had questioned how a man had come to power, and rejected his representing his country, more coups and counter-coups could have been discouraged. But the violent changes were regarded as "internal affairs" in world diplomacy.

In Nigeria, General Yakubu Gowon was in power for nine years (1966-1975), three of which he fought a civil war. During his regime, the Naira as a decimal currency was introduced. Mention has been made of the indigenisation decree. The physical face of Lagos, the capital of Nigeria, changed, with wide fly-overs, and the improvement of Tafawa Balewa square. More refineries were built and crude oil was pumped from Warri in the Delta to Kaduna refinery, some two thousand kilometres into the far-north.

The craze and fever of the demand for imported goods rose to a boiling point. Corruption unprecedented soaked into the army itself, the government and the civil-service, as was revealed later by the Murtala Mohammed purges. General Gowon who had promised a handover to the civilians in 1976, reneged, only because that year "was no longer practicable" for him.

In July 1975, while Gowon was attending an OAU conference in Kenya, his regime was toppled, in yet another coup by General Murtala Ramat Mohammed. Mohammed's short, less than one year rule was the most spectacular in Nigerian history. He attacked corruption with the vigour and courage, no other ruler ever had. Of the eleven Governors and one Administrator of Gowon's twelve states, only Brigadier Mobalaji Johnson of Lagos State and Brigadier Oluwole Rotimi of Western State were absolved of corruption. Total value of assets confiscated, following investigations, was worth over N10 million. The nine Governors and the Administrator of the East Central State were dismissed "with immediate effect", and the Head of State, in a dawn broadcast on 3rd February, 1975, said "they should be ashamed of themselves for betraying the trust and confidence reposed on them by the nation". The purge affected the civil service too, and the affected officers were retired or dismissed, also "with immediate effect".

General Mohammed created seven new states (Ogun, Ondo, Benue, Gongola, Niger, Bauchi, and Imo) to bring the number to 19 to further ensure the stability of the nation. He then announced that the new capital of Nigeria would be Abuja. Both the States creation and Federal Capital panels were headed by Justices Ayo Irikefe and Akinola Aguda respectively.

The memorandum signed by me and many other prominent Igbo leaders argued successfully for the creation of two States from the East Central State, namely Imo and Anambra. The same was true for the struggle for the citing of the capital of Imo State at Owerri.

I cannot forget the efforts, sleepless nights, meetings, and
vels of Chief J.O. Udoji, Chief M.N. Ugochukwu, Chief
llins Obih, Chief Evan Enwerem, Chief Kanu Offonry of the
gos front, or the noble pressures from the home front,
arheaded by the late Chief S.E. Onukogu, Eze Patrick
holonu, the Igwe of Orlu, other Ezes and the leaders of Imo
the citing of the headquarters at Owerri.

To further heal the wounds of the civil war, General
)hammed took another bold step; not only did he order the
urn of the so called "abandoned properties" to their rightful
'ners, he also allocated N14 million to the Governments of
/ers and South Eastern States to pay a flat rate of N500.00 to
:ry building property as rent arrears yearly for a period of five
urs from 1970 to 1975.

On the political level, General Murtala Mohammed, in
lition, launched a transition programme which eventually
urned the country to civilian administration in 1979. He did
t live to hand over personally, because he was assassinated in
: another abortive coup on February 13th 1976. But he made
. mark.

When the life and rule of Mohammed was cut short on an
en-day robbery of power, organised by Col. Dimka, the
licies of the regime were inherited by the next in command.
l Gen. Olusegun Obasanjo, who promised to continue from
lere Mohammed stopped. Obasanjo kept his word.

He set up the Constitution Drafting Committee (C.D.C.) of
ty-nine wise men under the chairmanship of Chief F.R.A.'
illiams (SAN). I was privileged to be appointed by
)vernment to serve in this Committee of hope. It was in this
mmittee that Chief Obafemi Awolowo publicly refused to
rve. Obasanjo's regime was also known for the local
vernment reforms of 1976, the Land-use Decree of 1978, and
: "low profile" policy in public life, after governement realised
it the oil boom had ebbed like a tide.

After the forty-nine "wise men" submitted the Draft
nstitution to the Government and the Constituent Assembly

was set up, I gave an interview to the *Newbreed Magazine* published in the December 1977 issue. Mr. Tony Amadi, the Assistant Editor, threw the first question to me, "What area of the Draft Constitution are you going to lobby for adoption by the Constituent Assembly?" My answer; "I will lobby for Nigerian Unity, not for specific points in the Draft". On coups. I answered him; "If you serve your people well, forget about coups. Even if it is attempted, it will fail before you know it." Those statements which I made to *Newbreed Magazine* in 1977 still stand today for me.

Chapter 22

The Transition Period

The African scene, the ideological divide of the world, and the failure of Nigeria's first Republic and of the Parliamentary system of government had given me much concern. I had looked for an appropriate opportunity to air my views. Then I got an invitation by the Economic Society of the University of Nigeria, Nsukka, for an address on 15th October, 1974. In this, I outlined my views of the Second Republic which included the Presidential System, the choice of the President, the Separation of Powers and other issues which eventually found their way into the 1979 Constitution. It was a widely publicised lecture. Excerpts:

The Case for Rotation

The Igbo man is an Igbo man, though he wants to belong to a bigger Nigeria with Hausas, Yorubas and others. The same is true of the Hausa, the Yoruba, and other groups. This is true of every ethnic group in the country including even the smallest of the minority groups.

This fact is fundamental to our Nigerianness and ought to be recognised and entrenched in our constitution, so that there must be provision for all sections of this country at one time or the other, on a principle of rotation, to have an access to the highest office in this great land. National political parties must also entrench this in their constitution and will in fact be compelled to do so if entrenched in our National Constitution. Under such a system, the ethnic background of any individual President of the nation will be irrelevant to the degree of loyalty, honour and support he will enjoy nation-wide. This is because every group knows that its turn will come. Such is the nature of Nigerian realities. Any other type of constitution will be quite unrealistic. The essence of my proposal is that we return to our traditional methods of sharing resources and privileges in such a way that equity is always achieved.

Take our village councils, for example. This applies everywhere in this country. If a village is assigned four council seats amongst themselves, our fathers who never went to school will share that out to the satisfaction of all - without elections, and without recriminations - on the basis of a rotating access to the privilege by selecting the required councillors for stated and limited periods of time. Where seven villages are involved in sharing four positions, the first four will enjoy the privilege for the time being, but the other three are also certain that their time will come.

What we need is originality. We borrow too much. Our fore-fathers left us a structure, a system of doing things. I have been present at a village mass meeting where 7,000 people had only one carton of beer to divide amongst themselves. One Chief was able to divide this carton of bear among 7,000 people to the complete satisfaction of all. Each area appointed a representative to obtain a share on their behalf. The representative probably drank the beer himself alone. His people did not care. Their name had been mentioned and a share assigned to them. Their representative's share was symbolic of their obtaining their quota.

The educated man, loaded down with degrees from expatriate schools, would never approach the problem in that manner. He will try to divide the beer literally among 7,000 people. Dissatisfaction will reign supreme, and there will be breaking of bottles, and a general fracas will result over the matter.

We have to return to our roots to study our traditional political system. Once we do this, we will be a secure nation. In America, with their long established tradition of higher education, the simple fact that no single person can rule perpetually is recognised. There are always other ambitious people. After the election of the late President Roosevelt for the fourth term, (because of the second world war position) the congress passed an Act, an amendment to the U.S. Constitution, stipulating that no person can occupy the Presidency for more than two terms.

These people had their independence almost two hundred and thirty years ago. They are still adjusting their Constitution in the light of American realities. How much more ourselves who have just attained nationhood. We have to learn from experience. In the first Republic, our President was a purely ceremonial figure.

Is there anything in African history, or African society suggesting that there was ever a ceremonial head of any village. Of course, not. The Chiefs, Ezes, Igwes, Obis, Emirs, are executive heads of their areas. Why must we abandon these time-tested traditional systems in favour of a character who merely signs documents, implementing the decisions of his subordinates and officers of his government. We must have an executive president who can take decisions and have them implemented. A President who can cancel rigged elections, sack an incompetent Prime Minister, order fresh elections, in short, a President with the power to rule. Such a President is essential to the stability of this country. He should be both an executive and ceremonial head of his country. The only provision is that there must be a time limit to any Presidency.

Rotation of the Presidency

To ensure equal opportunity of access to this high office for all Nigerians, regardless of ethnic background, the office of the President should rotate round Presidential Electoral Zones. For this purpose the country shall be divided into 5 electoral zones, namely:

(1) *Zone A*, Comprising the present North-Western, North Central and Kano States.

(2) *Zone B*, Comprising the present East Central, South-East States.

(3) *Zone C*, Comprising the present Western, Lagos and Kwara States.

(4) *Zone D*, Comprising the present North-Eastern and Benue-Plateau States.

(5) *Zone E*, Comprising the present Mid-West and Rivers States.

Suffice it to say that in 1978, my party, the National Party of Nigeria, adopted the zoning system in line with the suggestions above. If Shehu Shagari had completed his term in 1987, no person from his zone would have been nominated by the party for President.

I actively participated in the new Constitution making bodies, the CDC (1977) and the Constituent Assembly (1978). I won an election to represent the Ideato/Nkwere/Isu Local Government Areas of Imo State in 1978. I had participated fully in all the pre-independence Constitutional Conferences in London and in Lagos. At that time, we adopted the British type. It was not bad in itself. But the intolerance, the naked greed for power, and the indistinction between the Legislature, the Judiciary and the Executive, combined to strangle it to death. The paper work was okay. What was not okay was some of the persons called upon to execute the Constitution. The American type Presidential system very much appealed to me, not only because of its system of clearer division of powers, with checks and balances, but because of its unique nature in the emergence of one strong leader to bring all sections of Nigeria together in a patriotic march to greatness.

I need to recall an incident during my days at the Constitution Drafting Committee in 1977. It was in the debate for the election of the President. Some pressing family engagements had made me travel to the East one weekend on Friday. I was to return on the following Sunday. I came to the Enugu Airport. To my great disappointment, there was no flight. It was during those days of the monopoly of the Nigerian Airways and their attendant cancellations of flights. I drove back. On Monday morning, I came back. Till 2.00 p.m. no flight came. Eventually, the day's scheduled flights were cancelled. That Monday was the day for the last debate and passing of the resolution on the Section of the Constitution stipulating how a President would be chosen. The CDC agreed it would be by a simple majority, and passed on.

On Tuesday, I managed to get a flight back to Lagos. It was too late for me to participate in the debate of the previous day. I asked how the decision went and I was told. I cried. I lamented. I thought of what to do to reverse the decision. I immediately talked to my colleagues. I told them that by a simple majority the carrying of Nigeria as a whole was doubtful because one section with a large population could influence the election. It will amount to electing a minority President, instead of a President for the whole country. I had prepared a memorandum in a way of contribution to the debate. How could I set the hand of the clock back, as it were? Who was I to upturn the unanimous decision of the whole House? I remembered my dictum that impossibility is found in the dictionary of the undetermined. I requested to address the House. I was given the chance. It was out of respect, generosity and the confidence in the fact that I never cried wolf when there was none.

I held the House for over thirty minutes. The mood started from mere nodding in assent to an overwhelming acclamation. The former decision of the simple majority was amended to be, "that the President, in addition to a simple majority win, must also have 25% votes in at least two-thirds of the States of the Federation. That stamp of fair spread, national acceptability and popularity for the President found its way into the 1979 Constitution.

The text of the address is as follows:

My Dear Colleagues,

1. I crave your indulgence and humbly request you to examine thoroughly this memorandum with open mindedness, characteristic of great men who have nothing but the interest of their country at heart.

2. Circumstances beyond my control necessitated the re-opening of this question of the election of the president, as communicated to you previously in a letter I circularised to members.

3. I have studied most diligently the debates of May 20 and 21 by this august body on the election of the President. No one who has read them very closely will fail to appreciate the seriousness of this question. I have learnt a lot from these debates and I have gained a lot too.

4. The election of the President is one of the most fundamental issues of our new Constitution and upon it will determine the success of the Constitution which we present to the country or lead to the defeat of the Constitution from its very beginning. The people will like to know, from the day the Constitution is presented to them, how they are to be ruled, by whom and by what process does the person come to power.

5. The main decision which has to be reached in connection with the election of the President is:
   a: Whether it should be based on the popular vote, or
   b. Whether its acceptability to the masses of Nigeria is through the broadspread of election in the states, or further still
   c. Whether by the combination of both factors (a) and (b) above.

Our committee reached a decision that the President shall be elected if he secured 50 per cent of the overall majority plus one of all the votes cast in the election or 25 per cent of the total votes cast in two-thirds of the States.

6. *Submission*

My colleagues, I submit:

If the word "or" was amended to "and", I would have welcomed t▮ recommendation as a triumph of a formula for the unity of our coun▮ and a concept of a new Constitution which differs entirely from the ▮ one. I again humbly appeal to you all that for the excellent work whi▮ you have done and for this country to earn it and use it to save itself ▮ the generation now and the generations to come, that you accept ▮ amendment of "or", to "and" for the following reasons:

7. *Simple Majority as Basis*

Adopting simple majority as the principal basis for electing t▮ President, will tantamount to offering this country the same o▮ Constitution. This country called us to devise a new Constitution f▮ it. In the address of the late Head of State, General Murtala Ram▮ Mohammed at the inaugural meeting of this Committee, he said amo▮ other things: "While it is evident that some of our difficulties may ʰa▮ been created by political leaders who operated the Constitution, it clear that some of the provisions of the Constitution, facilitated t▮ periodic political crisis this country went through". The Head of Sta▮ went on: "Winning elections became a life and death struggle whic▮ justified all means - whether fair or foul. So vile was the abuse of th▮ electoral process that this has raised the question as to whether we nee▮ continue to accept *simple majority as basis for political selectio*▮ *especially at the Centre*".

8. We are now by our decision telling the Military Government th▮ accepting any simple majority merely is a wise one, but this ▮ what they have told us to examine. There are other evil effects o▮ accepting any type of majority which are as follows:-

   (a) By accepting simple majorities as the basis for futur▮ elections of the President, we are recalling regionalism an▮ tribalism to the forefront.

   (b) We are also giving prominence and place of honour b▮ politicising population census, the same factor which brough▮ catastrophe and civil war to this country. We are doing th▮ very thing which the Military Government appointing us warned in the inaugural address, in the following words▮ "Considering our past difficulties over population counts, we should endeavour to devise measures which will have the effect of depoliticising population census in the country which we all know has caused interminable disputes at home and▮

created embarrassment elsewhere on more than one occasion". If this is all we can offer, then Sirs, the last best hope for Nigeria is gone. The disillusionment that may result cannot be compensated for by the monumental work which we may have produced in other sections of this document. Who rules Nigeria and how he is produced is the single dominant factor in the whole Constitution. Lose its acceptability, the whole Constitution is lost. We have-time to save it. Let us march boldly to it.

9. Based upon the above, my colleagues, I submit that states should be the primary basis for the election of the President and this will conform with the address of the late Head of State which is very wise in all concepts. He said among other things; "Three major political parties emerged with regional and ethnic support, and at the Centre, only an uneasy coalition of two of these parties was possible at any one time". He continued, "But the fear of predominance of one region over another has, for instance, been removed to a large extent by the simple Constitutional act of creating more states".

10. The Head of State and the Military Government who invited us to this exercise called upon us to strengthen the states as the first means of eliminating predominance of one Region over another and also eliminating fear. Any election which cannot excite the sensitivity of the States can surely not excite the depth of Nigerian unity. To extend the election to the State level is the greatest key to focus attention to Nigerian oneness, and a clear conscious step to blend the heterogeneous nature of our people to an organic national entity.

11. The absence of elements of states in our last Constitution was responsible for a political party to win in a more densely populated area in order to give it a majority without really touching the vastness of the Nigerian territory. Thus the wound of the minority areas became aggravated and resulted in a national issue, hence the creation of more States became inevitable.

12 *The Appeal*

I appeal to my colleagues to use the States as a measure of acceptability of the President who must win 25% in two-thirds of the States. I disagree with those who feel that it will be an impossible exercise. If a person wants to be great, to be a President of a nation, certainly, he must pay the price of that greatness. He must go beyond his own boundary to appeal to others. We need not tell him how to do it. The desire to be great will dictate how he wins his territory and many other territories to be acceptable.

13. By relying on states, the President will emerge as a Symbol of National Unity. The question of tribe and ethnicity would have been minimised. Whoever is accepted by the Nigerian people becomes a hero of the day, irrespective of his tribal or ethnic origin. Our unity in diversity would have been strengthened.

14. We directed that the formation of political parties be on national basis by going across States. By involving Presidential elections with states, it will strengthen the national spread of the political parties.

15. Finally, I submit to the Committee to accept that for a person to be elected President:-

    (a) He MUST carry 50% plus one of the popular votes cast and 25% of the votes cast in two-thirds of the States. Or

    (b) Accept the recommendation of the Sub-Committee on Executive and Legislature that the President shall be elected on simple majority of all the votes cast and a simple majority of votes cast in two-third of the States.

16. One may consider the first, (a), very stringent and very complicating; but, (b), the other recommendation of the sub-committee, is clearer and more understandable to a vast majority of people of this country. If no one satisfies (a) and (b), then there will be a run-off election. But the principle of acceptability applies. In the run-off, the person who wins the majority of the States wins the Presidential election. My colleagues, I humbly submit.

Chapter 23

New Political Parties

The Federal Military Government under General Obasanjo kept to its transition programme and lifted the ban on politics in 1978. However, subterratnean moves had been going on in way of Clubs, Movements, Committees. Contact with the surviving leaders of the defunct political parties during the Constituent Assembly days. provided opportunities for discussions, re-alignments and amalgamations. Chief Obafemi Awolowo who did not participate in the CDC or the Constituent Assembly, utilised that period to organise a Committee of Friends, mainly made up of his erstwhile members of the former Action Group, which he announced as the Unity Party of Nigeria (UPN), only hours after the ban was lifted.

For the other major groups and clubs, the situation was as follows. I had contacted former colleagues in the NPC and NCNC during the Constituent Assembly meetings and discussed the possibility of the members of the former alliance in the previous coalition government to form one political party with a national outlook. It was agreed that the former members of the NPC in the Assembly shall gather former members in the North, while former NCNC members should do the same in the South. The Northern group organised themselves into the National Movement, while the South formed a Committee on National Unity (CNU). I was elected the Chairman, and Chief Adeniran Ogunsanya, Secretary.

Meanwhile, Club 19, the Progressive Club and the Friendship Circle were organising in the East. So were their counterparts in the West and Mid-West organising. When these Progressives joined, the name was changed to Committee on National Unity and Progress (CNUP). This with other smaller groups went to negotiate a merger with the National Movement. Chief Dennis Osadebay was elected Chairman of the Joint Negotiating Committee. Others were:- Dr. Nwigwe, Dr. J.C. C₂bonnaya, Mr. Femi Okunnu and my humble self. On the National Movement side were Alhaji Shehu Shagari, Alhaji Ali Monguno, and Alhaji Ibrahim Dasuki. The first meeting was on September 21st 1978. The negotiation ended in total agreement in all issues. It was triumph for both sides.

On the morning of 22nd September, when Chief D.C. Osadebay was to report formally the outcome of the negotiation to CNUP members, unknown to him and to myself, was the launching of the NPP - Nigerian People's Party. We disassociated ourselves from the new party. I put Chief Adeniran Ogunsanya to task. Anything born in treachery and deceit must end up in treachery and disintegration. Soon the NPP (Nigerian People's Party) split into two, one faction, under Alhaji Ibrahim Waziri, named itself the Great Nigerian People's Party (GNPP). The other faction under Ogunsanya continued with the name NPP.

After Chief Osadebay's report, we all agreed to form one party with the National Movement, a party that would cut across the North and the South, a party that would remove all the obstacles to a strong united Nigeria. At the Satellite Village on Badagry Road, where the party was born, I coined the name NPN. I sold the idea to some of my close colleagues. Within days a nucleus each of the parties was formed in all the States of the Federation.

Not long after, Dr. Nnamdi Azikiwe, the "most beautiful political bride" of that year declared for the NPP. That in itself suddenly changed the texture of the political parties. Added to the fact that Chief Awolowo was already leading the UPN which had a strong footing in Yoruba land, Zik's entry made the NPP an Igbo Party, as the UPN became a Yoruba party. The NPN cannot be described as an Hausa Party because Aminu Kano's People's Redemption Party (PRP) held Kano as Alhaji Waziri's GNPP entrenched itself in Borno State. Though, Bendel in the 1979 elections voted for the UPN, and Plateau chose NPP, the pattern of a two party system could have naturally evolved where NPN pitted against the rest combined.

In drawing up the consitution of the NPN, we not only insisted that it reflected our original agreements of the formation, namely one nation, no north-south dichotomy, secular state, equal opportunities, but we insisted and agreed on "zoning" system. This last was most attractive and appealing. It also reflected my thinking on the present Nigeria as I explained in my lecture at Nsukka on October 15th, 1974. If all my proposed rotational zones, in their turn, produced Presidents over the years the need for zoning could perhaps no longer arise, and we would have "zoned to unzone".

The campaigns for the party support soon followed. At a rally in Owerri on 18th November, 1978 I said:-

"Unity has become very important in our lives, in the life of this great country, in the life of this generation and in the life of the future generation. Without this solo-word "UNITY", nothing can prosper, nothing can go forward.

I invite you to check all the Political Parties that now exist. Not one of them fulfils the qualifications to usher in peace, unity and progress for this country as the National Party of Nigeria. It is the only Party which can lead us to the promised land.

What does the NPN offer to the Nigerian society at large? It offers the followings:-

(a)   One nation, one destiny.
      A unity born out of faith - a unity born out of diversities - a unity born out of common experience and the desire to be one united nation.

(b)   We have answers for all human ills and human needs; but we shall make the vitality of the rural area our starting point. We want to ensure in this land that the era of the common man has emerged. We want to show the common man that in truth, he is now free and that he is now independent in reality. We like to show him that life is now to change for the better. We offer the common man *food and shelter in abundance*, for a hungry man is an angry person.

(c)   We shall make life comfortable in the rural areas. The NPN will provide for them a public sanitation programme, and other facilities.

The NPN will *electrify the Rural Areas.* The NPN will establish at least one Industry in each Local Government Area to curb the drift of young men to urban areas.

The NPN will put up at least one *Hospital* and one *Health Centre* in each Local Government Area. There shall be *Pipe-borne Water* for all. There shall be *Co-operative Bank* in each Local Government Area.

(d)   There shall be a *cultural square* for the presentation of Arts and Culture during Festival Periods. The position of Chiefs and traditional rulers will be enhancedand made as respectable as they will be well catered for.

There will be *Mental Homes* for the mentally afflicted. There shall be more schools and colleges all over the areas,

(e) *The Place of the Local Government Councils*

In order to achieve all these things within the rural area, we shall strengthen the local government as a Third Tier of the Federal System of our government structure.

Never again shall the Local Government and those who lead them go, cap in hand, for subsistence allowance in order to keep the work of the Local Government going.

Never again shall the State Government determine the destiny of the Local Governments because they have been entrenched in the Constitution as functionaries of the third tier of the Federal System.

Never again will the Local Governments be subjected to the manipulations of the State Government. The Consitution has provided for the Local Government's independent revenue sources. If this is not enough, the Federal Government shall give them subsidy in the same way that it has come to the rescue of the States.

(f)   In our relationship with our African brothers in other distant parts, we shall be firm and resolute in support of their self direction and self determination. We shall proclaim once again that no section of Africa shall be in bondage. We are not free and independent until every square meter of Africa is truly independent. We shall carry on the Federal Government's Foreign policy on South Africa, Zimbabwe, Namibia and other spots in Africa where our people are humiliated and dehumanised by apartheid regimes. The African High Command will become a reality. We shall equip our Armed Forces with the most modern weapons and with a strong striking force, even though we are dedicated to peace around the world.

(g) To our young men in schools, we will ensure more technical education to them, so that they may be endurable and adjustable to the practical demonstrable priorities of life.

We shall no longer be vineyards for raw materials collected for export. We shall release the energies and the endowments of our youths to inventive products. We shall finance geniuses. We shall export knowledge to other parts of Africa and the world, while gaining ideas and knowledge for those we have not yet acquired.

In other words, all our experiences will be galvanized and geared up for action so that the position of Nigeria in the Continent of Africa and the World will be on a high pedestal.

This is the most challenging time for us. This is the most exciting moment to be alive. Those of us who are alive and in the treshold of these events will now give all our best efforts, our talents and experiences to the service of our own people, inspiring the youths to actions, inspiring the youths to inventive heights so that they can scan the depth of our oceans and extract the wealth therein, so that the mountain tops can be explored and excavated. This and other things we wish to usher in".

Chapter 24

The Administration Of Shehu Shagari

The Second Republic began formally with the inauguration of Alhaji Aliyu Usman Shehu Shagari in October, 1979, as President. This ended a 13-year military rule in a country nineteen years old as an independent nation.

Shagari had campaigned widely, visited all the nooks and corners of this great country which is his one constituency and had met the electoral and constitutional requirements of,

(a) overall majority of the votes cast and
(b) one quarter votes of two thirds of the number of States in the Federation.

The next second best of the Presidential candidates was Chief Obafemi Awolowo of the UPN, who in vain contested Shagari's election, in court. The NPP Presidential candidate, Dr. Nnamdi Azikiwe, came third in the race. Following the court ruling, I addressed a Press Conference on 28th September 1979; here is the text:

Gentlemen of the Press,

It is a great pleasure to address you today. As you are all aware, the Supreme Court has given a momentous decision in favour of Alhaji Shehu Shagari as the duly elected President of our great country. This decision, no doubt, ratifies the verdict of the majority of the electorates of this country at the polls. In addition, the decision of the court is a vindication of the unshakable belief of our people in the rule of law. There is a yet a deeper meaning to this verdict. It is the enthronement of the supremacy of an indivisible nation. The spontaneous joy which sparked off at this verdict is the celebration of the triumph of a NEW NATION, NIGERIA. Today, the aspiration of ONE NATION, ONE

DESTINY, ONE GOD, is born. Shehu Shagari is now given a full mandate to nurse and consolidate this national objective.

Alhaji Shehu Shagari is a humble, patriotic and imaginative man, and having intimately known him for many years, he will, I am sure, serve this nation with a crusading zeal and without any clog of selfishness. He will prove a constructive administrator and statesman and, thus, establish himself in the minds of the people of this country.

We should not expect him to work miracles in a day, we should give him our sympathy, our understanding, realizing that he is assuming office at the most critical period of our economic life. The problems which fall on his shoulders are staggering, but with time and patience, he shall overcome them. In any contest some will win and some will lose. Whether we win or lose, NIGERIA FIRST must be the supreme goal; as long as this objective endures, there is hope for every ethnic group within the framework of one Nigeria. It is in this spirit that all parties and individuals must reciprocate the hand of fellowship outstretched by the President-elect to join in the task of nation-building.

When the curtain is drawn on October 1, General Obasanjo will go down in history as a hero and a great man and his team of military argonauts will long be remembered as men who went in search for a NEW NATION, celebrated its founding this October 1, and handed it to Alhaji Shehu Shagari, on its onward march to greatness which comes with prosperity and stability".

Alhaji Shehu Shagari chose for his running mate and Vice-President, Dr. Alex I. Ekwueme, a young man I fondly describe as a "Human Computer". In the National Assembly, Shagari's party, the NPN, did not have an overall majority which was necessary for the presidential bills to pass easily into law. To obtain this working majority, the NPN and the NPP had to go into a working "accord" at the National Assembly.

On the inauguration day, the President had pledged:

Before God and you all, I will fulfill my oath of office and do my utmost best to serve without fear or favour. This occasion is a national event in which I call on all Nigerians to join hands with me in nation-building to the glory of our fatherland.

The problem of creating a national government, a viable economic base, and the integration of various ethnic groups in Nigeria, in fairness and without acrimony overwhelmed the first Republic. These problems are still with us. And it is our determination to do our utmost to contribute to their solution. This administration is determined that the slogan of One Nation, One Destiny, shall be translated into reality.

The first thing is for all who have participated in the recent elections to work together, whether they gained or lost. Now that the elections are over we must act like sportsmen, set aside differences and harness our energies to the task of nation building...

I would like to re-iterate my Government's commitment to *feed, house* and *educate* the people....

In the area of foreign policy, as your President, I will continue to advance and defend the cause of our great country before the world community of Nations. It is our national will that Africa shall remain the corner-stone of our foreign policy. Also, it is our national will, that Africa shall be free, of racial bigotry, free of oppression, and free of vestiges of colonialism. My Government is determined to see the cause of justice and human decency prevail in Namibia, Zimbabwe, and South Africa. We shall continue to support all forces of progress and oppose all forces of oppression in Africa and elsewhere..."

The President invited me to assist his Administration in the capacity of Presidential Adviser on National Assembly Affairs. I accepted. The assignment was a most critical one at a time when the new 1979 Constitution, and the system of government which it recommended, were being tried for the first time. The fulcrum of this new system was the separation of the Executive, the Legislative and the Judiciary powers of government. My duty was to represent the Executive interest in the Legislature and to dilute the hostility of the rival political parties (UPN, NPP, GNPP, and PRP) towards the Executive. By my adroit political manoeuvres Executive bills, programmes and recommendations usually received support across the parties. Serious disagreements and crises between the two bodies were avoided.

As NPN's zoning policy worked, so did its other cardinal manifesto promises; namely, food and shelter. Low-cost houses were built all over the States of the Federation to ease accommodation problems for the low income earners. Rice and other items were imported to supplement local production. The River Basin Authorities were equipped to intensify efforts to produce more food. Though austerity measures were introduced ater, Nigerians everywhere felt the pride of belonging to One Nation, One God, One Destiny, during the Shagari Administration.

In his letter dated 25th September, 1983, accepting my resignation as Special Adviser on National Assembly Affairs, President Shagari had this to say:

"My dear K.O.,"

...The successful implementation of the Presidential System was due largely among others to the reliable and strong chain link forged between the Executive and the Legislature by the office of the Special Adviser on National Assembly Affairs. As the head of that office, the glory of that achievement is undoubtedly yours.

On my part, I wish now to place on record my gratitude to you and to your staff for the relentless effort you invested in developing amicable and successful relationship between the Legislature and the Executive during my first term of office as President of the Federal Republic of Nigeria..."

Chapter 25

The Progressive Parties Alliance

The split of the Nigerian People's Party at the National Assembly permeated the rank and file. One faction was led by Senator Nathaniel Anah and the other continued its loyalty to Dr. Azikiwe. The grouse of the former was centred on the shoddy manner the accord between NPN and NPP was broken by NPP coupled with the excesses of some State Governors of the NPP, with particular reference to dispossessing individuals of their landed property. The Zik-led group started to hob-nob with the UPN in a solid opposition to Mr. President. The Unity Party of Nigeria, since their leader lost the Presidential election, had seen nothing good in Shagari's Administration.

Before the 1983 general elections, therefore, the UPN and the NPP formed an alliance they called the "Progressive Parties Alliance" (PPA). In a well publicised Press Conference which I held at the Federal Palace Hotel on 28th April, 1982, I warned against the move.

The Presidential election that followed showed the struggle between two objectives; the struggle between tribalism and national unity. In that election, the National Party of Nigeria won the day. The lesson to be derived from it was ample for those who can read the handwriting on the wall. No longer in the history of this country can any ethnic group, working in isolation of other groups, win the Presidency of this country, much less any single person from the ethnic group. The new Constitution which the country was operating has closed the era of regionalism, tribalism and ethnicity. It had opened the dawn of a new nation under God.

The NPN was not alone in the march towards national integration. It was true that the NPN/NPP accord was broken, but Nigerians have matured with time. They could no longer be led by the nose. As the NPP led by Zik allied itself with the UPN, the NPP faction led by Senator Anah kept its faith with the NPN. Factions of GNPP and PRP joined and a stronger accord emerged. It is known as *Accord Concordiale*. The accord cut across political parties, having as its chief motivating force "Nigeria first" with all it implies: Unity and indivisibility of Nigeria.

The combined march for national integration is on. Any tree on its way must be uprooted. Any known impediment on its route of march will be dismantled and overcome.

Chapter 26

Shagari's Second Term And The Military's Second Coming

While the NPN held rallies, toured places and appealed to the electorate the other parties which failed to agree on a common platform against the NPN resorted to perfecting unorthodox means to rig the elections. The electorate resisted in most areas. Yet President Shehu Shagari was returned for another term with more States spread and a larger majority than in 1979. He settled to nominate his cabinet for Senate approval. The confirmations were a lot more easier and straightforward than at his first term in office.

He nominated me as Ambassador Extraordinary and Plenipotentiary. The Senate okayed it. This unique diplomatic appointment involved representing President Shagari and the Nigerian Government at the highest international levels. The assignment would take me around the world, conferring with Kings, Queens, Presidents and Prime Ministers. I was to address international organisations, mediate on inter-state, disputes and negotiate with other governments, as the case arose, with the approval of the President, to whom I would personally report and not to the Ministry of External Affairs.

He possibly considered my background experience from my days as a student in the United States, my ability as a Minister in the first Republic, my role as Adviser to the Prime Minister, late Alhaji Abubakar Tafawa Balewa, on African Affairs, and my personal knowledge and contact with world leaders. I took up the appointment as another and more fitting rostrum to place Nigeria on the gallery of great nations. Personally, I was satisfied. I relished a contentment as a politician.

The NPN, Imo State signed a resolution appointing me Patron and mandating me their spokesman to act on their behalf. The nation could not offer me a better chance. I mapped my plan of action, watching closely world events.

But I had hardly carried out the first assignment under the new dispensation before the Army struck again. The Shagari administration came to an abrupt end on 31st December, 1983.

The Military's Second Coming

The nation had not quite recovered from the throes of the disruption caused to an evolutionary process of democracy by the first *coup d'etat* of 1966, before there was yet another jolt. Who are you not to be cowed by the threat of the gun. A culture was inadvertently being established of the barrel of the gun as the easiest and quickest road to the seat of government.

The civilian population hail a successful coup with the same excitement as they boo a foiled one. The new Military junta often start by soliciting the co-operation of the traditional rulers. What can discourage these coups? Perhaps conscience, perhaps constitutional provision, perhaps a concensus of the populace for a civil disobedience. But there is no way you stop one that has succeeded.

True, there were a lot of problems in the country by 1983. The economy had slumped. There were some corruption. Political contest was a do or die matter. The state of the economy was not caused by President Shagari, who infact, had introduced austerity measures in recognition of the enormity of the problem.

Corruption was not restricted to the civilians, as General Murtala Mohammed's probes in 1975 showed. Naked pursuit of power was worse in the army ,as the Dimka's, Vasta's, Orka's coups clearly demonstrated. Infact, it is thought in some quarters that the reason why the Military keep postponing targets of handover to civilians is that they are not sure if the incoming administration would investigate them and those millionaire Generals who retired before attaining the age of 50 years.

One commentator said that if Nigeria's march to nationhood had not been disturbed by the coups since January 15th 1966, the country could have by now passed from the tutelage of experiments into the path of achievement. India was cited as an example of such evolution rather than revolution by the barrel of the gun. My constant appeal is for this great country to be spared any more *coup d'etat*.

From Buhari to Babangida

Nigerians are now used to the common phenomenon of a military coup. As the nation rises early in the morning, martial music takes up the usual programmes in the national radio stations. Then, there is a pause. Then a voice in tones, "Fellow Nigerians ... the last government has been overthrown". The speaker lists a catalogue of sins of the previous administration. He makes utopian promises to right every wrong. He pledges, on behalf of his group not to stay "one day longer than necessary". Finally he appeals to the people to remain calm. The voice you hear is often that of a fairly senior army officer who soon gives way to the strong man of the putsch.

That was how Lt. Col. Dogonyaro announced the advent of Major-General Mohammadu Buhari, who by force of arms toppled the elected government of President Shehu Shagari to usher in Nigeria's fifth *coup d'etat* in seventeen years. The unthoughtful crowd trooped to the streets and rang their bells in jubilation, but they were soon to wring their hands in regrets.

Draconian decrees started soon to rain. Decree One suspended the Constitution; Decree Two authorised detention without trial; Decree Four muzzled the press. Then wars were declared: "War against Indispline", "War against foreign currency", War against drug", War against inactivity", "War against uncleanliness", "War against foreign debt".

This was the rule of a twosome you did not know who was in charge - Buhari, the Head of State or Idiagbon, the Chief of Staff, Supreme Headquarters. Most of the battles of the war were fought and lost. There are however, some remnants of the war against indiscipline (WAI) and a regular monthly national "clean up exercise" which hang on, though the strictness is no longer there.

Idiagbon's whip, driving us to demolish "illegal structures" and to keep surroundings clean reminded me of my own days of the Lagos Slum Clearance of 30 years ago. I did it then, not with a whip or the barrel of the gun, but with legal backing and due notice. All it needed was the will to achieve and the people to appreciate that it was in their own best interest.

The harshness of Buhari/Idiagbon rule had upset the nation and embarrassed their colleagues in the army. Political detainees filled Nigerian prisons. There was no plan for a return to civil rule. National debt burden was crippling the country. About forty-four per cent of the foreign reserves went to it. Factories were virtually shut, as essential goods deserted market stalls. The Armed Forces themselves felt their leaders were no longer approachable or sensitive to the bleak situation.

In the early hours of Tuesday 27th August 1985, yet another coup, which the press described as a "palace coup", took place. Major-General Ibrahim Badamasi Babangida emerged as PRESIDENT and Commander-in-Chief of the Armed Forces. His maiden speech had streaks and rays of hope, but Nigerians received it with cautious optimism.

Some editorials in the National Newspapers within two or three days of the coup said it all. Excerpts:-

National Concord; (30/8/85)

"Nigerians might not have been jubilating in the streets since the country's latest military coup d'etat but that is certainly not because they disapprove of the latest change of government... They have found themselves where they are, wary of seemingly new heroes... finding no faith in civilian rule, and betrayed by successive military regimes, it is easy for such a disappointed people to be apathetic to events which must necessarily influence their lives and those of generations unborn".

The Guardian (30/8/85)

"It should be perfectly understandable if in the wake of the most recent coup, Nigerians seem a great deal more sceptical about their prospects...

Practically every segment of society, except, perhaps, the armed force: was antagonised, sometimes humiliated... Civil liberties were alway. precarious in military regimes. But the Buhari regime perfected the attrition of elementary freedoms to the points where the average civiliar was driven to see himself, often against his will, as a pariah. He had nc rights that the government and its secret police were obliged to respect, and he lived in perpetual fear of being hauled into jail without even : token charge being made against him. Ethnicity became a principle of state policy.... Ultimately, it was the arrogance of the Buhari administration that led to its downfall.

General Babangida is yet to vouchsafe a detailed blue-print of his intentions. But he knows as we do, that his task is well cut for him".

The New Nigerian (29/8/85)

"Given the nightmarish experience of the recent past, especially the systematic intimidation of people and the derogation of their fundamental human rights, the Nigerian media and people cannot but welcome the coup that saw General Ibrahim Babangida bestowed with the rulership of our beloved country. To cynics and critics the foregoing may elicit a smirk and a "de ja vu" shrug with justification. While awaiting the new regime's programme of action we may suggest the following:-

An immediate stop of the importation of rice and a phasing out of the importation of all other food items; a re-examination of the counter-trade survival tactics, with a view to restricting it to the execution of core capital projects as well as giving us a fairer deal.

We are not naive enough to believe that miracles are possible. Nevertheless, we expect that sooner than *20 months* of the new regime, hospitals will cease to be mere consulting clinics and armed robbers will cease to rule our streets and homes by day and by night".

Daily Times (29/8/85)

"The bloodless and apparently smooth change in the country's leadership can, in the main be taken as evidence of acute dissatisfaction of some top architects of the December, 1983 coup with the overall performance of the ousted administration...President Babangida and his lieutenants should therefore do everything possible to make their stay in office effective and profitable for all Nigerians. Every Nigerian should be made to have a sense of belonging in the most elaborate meaning of the word....

Even if we admit that a military regime is an aberration, there is still the need for some degree of responsiveness in running the government. Lack of recognition of these facts was the undoing of the ousted administration".

General Ibrahim Babangida is a man of surprises. First he assumed the title "President", the only military ruler in the country to be so addressed. Then he announced a "human rights" policy, also unheard of in military regimes, even though subsequent action belied all. He opened the prison gates for political prisoners and ordered the rearrest of those who needed it. The NSO (National Security Organisation) which was the "Secret Police" used by the Buhari high-handed rule to harrass the populace, was exposed and re-organised.

The President then ordered a public debate on whether we could accept an International Monetary Fund (IMF) loan as a panacea for our economic ills. Though, the nation rejected the IMF, that organisation still haunts us from the heap of memoranda and old newspaper cuttings lying in our archives, rejecting it. The surprises continue till today.

He announced a transition to civil rule programme, which could have terminated in 1990, and set up the Constituent Assembly. His Armed Force Ruling Council, set aside the conclusions of the Constituent Assembly and gave Nigeria the 1989 Constitution of its choice. Under the revised programme, two local government elections were to precede the hand-over in 1992, but the first democratically elected local government councils were scrapped one year after. And observers feel that State Assemblies, if elected in 1991 could be so unilaterally dismissed.

He lifted the ban on politics and asked people to organise parties, but rejected all they presented and imposed a two party system. Newspaper columnists daub him "Maradona", a reference to the Argentine football dribbler. They may not be right, but the nation is no longer surprised at any surprises.

For sure, President Ibrahim Babangida is a leader who is determined to take his people to a goal of self sufficiency and greatness what ever the cost. The road is full of obstacles. He made this fact known early in the day.

Babangida has survived two abortive coups against him. The first was headed by Air Vice-Marshal Mamman Vatsa in 1985, and the other in 1990 by Major General Gideon Orkar. What worries Nigeria is a situation, where Babangida will be unwilling to step down in 1992, as frequently canvassed by some Nigerians and frequently reassured by him. I personally believe he will keep his words.

Chapter 27

The Structural Adjustment Programme (SAP); The Transition To Civil Rule, 1992

Comment on the salient features of Babangida's regime will first focus on SAP. Within the space of five years, a lot took place which affected the very lives of the people, and Nigeria as a sovereign nation, in which the world may have confidence, provided it is no longer jolted by further coups.

Although the Structural Adjustment Programme (SAP) is a sound economic policy, the pains should be well-spread among the populace so as to ensure that no group or class of people suffers more than the other. At this period of food scarcity, efforts should be made to bring food to save people from hunger, so that they will be in a position to continue to contribute towards the success of SAP. I believe that our people are not so strongly opposed to SAP as to its application. What they are saying is that the pains brought about by this economic policy were allowed to weigh more on the down-trodden masses than on the rich who now appear to enjoy obvious affluence. Most of the hospitals are lacking basic medical facilities like drugs and some vital equipment. Efforts should be made to equip these hospitals since majority of our people cannot afford to go outside this country to treat themselves.

There is no country in the world which leaves its foreign exchange to be determined only by the vagaries of market forces. There ought to be one form of control or the other to ensure that our money is not completely lost out in value to other currencies. Government should announce a five year recovery of the Naira.

Economic emergency should be declared. It is my view that States should suspend white elephant projects so that money saved could be invested in more realistic ventures that could put the economy on a sound footing. There should be no more borrowing, by whatever name it is called, for five years.

SAP is the main factor which makes the present Military regime unpopular and which the people now allege brings worse experience to them than during the period of imperialism. During imperialism, we tried to send away Europeans. With this economic hardship, they now dictate to us from their homeland. They have virtually recaptured us though the IMF and the World Bank. It is pure neo-colonialism in action.

The nation, after a debate rejected the IMF Loan. What do we see every day? Loans and loans. That is one more reason why Babangida's regime should be the last Military rule.

We should re-visit the SAP protests, and admit that SAP application is too hard on the people. We should listen to the labour unions and the complaints of workers. Children are dying of *Kwashiokor,* a disease prevalent during the last civil war. There is no reason why this should continue to happen. Prices of commodities are sky-rocketing daily without a check. The middle class barely survives, and the low-income earner is completely sapped.

The Structural Adjustment Programme would have been a successful sound economic policy, if we had guarded the exchange rate of the Naira to other currencies. We are an oil producing country, a rare luck not many nations have, yet we still borrow from the World Bank and the IMF. If the dollar from these two sources had been used to fund FEM (Foreign Exchange Market), the economic law of supply and demand would have forced an improved rate of the Naira. Rather we get the oil money and the continuous loans for grandiose projects.

Money, as legal tender, is the measure for labour and the value of production. But from the difference in the value of our Naira between 1983 and 1990, it would appear that today our sweat, time and energy have no value at all. This is where government intervention is necessary. This is why people cry foul of SAP.

A former Head of State had advised that SAP should have a human face onto it. If my proposed state of Economic Emergency is declared, all arms of the Administration will be involved and all States should be compelled to revise their budgets. There is nothing that is impossible in the affairs of man. Let our slogan be "the most essential we do immediately, the less important to stay". With the right type of people, with the right type of knowledge, pushing away mediocrity, there will be results, and we all will be back on real recovery.

In 1986, I stated in an address and warned the Government to intervene I said:

> "It is for this consideration that I opt that whatever happens, the rate of exchange of the Naira should now be fixed at N3.00 so that it will continue to provide a little surplus for the development of the agricultural sector, otherwise, there is no reason why it should not be pegged at N2.50 to the dollar.
>
> It is even a matter of clear reasoning that a currency which was rated N1.00 to $1.50 in 1983 should not depreciate so fast as to tumble to N4.00 to $1 in so short a time. It is nothing but upsetting the whole economic base which I am sure is not the intention of the Structural Adjustment Programme (SAP)".

That was in 1986. And on 27th June, 1987, I issued another press statement which is still universally relevant. It reads:

Depreciation of the Naira; FGN should intervene now

I was determined to be silent on the present economic drift in the Nigerian economy which looks bleak, in the hope that the government or any of its many agencies would have awakened to the grave situation and taken steps to apply immediate remedial measures. I have waited for this to happen and since this has not been the case, I am compelled, in the interest and welfare of this country, to appraise the government and the people about the urgency of taking immediate remedial action.

The Nigerian economy is in a very critical stage of deterioration and, unless something very drastic is done to alter this trend, we face a bleak future. The Nigerian economic destiny is threatened as never before. It should pose a great challenge to the Federal Military Government.

The idea behind the SAP and SFEM Programmes was laudable as our alternative to taking the IMF loan. To evolve exchange mechanism for the purposes of translating our currency into any of the foreign hard currencies and thereby eliminating the import licensing process that has helped to falsify our economic worth as a nation, is indeed a progressive step forward.

We congratulate those whose imagination and foresight brought this about.

If the above observation is correct, where then lies the disaster to our economy that I spoke about? The disaster arises from the operation of the EXCHANGE RATE when the Naira is converted to other currencies. The depreciation of the Naira to the dollar and other currencies has progressed from bad to worse. From September 26th, 1986, when the auction started, the rate was established by taking the average of all the biddings by successful banks. This system continued till April, 1987 when the Dutch auction was introduced. The average rate of all the biddings for these eight months was around N3.50 to the dollar. At one stage, the Federal Government's intervention forced the rate down to N3.00 to the dollar. This is what it should be.

When the Central Bank introduced the Dutch auction, it was hailed as a move to stem the excessive rates. The results which this Dutch auction produced dashed the cherished hopes of many who actually yearned for the economic well-being of this country. Before this last auction, the Naira got as much as N4.32 to the dollar!

Why has it not dawned yet upon our Central Bank and our bankers that met at the auction to buy foreign exchange that the generated rate is a disaster to the entire economy and the well-being of our people? By one stroke; they have combined to destabilise our economic equilibrium.

All the banks should have recalled that before the SFEM started in September, 1986, the rate of exchange was around N1 to the dollar or even 90k to the dollar.

Under the Second Tier Foreign Exchange Market, SFEM, the rate went up sharply to over N3.50 to the dollar. The consequences that followed were sweeping. Cars, within the reach of the common man, like the Volkswagen Beetle and Peugeot 504 which sold for N7,000.00 and N13,000.00 respectively sky-rocketed to N24,000,00 and N40,000.00 respectively. The rise was over 300%. Other products followed similar lines.

When we rejected the IMF loan, we knew that this country would be called upon to make sacrifices by at least 50%. Even at the worst, we could never imagine it exceeding 100%. No one anticipated a suicidal economic measure capable of destroying the goose that lays the golden egg.

The IMF would not have dared to introduce its scheme with more than 60% devaluation, if we accepted it after our debate. Yet we rejected this. How come then that our own people handling the SAP Scheme as our answer to the IMF alternative produced all at once a devaluation of more than 300%?.

It will be recalled that on the 5th of November, 1985, I wrote the President in support of the rejection of IMF loan on a different basis. I hinged my argument on the incompetence of our experts to manage the loans if obtained. I said:-

> Many spoke against the acceptance of the IMF loan because of loss of confidence in those to handle the loan successfully and apply it for the purpose for which it is intended, that is, reviving the economy. It is feared that any mismanagement of this loan will plunge the country into a greater economic catastrophe. Rather than see this happen let us forego the loan...
>
> The process of negotiation (with the IMF) without achieving its goal has already inflicted a devaluation of over 28% on the Naira. Therefore there is no basis for further devaluation of the Naira, by delayed negotiations. As far as Nigeria's self-interest is concerned the irreducible minimum should be N1 to $1 which will bring total devaluation to 30%.

It is my contention that there is a great mistake in the medium employed to arrive at the rate of exchange, through the collection of bankers for an exercise in auction. The language of an auction is bad enough. No nation worth its salt would gather to auction its economic soul. To do it with bankers is a new strange economic phenomenon. It is an exercise which carries foreign exchange to the money market and the banks who have great thirst for foreign currencies and who are ready to pay anything for them. Thus we have created a new society of the "haves: which represent the money barons, and the "have nots", the rest of us. This group of "haves", but for fear of public opinion, is ready to pay anything from N8 to N10 to the dollar.

It is mere self-deceit if we say that such a system of auction will peg the market value of the Naira. It rather has the negative effect of producing a distorted and exploitative value in favour of the banks.

The Effect of the Depreciation of the Naira on the People

(a) It has sky-rocketed prices beyond the reach of the common man or the average middle class. When a car which sells at pre-SFEM for N13,000 now costs about N140,000 under SFEM, who will buy? This means that there are no more new cars for the middle class and below.

(b) What about cement and all items of building? House ownership by any average person as of now is a far cry. The average wage earner is merely existing, not living, because goods produced under SFEM are very expensive. Retrenchment is the order of the day.

I agreed with Mr. M. Oladimeji who wrote in the *Daily Times* of May 22nd, 1987 (page 9) about the depreciation of the Naira to the dollar when he said:

.... why would these experts ever depreciate the Naira against the US dollar at the time when the US dollar is at its lowest level in the world money market and several Western countries have had to purchase large quantities of the dollar from the market in order to stop its rapid decline?

The Americans themselves are very worried about this very rapid and unprecedented decline, yet our experts want us Nigerians and the rest of the world to believe that the Naira must continue to slide against the already badly sliding dollar!

The Place of the Central Bank

The Central Bank cannot absolve itself from the responsibility of the failure to find a reasonable rate for the Naira after conceiving such a fine scheme as the SFEM.

We concede the right of the Central Bank to experiment on its various options, but once it sees that the result, if applied, will be disastrous to the economy of the country it would have taken steps to remedy the situation without apologies to anyone for doing its duty to Nigeria.

To continue with astronomical high and different rates of the Naira to the dollar every fortnight would have demonstrated to them that no country can continue this way to a clear and known direction to suicide.

We welcomed the announcement that the SFEM was an exercise to find the market value of the Naira, but the method it has adopted in achieving that aim has no scientific application. The Central Bank has to rethink immediately.

Another faulty method is the programme of funding the scheme. The SFEM started with $50,000.00 per week, and later went up to $75m per week. After April, 1986 it changed to fortnightly intervals, and yet could only find $75 million. One would have imagined that fortnightly it could either be $100m or even $150m.

Bankers and SFEM

The bankers which assemble every week or fortnightly to bid at the SFEM auction owe a measure of patriotism to the country. They should consider the per capita income of the average citizen of Nigeria. They should be aware that their biddings can make for harmony in the economic evolution of this country. They should not take steps that spilt the country into the "haves" and the "have nots". For banks to reach a bidding of between N8 to N10 per dollar for a country which only yesterday was operating at the rate of N1 to the dollar is nothing but sheer economic madness.

On the 7th of October, 1986, I sent a written opinion to the Central Bank of Nigeria and other agencies of the government, giving my humble suggestion as to how to establish the exchange market. In that statement, I said in conclusion:

My contention is that Merchant and Commercial Bankers are not the only group to determine the value of such a complex market made up of very many forces at work. On the other hand, bankers could give an opinion on the rates established by the CBN. Added to the views of other experts, the rate of exchange will emanate, based upon what the CBN produces. Any other method is just a mechanical selling of the dollar to the banks. It does not give any prestige to the country, Nigeria.

I assume that it is never the intention of the CBN to sit over the liquidation of the Naira, nor employ its office to enthrone any foreign currency beyond its level, giving it a status that even the IMF never contemplated. The CBN is urged to think again and very quickly and restore sanity and confidence in the whole system.

The Way Out of the Dilemma

It is my humble suggestion that all our economic forces should meet; the Ministries of Finance and of National Planning, the Central Bank of Nigeria, the Chambers of Commerce, the Manufacturers Association of Nigeria, Economists, and any other groups or individuals that the government may deem fit to assemble. It should be an emergency session to determine the stability and the fair market value of the Naira and report to the President. It is a grave national issue now and must be tackled on that level. I suggest as follows:-

i. Take the average under the first auction exercise from September 26th, 1986 to April, 1987 to become the rate.

ii. Or take a flat rate of N3 as a base which was the rate at one time when the government intervened. Although there were agitations against the government's interference, the fact remains that the government was perfectly right because it is its ultimate responsibility. Making the base N3 is not the end by itself. It is in accordance with the Chinese proverb that in the journey of a thousand miles, you should take the first step. Everything considered, N3 will give us sufficient margin and is enough sacrifice to make for financing our own greatness.

The state of our economy will determine how the rate appreciates or depreciates. If we put out say $400m in a month, to be expended on our foreign exchange, then we shall watch what our crude oil and other export commodities produce within that period. If they produce more than we have expended, it is then known as favourable balance of payment, and then the Naira will again appreciate, i.e. less than N3 to the dollar depending upon the rate of the favourable balance. If, on the other hand, our outlay exceeds our income then the picture will result in unfavourable balance of payment. To that extent the Naira is further depreciated, i.e. an increase to N3.20 or N3.50 depending upon the rate of the unfavourable balance. By this way, the country is kept abreast of its economic growth.

Right now we are in the dark. There is no light in the tunnel. It is this darkness that must be cleared immediately. This approach is more scientific than our present adhoc method which has no base and no measuring data of growth.

One agrees easily with Mr. M. Oladimeji when he concluded:-

> We know the factors that have continued to lead to the appreciated value of the pound sterling. The solid industrial base of Britain, the favourable balance of payment, the improving value of the crude oil are among the contributory factors. Any slight drop in crude oil value, for instance, leads to a slight drop in the pound sterling value and vice versa. Here in Nigeria, even when the value of our crude has improved, our experts believe the Naira must continue to sink!.

Today, in 1990, the exchange rate is over N9.00 to the dollar. Every marketable stock, trade and merchandise is based on the current value of the Naira. I advise the present administration again to do something drastic to close the gap between the naira and other currencies. It may not be done in a swoop. It should be taken step by step. We can make it a three year programme. We should strive to close the gap substantially each year. For instance in the first year, we can battle to reduce it by N2.00 which will give us N7.00 to the dollar; then in the second year by N1.50 bringing it to N5.50 and finally by the third year to N4.00 to the dollar. It is admitted that the Naira was over-valued and that there is a general world recession, but $1 U.S. for N9.00 is preposterous in economic calculations.

In a press conference in 1986, at my 69th Birthday anniversary, I declared that I had retired from active partisan politics, but promised that, as long as God spared my life, I would neither be silent nor neutral on major issues concerning my fatherland, especially if they will lead to the greatness, unity and prosperity of Nigeria. I do not, therefore, address only press conferences or grant press interviews; I also directly address letters embodying my thoughts to the government.

As soon as General Ibrahim Babangida came to power in 1985, I addressed him and poured my feelings to him. In a welcome acceptance of that gesture and my proposals, he gracefully replied as follows in a letter dated 27th December, 1985:

1. It is with deep sense of appreciation that I write to thank you most sincerely for your letter of 6th November, 1985 in which you reflected deeply on some of the current problems facing our great country.
2. I wish to inform you that I have spared some time to go through the submission which I have found to be extremely useful. It is my belief that an elder statesmen like you who have accumulated experience over the years in the service of our nation should be hearkened to whenever you wish to offer some advice. In that regard therefore, I look forward to receiving more contributions from your very good self.
3. Once more, thank you very much for sparing your time to write me and may the blessings of the season be bestowed on you and your family.

Four years later, on 20th September, 1989, I addressed a well publicised press conference at the "Light House", Victoria Island, Lagos, in which I touched on very many aspects of Nigerian life: the economy, the society, military disengagement, politics, religion etc. I wrote again to Mr President enclosing the text of the press conference and highlighted my vision for the third Republic and proposed concrete steps to attain them. I wish to place on record the great respect the President has for the views of the Elders as expressed in a reply to me dated 10th October, 1989:

My dear Elder,

I wish to thank you for finding the time to write to me on matters which affect the well-being of our country. I am grateful to you for lending your personal experience and know-how to the subject matter of your letter: Armed Robbery, Abandoned Property and Boundary Adjustment.

I am at one with you that this nation needs a sound economic base and indeed an integrative political culture that can ensure happiness and peaceful co-existence among our people. the policies of this Administration particularly the Structural Adjustment programme, are intended to open up new economic and political frontiers.

I wish to thank you, most sincerely, for constantly making available to me the benefit of your experience. As you are aware, I have publicly admitted that this Administration does not claim to have all the answers to all our problems and we shall always welcome the words of wisdom of our elders in our task of bringing about a new Nigeria that will be the pride of us all.

Thank you.

Yours sincerely

(General Ibrahim Badamasi Babangida)

President, Commander-in-chief of the Nigerian Armed Forces.

The Transition to 1992

After he set the wheels of economic recovery moving, harsh and slowly, President Babangida turned to the political front. He set up a Constitution Drafting Committee and mandated it to fashion out a Constitution that is locally based, since it would appear that the British and the American systems had both failed to be operated successfully by Nigerians. This Political Bureau was headed by Professor S.J. Cookey. Then the President announced the time-table of hand-over in 1990, which later was modified to stand in this order:

Local Government Elections - non-party, 1987
Constituent Assembly
Lifting of the ban on politics
Formation of Political Parties
Local Government Elections (on Party Basis)
State Legislature Assembly
State Governor's Elections
The Census

National Assembly Elections

The inauguration of a Civilian President - October 1st, 1992.

Decrees and administrative directives guide and qualify these measures. For instance Decree No. 25 of 1987 placed a total ban, or disqualification till 1992, on certain Nigerian former office holders and a section of the members of the National Assembly. For certain categories of persons, it was an unfair blanket ban. A case in point is the disqualification placed on members of the National Assembly, who neither were found guilty of any wrong doing, nor headed any House Committees. The legal draftsmen may not have addressed their attention to the contents of the Constitution of the defunct political parties in order to ascertain whether all of them provided that members of the National Assembly were *ipso facto* members of their Party National or State Executives before placing them on the banned list. The Decree No. 25 of 1987 disqualified these persons, but it turned out that only one party, the NPN and possibly the NPP for Senators, provided in their debatable Constitutions, that a member of the National Assembly is qualified for membership of the State or National Executive Committee. Thus, an injustice that has not been repaired is inflicted on innocent citizens.

One other jolt to the conscience of the public was in the areas of political party registration, mentioned above, Nigerians were given stringent guidelines on which they would have registered associations into political parties, in five months time. They went to places, spent huge sums of money hiring offices, buying vehicles and paying staff as was required.

At the close of the exercise, thirteen associations filed application papers. Four were said to have done better than others. But in a marathon speech lasting some ninety minutes, the President announced the decision of the Armed Forces Ruling Council (AFRC) that none of the 13 parties would be registered and that Government was creating its own two political parties for Nigeria "one a little to the right and the other a little to the left". The nation was shocked but absorbed it with the resignation they are used to.

But all hopes are not lost to Nigerians as they still look up to the target date of 1992 for a return to civilian rule. The Directorate of Social Mobilisation and Economic Recovery (MAMSER) took up the gospel of the two government "grass roots" political parties to the nooks and corners of the country. Nigerians hope to make the parties their own and not army-created after 1992.

On the issue of the so-called "new breed" politicians to have this to say. Some of these "new breed" are persons who either had been failing elections in their constituencies or never had any party nomination. You can never completely isolate the "old from the new" so long as the old are alive and kicking and the new are the offsprings or relations of the old. It is also arguable whether the "new breed" politicians will be more patriotic and less greedy than their predecessors, in the same way as one may not swear that all in military uniform are more innocent and cleaner than their civilian counterparts. We who are retired from active partisan politics are only praying hard for a better crop of people to hold the mantle of leadership in this country.

Part VI

Vision For The Third Republic

President Ibrahim Badamasi Babangida addressing the Nation on the Structural Adjustment Programme (SAP) and the Transition to Civil Rule.

Chapter 28

The Military In The Third Republic

It is thirty solid years of independence. But what has Nigeria got to show for it?

The giant of Africa continues to grope in the dark for a foothold in the comity of advanced nations of this world. We all believe that Nigeria is destined not to be in the present doldrum for long. Not with the ever flowing resources, human and otherwise, waiting to be exploited for the good of all Nigerians, and the world as a whole.

There is no doubt that somewhere around the corner in our march since nationhood we had made mistakes. We had allowed our economy to run haywire with the strings being pulled from outside our borders. We have always abandoned our traditional values, hence today no one is his or her brother's keeper.

Education, a legacy that is bequeathed to generations after generations in all orderly societies have become a thing to be purchased by the few who can afford it. Free health medicare is fast becoming part of a history of the past.

Our clinics and hospitals still remain unequipped and lack skilled manpower, drugs and modern tools. The few who can afford it under SAP's costly pricing system rush abroad only to be treated by Nigerian hands in a new SAP - induced diaspora. How much have we achieved technologically for genuine indigenous industrial revolution?

On the social level, our man-to-man relationship is yet to be examined to find out why we are still behaving like the cat and the mouse to each other. Brother Taiwo still does not seem at ease finding himself in the same political boat with Nzegwu. Mallam Umaru's association is still detested by Effiong. Yet we are citizens of one indivisible country with one common bond of unity and one brotherhood!

No wonder we stumble. Political stability, a precursor to economic development, had all the time eluded us. We face multiple crises all year round. Not only in civil democracy but even the military juntas have we had to go through one upheaval or the other. What we wonder at most is that some of these problems needed not to have confronted us, not to talk of confounding our leaders, if we meart to serve our country honestly and selflessly.

I still repeat it that we started very well during the early years of independence. The leadership was close-knit, well-meaning, honest, and responsive. At a stage during our forward march, I admit, the keel which balanced the boat received a jolt. By the time any attempt was made to return it to course, the unexpected had happened, and everyone was thrown overboard. We are still marooned.

Since then we had had several self-acclaimed saviours. But our socio-political problems remain unsolved. It is now worsened with the economic instability which is sending lots of men into untimely graves unceremoniously.

It is thirty years since independence, and we are still looking for direction from those we wrested power from. We still want them to be controllers of our own destiny. We indirectly go round once again begging to be allowed the use of the erstwhile noose with which the colonialists hung us to their home economy. We still want to go back, begging the so-called benefactors who still enjoy the resources they once pillaged from our shores.

Why indeed are we still so slow to development internally? All third world nations are striving to build stable economies and polities. They are trying to rediscover themselves so that they can utilise what they have in order to gain what they need to become great. It is time Nigeria goes soul-searching, seeking and acquiring knowledge for technology, for creativity, for originality, so as to hold its own among the great nations of the world. What then is the way out, one may ask?

For more than 40 years of active political life I have taken part in constitution making. I have also taken a fore-front position in the usage and application of such constitutions. I can now discuss authoritatively the much expected change in our attitude as a nation for us to have stability and progress.

Although some years ago, I announced my retirement from active partisan politics, I say it again, that much as I would no more be involved in political brickbats, I would not be neutral on issues involving the socio-political development of my country. As we now move towards the Third Republic I regard it a duty thrust on me by Providence to present to the nation my memoirs, and to give a visionary description of my hope for the future Nigeria. This is what I style my *"Handingover Notes"* to Political Activists, and other citizens of this country. They are detailed comments on issues of the moment, suggestions for future political stability, and a way out of the present economic morass in which we find ourselves.

After sober reflections of the joys and sorrows, the gains and losses, the ups and downs, the hopes and fears, from the Babangida administration which is the latest military rule, and hopefully the last in Nigeria. I called yet another Press Conference on 20th September, 1989, at the Light House, Victoria Island, Lagos. The theme was "A New Vision for the Third Republic: A call for Action".

My mind had been agitated by the plight of the working class *vis-a-vis* the sky-rocketing prices of every day need. The Shagari Administration had given the worker a minimum wage of N125.00. In 1989, the wages remained the same when prices went up at least 10 times. A tin of milk which cost 30 kobo in 1983 cost N3.50 in 1989, a peugeot 504 car which cost N10,000, six years before now costs N110,000. From tooth paste to television sets, the proportional increase is the same, 1000 percent.

Government Parastatals were being privatised and those left to be commercialised were compelled to be self-reliant. As a result we pay 1500 percent increase in telephone bills, and an equal percentage rise for electric power and air travel. Petrol, produced in our country, rose by 200 percent. So is the cost of gari, produced locally, too.

We became good boys to industrialised countries and International Monetary Organisations. Though old debts were being rescheduled for payment we accepted more loans. Otherwise, why did we reject IMF loan in 1986, after a national debate, only to have an IMF loan of $120 million dollars for Universities and $100 million for Secondary education in 1990? Yet the President told the Nation that fuel subsidy was removed to utilise the saving for funding education.

Let us admit, however, that there is an intensified effort at rural development, often based on rural people's own contributions, self-help efforts and community launching of projects where thousands of naira are voluntarily donated by indigenes. The Local Government which should involve itself in these actual rural development is overburdened by the State and the Federal Governments, on things like maintenance of political party offices and primary education.

Internationally, Nigeria was placed on a bright world map by diplomatic successes and sports. Our role in the liberation of Southern Africa is historic and worthwhile. Two Nigerians became the Chairman and Secretary-General of the United Nations General Assembly and of the Commonwealth respectively.

Having considered our balance sheet so far, I thought I should now address the nation, crystallizing my ideas of the Third Republic and outlining my promised hand-over notes to the new generation.

My premonitions, prophesies and forebodings expressed in a similar address in 1974, at Nsukka, were later amply reflected on the 1979 Constitution and the manifestoes of some, now defunct, political parties. I hope this exposure of my visions for the Third Republic will in no small measure inspire the new generation. The guide posts are summarised below:

(A) **Why Military Rule must be Terminated**

Before an issue of this magnitude is proposed, it is necessary to briefly trace again the genesis of military rule in Nigeria. As an actor on the stage then, I qualify to do this and to show the reversals of intent on what would have been a temporary corrective phenomenon.

When I and Late Hon. Zana Bukar Dipcharima, representing the Federal Government, handed over power to the Military on January 16th, 1966, it was on a solemn pledge from the army. The written pledge was "to bring about peace and stability in Nigeria, and that the welfare of our people shall be their paramount task". The three operative words are firstly peace, secondly stability, and thirdly the welfare of our people. The Council of Ministers which decided on the transfer of power to the army could have appointed one of themselves in place of the Prime Minister, then reported kidnapped, (and later dead) and rallied the loyal soldiers, led by Major-General J.T.U. Aguiyi-Ironsi to crush the rebellion and let the civilian government continue. We did not take that line of action because we loathed bloodbath as an avenue to attain or continue in power.

We thought that the stability of the country would be shaken, because at that time we had a national army which was not to be seen as serving the interests of one or two political parties. We rightly thought that the peace and unity of the country would be completely shattered if the civilian government continued in disregard of the great impact of the deaths of the Prime Minister and two Regional Premiers. So the military gave a pledge for peace, stability and welfare of our great nation which had five years of Independence and three years of being a Republic.

What happened soon after? We soon discovered to our chagrin that the saying that, "a man's word is his bond", has no place in the thinking faculty of some Nigerian soldiers. Soon, the thoughts of peace, stability and welfare of Nigerians were erased from their minds and were replaced with power, suspicion and wealth. Patriotism was given a warped interpretation. Internal infighting in the army took over from the purpose of government. The eyes of many soldiers, for one quarter of a century of Nigeria's nationhood, became focused on Marina or Dodan Barracks, the seat of Government. Not engaged in the defence of our territorial boundaries, their exercise of tactical manouvres became how to topple the next government by force of arms.

Major Chukwuma Nzeogwu led the first coup which brought Major General Aguiyi Ironsi to power. Ironsi was killed on the 29th of July 1966 in the second coup which saw Lt. Col. Yakubu Gowon as Head of State. Major-General Murtala Muhammed, in turn overthrew Gowon in the third coup. The fourth coup of Lt. Col. Dimka saw Muhammed dead. Murtala/Obasanjo's regime handed over government to a civilian administration, headed by Alhaji Shehu Shagari. On December 31st, 1983, in yet a fifth *coup d'etat* in Nigeria Major-General Buhari shot out the civilian government. The sixth coup was masterminded by Major-General Ibrahim Babangida on August 27th 1985. Six months after, Nigeria's seventh coup-bid was crushed and Air Marshal Mamman Vatsa and group were shot by a firing squad. The eighth was headed by Major Gideon Orkar on April 22nd 1990. Nigerians in one voice said, "this is the last."

It is relevant to state that this issue was recently discussed authoritatively, by some of the actors themselves. At an army week seminar in Lagos in 1986, retired Major-General Ibrahim Haruna postulated that, "if the soldier accepts that his first task on assumption of political leadership in Nigeria was to solve Nigeria's socio-economic problems, then the military must admit that it had not performed exceptionally well in this direction".

General Peter Ademokhai (retired), one-time General Officer Commanding One Mechanised Division, Nigerian Army, once submitted:

> While a soldier has no option but to be patriotic, I do not believe that soldiers should be involved in politics, it violates the spirit of professionalism of the military.

Putsches have not even meant well for the military itself. Lamenting the effect of military uprisings retired General T. Y. Danjuma's memorandum to the defunct Political Bureau states:-

> The first casuality of most coups is not the constituted civilian government that is being removed, but the destablisation and the overthrow of the established hierarchy of the military set up. No civilian who has never served in the military, can adequately guage the kind of volcanic tremors that coups can inflict upon the armed forces:

A soldier who nurses an anger as a result of one coup spends the better part of his time planning a counter-coup. The cycle continues. The General reminds us of the many young Generals, Brigadiers, Colonels, even Majors, now in Nigeria's pay roll as "retired", but not tired young men, not to talk of the unfortunate ones who lost their lives in those coups and subsequent uprisings. One can count many of these retired men.

Lately, the former Head of State, General Yakubu Gowon (also on the retired list) added his weight to the call for the military to hands off permanently. In a speech delivered at the annual lecture of the Oxford and Cambridge Club of Nigeria, on 31st May 1990, he argued that capital flight from Nigeria, lack of zeal for investment by foreigners, and abhorence of repatriating honest funds from abroad by wealthy Nigerians are hinged on political instability due to coups.

Says Gowon:

> Our economic pundits emphasise that if large doses of foreign capital and investment (and I include fleeing Nigeria capital) are pumped back into our economy, our political stability would be sustained by such eventuality; but as it is, foreign investors appear reluctant mainly because of the reasons of instability, thereby giving rise to a vicious circle which must be broken if meaningful progress must be made on the political and economic fronts.

He recalls that:

> In January 1966, a number of young military officers, then highly politicized, began to see a so-called vision of the brighter future for the country, Nassarite type vision, that encouraged them to attempt the over- throwing of the fledgling democratic government of Nigeria, to plunge us into a vicious circle of instability, delusion and disunity.....
> Frequent military intervention creates instability which does not allow democracy to flourish and which in turn hampers economic and social development of the country

I go to this extent not because I grudge the military for what role providence assigned to them these years of turmoil. Maybe, we needed to learn from our mistakes for which the military had to come in. I go this extent to prove that it is not only the civil populace, including the politicians, who are calling for an end to military government. We must proceed with every necessary measures which will make the Babangida's regime the last of all military governments.

The Nigerian masses will no more entertain a self-proclaimed corrective military junta. We should allow the electorate the right to change bad, unpopular and unfit governments, through the ballot box, not through the intimidating barrel of a gun.

All the coups demonstrate the military's in-fighting and thirst for power, rather than the military's correction of the civilian excesses. The first coup fanned an unprecedented ethnic jingoism in Nigeria. Non-indigenes of the regions were entrapped in their places of domicile and executed en-masse. Survivors were forced to their tribal homes. The second coup resulted in the 30 months civil war in which thousands of innocent people lost their lives. The Military did not keep faith with civilians. It did not keep faith with itself on what they agreed at Aburi, Ghana. The third and fourth coups deepened the suspicions taking hold of the armed forces. The fifth coup murdered democracy and never gave rest to its perpetrators as shown in the sixth, seventh and the eighth coups. The aftermath of the coups was an unprecedented upsurge of armed robbery,

drug trafficking, economic sabotage of all forms, and all evils
and crimes hitherto unheard of in this land.

With the advent of coups, as a ladder to climb to power, two
groups of citizens emerged in Nigeria: the military and the
civilian. The soldier who has the gun looks at himself no longer
as the servant of his people, but as "lord and monarch of all he
surveys". He assumes monopoly of knowledge, of wisdom and
of expertise, to solve all Nigeria's problems. But it turns out that
he uses the sound of his gun and the threat of decrees to cover
ignorance and incompetence. He is more corrupt, more tribal and
more unscruplous than anybody else.

With the soldier's totting of the machinegun, the civilian
population, as the other group, is cowed into submission,
sometimes into singing praises to save his skin. Let it be said
clear and loud that the civilian is no inferior. He is the nationalist
the patriot, the technocrat, the tax-payer, the producer of goods
and services. The history of the independence of this country is
the story of civilian heroes who had high ideals, great vision,
and who sacrificed immensely for their fatherland. They see the
military junta as a bunch working for the Imperialists who did
not think we should really be free to experiment on democracy.
Unless, the military is re-oriented to be a people's army, or
people's airforce or people's police or people's navy; unless one
citizenship is evolved from the present army civilian dichotomy,
unless democracy is given a chance to thrive, our whole
independence as a nation is a sham.

Records show that breaking of pledges, breaches of faith,
and reneging on obligations are a constant feature of military
regimes in this country from 1966 to 1990. This is the reason
why there is consensus that there will be no more military rule in
Nigeria, ever.

Professor Ben Nwabueze, lecturing at Guardian Anniversary
on 25th July 1989 put it straight:

> In comparison with military absolutism, colonial absolutism may be
> said to have been glorious... There is no really acceptable and viable
> alternative to a government freely elected by the people and limited in

its powers by a supreme constitution. The best service the military will render this country is to accept this message and abandon any ambition to take over government.

And the *Guardian Newspaper* in its editorial the next day agreed:

> If the military has neither superior wisdom, nor judgement, nor morality, nor mandate, and certainly not superior competence, then to justify any military intervention for any period whatsoever, is to legitimatize violence and might, in the resolution of society's socio-political and economic problems ... An intervening military commits two immoralities. It abuses the public trust involved in allowing it monopoly control of the total coercive power of society for defending the general public against external aggression and internal subversion. Secondly, it exploits societal discontent to execute its own hidden and private desire. These two immoralities of which it is guilty, infact, disqualifies it from arrogating to itself the prerogative of passing judgement on the goodness and badness of government. Our rejection of military rule has been made so loud and clear that if the military has any respect for the people of this country, it should leave us alone, even when our elected governments fumble and fumble.

Without an intention to fumble, the crucial question remains, what then do we do to terminate military rule in Nigeria? Provision in the Constitution is not enough. Did not Chapter 1 section 2 of the 1979 Constitution provide as follows:

> The Federal Republic of Nigeria shall not be governed, nor shall any person or group of persons take control of the government of Nigeria except in accordance with the provisions of this Constitution.

An anti-coup clause, you may say, but on 31st December, 1983 the army (a group of persons) took over the government in clear violation of the country's Constitution.

If the 1989 Constitution missed a final word on the coup, the incoming civilian administration will not miss it, early in its reign.

The basis for the military's successful snatching of political power should be understood. It is the monopoly it has over our "collective violence" or coercive power. That monopoly can be broken by dispersing control of that coercive power of society. The United States, West Germany and Switzerland provide for dispersing such control. I shall include them in the options which now present to my country for terminating military rule.

a) **Option One**

The United States has three different arrangements which make military *coup d'etat* impossible.

. The National Army is entirely controlled by the President and the Federal Government. The State militias are controlled by the State Governors and the State Governments. If a part of the National Army rises to topple the Federal Government, the loyal troops and the State Militia will fight in defence of democracy. And it will be crazy for a State Militia or a combination of them to aim at a coup to topple the Federal Government.

i. The Police is decentralized. It cannot therefore be easily brought to support a coup as is often the case in Nigeria.

ii. Individuals - responsible citizens - are allowed to own private guns. This implies that they cannot be pushed around, neither by the army, nor by the militia, nor by the police. In Nigeria, on the other hand, the army and armed robbers hold the citizens to ransom.

b) **Option Two**

In West Germany, their 1949 Constitution requires all citizens to automatically go on a general strike against any body or group that illegally usurps the government of the land. Society here adopts an attitude of voluntary non-cooperation with any coup maker. Nigerians can do the same. Let us stop cheering any group - soldiers, students or market women - that topples an elected government with violence.

c) **Option Three**

As in Switzerland, the defence of the country is done by a universal military service. Every able bodied person receives military training. In a grave national emergency, like an aggression by a foreign troop, the National (universal) Army is called up. In peace time, only a microscopic professional army is

274 Rebirth of a Nation

maintained. Because everybody receives military training, n
group of professional soldiers will assume that it alone has
moral duty to fight or to correct the political ills of the society
Nigeria must reduce the size of the standing army and giv
military training to school leavers and fresh graduates.

(d) *Option Four*

This demands a serious consideration. Soon after independence
we nationalists abhored, cried against, and opposed any military
pact with Britain or any other country. To do so, at that time
would have amounted to our winning independence and selling i
back. Times have changed; the world is also fast changing and
experimenting with new ideas. In 1968, a grave emergency
situation arose by the inception of the civil war. To help it stay is
power, and ostensibly to assist it crush rebellion, the military
under General Gowon, signed military pacts with Britain and
Russia. With their armoury, Gowon was able to prevent Biafra's
separate existence.

A *coup d'etat* is as grave an emergency. The fourth option
therefore, would be for the next civilian administration to enter
into a military agreement with a friendly country of its choice ·
Anglophone or Francophone Africa, Britain, Russia or U.S.A.

Should any group of soldiers again strike in a coup, the pact
will be invoked in order to restore civilian rule and save
democracy in Nigeria. Any gangster who disturbs the natural
evolution of democracy in Nigeria should be immediately
arraigned and tried. No group of soldiers who came to power,
by force of arms have the moral or legal justification for sitting
over the trial of fellow soldiers who try, but only fail, in their
game of coups. But this is the practice of the military junta when
a coup fails.

(e) *Option Five*

Non-cooperation. If we know our rights , we would never cheer
any individual or group that dispossesses us of the right to
choose our governments through the ballot box. But often the
military, on seizing power, muzzles the holders of the conscience

of society by fat appointments. We must resist them. Civilian Ministers appointed by the Military should refuse. Commissioners enticed to serve should reject the offer. If any citizen is thirsty of political power, he should join a political party and get a mandate.

Non-civil servants appointed to any tribunals, commissions or boards by the military should look at them with disdain and turn their backs. Traditional Rulers and Religious Leaders, to whom the military first turns for support, should question them about their mandate. Businessmen, who are lured by promises of government loot, should turn to more honourable ventures. Only if the citizen disowns the coup maker can he (the citizen) us the power of the ballot to change a government he does not like, and instal the one of his choice.

I have tried above to show why military rule must be ended and the options for doing so. I have not in any way diminished the role of the armed forces of the country. I shall rather below show my vision of what their role in society and in the Republic will be. But for them to come again to goverrment, it is no!

(B) **The Place of the Military in the Third Republic**

With deliberate repetition, let me say immediately that militarism and military government are incompatible with national greatness. To say the least, it is repugnant to clear conscience and good morality when soldiers turn round against those they were under oath to protect and, at gun point, dictate and lord it over them. The coup which brought President Babangida to power should be the last coup in Nigeria, a coup to end all coups.

History has imposed on President Babangida a grave responsibility to steer Nigerian out of coup-prone situations. He has no choice. He could not have known that the turn of history would impose this task on him. He was among those who terminated the First and Second Republics: He is now involved in the move to usher in the Third Republic which will put a stop to all attempts to unlawfully topple governments,

When we fought England, with all her might, we had nothing but faith. Let us take the solemn oath today, all of us, men and women, and say that enough is enough. We should make provisions for the new military of the new Republic to emerge with pride, to forget about coups, to defend their fatherland and give us the pomp and pageantry of a People's Army.

Was President Babangida not welcomed by the British Army when he visited England recently? There has been no interference of the military in Britain. The only army intervention was determined by Cromwell and from that day there was no more military interference. I wish that President Babangida is the Nigerian Cromwell to stop the military from further interfering, politically so that Nigeria will emerge a great democracy.

The end of coups does not render the army irrelevant, but it will signal the beginning of a proud and magnificent army of the people, whose power, pomp and pageantry will be appreciated by all strata and segments of the society. It will be an independent and proud army whose place in the society is marked by honour and a readiness to defend the people and the territorial integrity of the nation. A new people's Army will be bequeathed to the Third Republic. It should be an army prepared and ever ready to serve the people, and their elected representatives

Let me summarise the guidelines for Army-Rebirth, the rebuilding of the Armed Forces, which can make us proud any day:

i.   In the first place, it has to be purely a Nigerian Force having no trappings of colonialism, no attachment to any foreign influence, and capable of belonging to Nigerians from all walks of life, the lowly and the privileged. Both the officer corps and the men should be quite representative of all Nigerians. This time, sons of the working class, the business entrepreneur, the financier, the labourer, the traditional ruler, should all be for recruitment and be selected without discrimination, to serve Nigeria.

ii. There should be no more concentration of the army personnel in one state or one area of the Federation. There must be an even spread of recruitment, training and deployment.

iii. There should be voluntary service in the Armed Forces for all able-bodied men. For some limited period, every man should be put in the colours so that at the end, no man is left out of the disciplined experience. This system will remove the tinge of feeling that the soldier is a different person from the rest of us.

iv. The new Armed Force should be functional. We inherited an octopus army which only sucked but did not replenish. We cannot continue this way for long without creating some tempting grounds for further mischief in the army. The devil, we are told, finds work for the idle hand. Had the army units been saddled with targetted production, they might not have had time to discuss politics at their mess. I agree with Chief Anthony Enahoro who argued that:

"In the Soviet Union, the military are part of the total mobilisation for modernisation, political indoctrination and agricultural development. By contrast, the military in ex-colonial territories at the most were idle, performing largely ceremonial roles during independence celebrations and similar occasions. The exercise of political power becomes an attractive outlet for their latent energies".

The Peoples' Military should train its men to mingle with ease with their menfolk outside the military. They should be able to interact with workers in the factories and schools. The army should compete with those outside it for ability to feed the nation.

v. The new Armed Forces should become purely professional and be cleansed of any propensity for ruling. As the new armed forces become a weapon for protecting the people, through their elected leaders, they should never hold their guns to terrorize those leaders.

Chapter 29

Politics In The Third Republic

Politics is an art in the government and administration of human beings in the society. It is one of the highest functions devised by man for the upliftment and orderly preservation of his well-being. It is painful, however, to see that this highest function of human beings in the society is so carelessly handled that it seems to have lost respectability.

Before lawyers become members of that profession, they are well trained, and pass some prescribed examinations. Those in the medical profession also have to undergo a long period of training and pass prescribed examinations before they are allowed to practise. The churches have their theological seminaries, where would-be priests undergo systematic training before being commissioned to preach.

Politicians who govern and coordinate the activities of these professionals should not come from nowhere, without being trained to assume leadership in the society. Before any person could reach the level of being a politician, whose responsibility covers the management of men and affairs, he or she will have been trained and seasoned. His above-average intelligence is taken for granted as a precondition of qualification for any training.

In the name of what is logical and what is sensible, how can people without training be made to direct and rule those who are more competent than themselves? These are some of the factors which contributed to make politics in the First and Second Republic to be misapplied by some over zealous upstarts.

In this Third Republic, we must effectively identify the ills of the past and cure them, if we must find a place of greatness for this nation. First and foremost, our political build-up must be imbued with the concept that politics is a noble game, a most noble occupation for those who are annointed and dedicated for human service. This concept should be preached and pressed upon the political parties before any other thing. We must henceforth tread cautiously into the Third Republic with the intent to create a new nation, a new conciousness, a new society, dedicated to selfless service, honesty and integrity. There must be a departure from the past misdeeds, from greed and grab, and from all kinds of corruption and nepotism. This is a big assignment, where you asked what you can do for the country and not what the country can do for you; where you find out that it is more blessed to give than to receive. Here, I also endorse a two-party system of government for Nigeria. That is the best that can happen to us now.

Each of these political parties must have a set policy and each member must strictly adhere to this objective. It should be compelling on all political associations to establish a centre for training. All functionaries should be required to pass through this training ground. Political education is a necessity for the next attempt at democracy so as to purge the nation of the abuses of the past: corruption, tribalism, nepotism, morbid ambition for power.

Going into the Third Republic without an ideology does not make sense. No nation moves without direction. Our direction is towards a WELFARE STATE. Welfarism is a thing suited to our own nature as a people. The Nigerian has been his brother's keeper all along. Today when you have one person on employment, go to his house, he is surrounded by more than ten persons, relatives, distant cousins for whom he cares. He may have in addition his aged father and mother who also depend on his meagre salary. Extending this to national life, one sees no application for "welfarism" in the complete withdrawal of subsidies on essential services. So we expect one of the parties to adopt the ideology of Welfarism now or in the future.

The system of rotation of the presidency should enter the constitution of each of the two political parties, in order to enforce a system which makes for continued unity of the country. This does not in any way suggest enthronement of mediocrity. If there are four to six zones for the rotation of the Presidency, it should be seen that Nigeria is so rich in human resources that you must have a nationally accepted leader emerging from each zone, at any given time.

When people know that there is an equal opportunity for all, they feel a sense of belonging. After the four recommended zones in the party constitution have all had their turns and chances to present the President, we end rotation and go for open and healthy competition. This is "zoning to unzone", as I described it earlier.

It took over fifty years for the Soviet Union to start changing their politics. They were protecting themselves from disintegration. Now that they are strong, united, and confident they can relax and go purely democratic. This is the spirit behind their glasnosts and perestroika. It will be the spirit behind our zoning philosophy.

Leadership and Followership

With the emergence of a visionary leader, a leader accepted nationally, forward-looking, honest and patriotic, the nation's problem of instability is removed. I believe our search for a new society will bring forth such a new leadership for the people. The New Society which will be dedicated to the equality of all people will entrust power to a highly responsible Peoples' Leader. The leadership shall, in return, hold power in trust for the greatest good of all Nigerians.

No one should be made to aspire to leadership or be entrusted with power unless he is qualified to hold it, unless he has something worthwhile for the people. I very much relish the often-quoted Northern scholar, the late Othman Dan Fodio, who wrote in his book, *Kitabul Faro*:-

No one should look after the affairs of men but one who is of sound mind, abundant knowledge, little conceit, great zeal, strong without weakness, generous but not a squanderer, fearing no blame of any person.

He also stipulated that a leader;

must have such strength that the killing of a man in the cause of truth would be to him like the killing of a swallow, and should have mildness, kindness, care and mercy which makes him fear to kill a bird without justice.

Furthermore, Dan Fodio stressed that the ruler,

must endeavour to ward off every cause of corruption and harm from befalling the people of his land, to secure everything for their welfare and substenance, and to protect and defend them against anyone who would want to cause them any harm.

That indeed summarizes what type of leadership Nigeria expects from its future rulers. Therefore the qualities expected of our new leadership include:

The new leader must, as a precondition, have the traits of leadership, namely, knowledge, humanity, public spiritedness, approachability, sincerity, keeping faith, selflessness and patriotism. He should appreciate the implications and applications of power. Apart from the constraints of tenure, as limited by the constitution, he should be ready to bow out if need be.

The leader should understand his worth; he should not be self-opinionated. He should be confident but not pompous. The new Nigerian expects his leader to have and exert power in the national interest. He should have before him achievable targets and pursue them with a sense of mission. The nation is prepared to give the new leader a toga of authority, but this should not be worn by power-drunk elements.

The new leader should be able to map out a new sense of direction modelled on adopted national goals. He should be visionary and make his vision and direction clear to his country men.

v.   The leader should present to the nation, a symbol of solidarity and oneness. Put in practice, this sweeps away corruption, nepotism and group interest.
Indeed he is an inspiration to us all. He is the one to ask not what Nigeria can do for him, but what he can do for Nigeria.

vi.   The leader should be an acme of all that is fine in language, bearing and pride. His presentation should not lack the finesse that belongs only to the best in Nigerian manhood.

But for leadership to succeed there should, of necessity, be a loyal followership. The follower, therefore should be expected:

(i)   To be a partner and fellow builder. He cannot afford to destroy what he is helping to build.

(ii)   The follower should criticise, if need be, and he should proffer solutions or alternatives, where possible. But once a decision is taken it must be given a chance to operate.

(iii)   Patriotism is as much a power-house for the leader as for the follower. The ruled must discourage sabotage and any attack on the national pride.

(iv)   We all have personal pride to maintain. The follower will not, therefore, demand gratification for doing his job or succumb to pressure not to do it. No candidate at election can buy a vote if he does not find a willing seller of a vote. Be proud of your franchise to choose or reject a ruler and install a government of your choice.

(v)   The follower must respect the leader, for the time being, but he must abhor sychophancy. Loyalty is a virtue, sychophancy is a vice.

Chapter 30

Technology In The Third Republic

For us to achieve greatness, we must usher in the Third Republic on a very sound technological base. Sound technological base embraces several ingredients.

Education

We must early develop a habit which must make us ever conscious of our goals, and propel us towards its attainment. If this is done we shall discover that basic primary education, capable of cultivating human resources from childhood, is a pre-requisite for sound technological development. From primary education, we can move to secondary, tertiary, and university levels, laying at each stage the foundations for sound technologies which will serve our self-determined goals and aspirations.

In entering the Third Republic, therefore, we should place great emphasis on technology. We can do this by selecting a most conspicuous site and develop it as a Technical Centre and there mount, for a symbol, a burning torch, just as the Americans, when they wanted to emphasise their desire for human liberty, mounted the Statue of Liberty.

I advocate that we must build this centre of technology to demonstrate that we have turned a new leaf on technology, and that both our elementary schools and universities are geared towards the full meaning and utilization of technology for the advancement of our country.

Things to Abhor

There are many things which we do as a people which when examined very critically make us look ridiculous. For instance, if we must acquire technology, we must go in for excellence and not mediocrity. All along we have been saying that we want the country to attain greatness, but instead of investing and financing greatness, we have consistently and unashamedly been financing mediorcrity. The two things cannot interchange.

Our educational system and the national policy on it have not strictly hammered the nail at the head, either. Take university admissions, for example. We have messed it up through the policy adopted by JAMB (Joint Admissions and Matriculations Board). JAMB has developed uneven cut-off points, thereby injecting the element of discrimination in our admissions policy. Some States are favoured more than others. This is an outdated policy. We must from now on eschew discrimination in giving admissions to students in our institutions of higher learning, irrespective of ethnicity or State of origin. There are other methods of assisting disadvantaged groups in society, without bastardizing education. We should abolish retardation policies without delay, or be held responsible for putting this country backwards. We have to apologise for the degradation of the manhood of this nation by our discriminatory methods.

Our people have wings as the Eagles and are being told that they are incapable of flying. They do not want to be fed with the chicken's food because they are Eagles. We must render to our society the services which they deserve, if we must escape the condemnation of posterity.

If I should be asked where next my contributions should lie in the advancement of this country, I would readily wish to state that my humble contribution be in the field of technological development of this nation. I have done some preliminary work already. Let me restate how far I have gone.

Arrangement of Technological Development for Nigeria

By way of introduction, during my student days in the United States, I founded the African Academy of Arts and Research and bought the Africa House in 1945, with Mrs Roosevelt (wife of he former President of the United States) as Chief Patroness, and co-sponsored by Mrs Mary Mcloud Bethune, a great African-American.

The current phase of Africa House can be dated from 1976 to 1989. In 1976, we began the preparation for City College participation in the FESTAC. And it was in 1977 during the Festac festivities that the meeting of minds between President Marshak, then the President of City College, New York, and myself was achieved. On the basis of our shared vision we organised a Nigerian-American structure for the revitalisation of the Academy and Africa House. The twin hopes of the thinking in 1977 were centred around:

i. cultural enrichment of the Black Studies curriculum of City College, through the creation of an Mbadiwe Museum to be housed in Africa House.

ii. the fostering of economic link between Nigeria and the United States, through the collaboration of both sides for Technological Development in Nigeria.

When the American Ambassador, His Excellency, Dr. Princeton Lymann made a valedictory call on me, as he was returning to the United States, I addressed him as follows:

"Following the end of the civil war, I invited Dr. Robert Marshak, then President of the City College of the City University of New York, to be my guest in Nigeria. He inspired our discussions on my pet dream that there must be something tangible to commemorate in Nigeria the special relationship between America and Nigeria, the dream that one day a strong Nigeria will emerge as a natural ally of America, more so because part of American human resources is made up of people from this part of the world.

I am happy to report to you that Dr. Robert Marshak shared my views, shared my dreams and shared my vision in this respect. In furtherance of our talk, I connected him to the then Federal Minister of Education, Col. (Dr.) A.A. Ali and added unto that, was Professor Jubril Aminu, who was then the Secretary of the National Universities Commission (NUC). He joined in exploratory talks with Dr. Marshak.

He returned to America and pursued the subject of finding something tangible to show for American/Nigerian relationship, in Nigeria, with the greatest speed at his disposal. Thus, he instituted a workshop on Technological Transfer for Nigeria, jointly sponsored by the Nigerian Government, the US Academy of Sciences in City College and the US State Department, Washington D.C.

A voluminous Report of 852 pages was published on the outcome of this workshop with vast recommendations for the establishment of a Technological Centre in Nigeria to carry on the work.

Your Excellency, you can see that my dream for the American torch of technology for Nigeria has started, it can only be slowed down, but cannot be quenched."

The authoritative document can be picked up any day by any group which shares this dream and imagination through this new vision.

I was surprised when the Ambassador took hold of the book from me and showed me that he (Dr. Lyman) was present at the plenary session, in his capacity then as the Deputy Director, Institute for Technological Cooperation, in former President Carter's Government. He said that he would do everything that lies in his power to revitalise the recommendations arrived at that conference.

I am now addressing my countrymen from the point of view of a layman in technology, but from a strong point of view of an inspirer.

A task force could take over quickly the realisation of these dreams. The great role of technology in the world today cannot be over emphasised.

Dr. Frank Press, writing on development in technology remarked that, "over the next decades, we may be in a race with catastrophe. We must therefore build future development from the current base of poverty." That base of poverty in Nigeria today involves more than eighty million people who are caught in the so called "poverty trap". This is in spite of our oil revenue and yearly budgets or billions of naira of recent times by the central government. Appropriate technology is our savior.

The natural endowment and human potentials are here with us in Nigeria. All that needs, for us to develop, is direct and purposeful orientation and steady practical application of acquired skills. Though Universities of Technology and the

Polytechnics abound in Nigeria today, compared with the position in 1977 when I addressed the American Ambassador, there appears not yet to be an institution quite suited to the solutions of our technological problems. Hence the need for an organisation to blaze a new trail in this direction so that in the decades to come, Nigeria will be the Japan of Africa. The Laboratory, the Theatre, the Stage, the Training and Practical Workshop for this technological take-off, with a marked difference, will have to be established in Nigeria, as a National Institute of Technology. Its stature might be that of the Massachusettes Institute of Technology (M.I.T), but its hands will be the dexterious, efficient fingers of Japan, Korea and Taiwan.

Chapter 31

Handover Notes

I have said a lot about the armed forces, the politics and the economy of the Third Republic. I shall now give my handover notes to the nation through selected interest groups, namely the churches, journalists, trade unions, professional bodies, traditional rulers, women, the youths, the business community, the self-employed.

(i) *To Journalists*

It is generally held that the Press is the Fourth Estate of the Realm. The three other powers are the Executive, the Legislature and the Judiciary. The role of the Press as the informer, the educator, the critic and the entertainer in society cannot be over-emphasised. The press can pull down individuals or governments. It could popularise or condemn policies. Hence the saying that the pen is mightier than the sword.

Nigeria's independence was won, not by the shot of the gun, as in Kenya or Zimbabwe or Namibia, but by the sweat of the Nationalists and the ink of the Nigerian Press. Had a section of the press not fanned the embers of tribalism, that word should not have entered the dictionary of Nigerian politics. Had the Press not hailed a military take-over of the government from elected civilians, the culture of army-rule in Nigeria would not have been a phenomenon. Had the Press not been the Nation's watchdog, the wind of corruption, the flood of SAP and the blitz of crime, should have swept corporate Nigeria from existence.

My handover advice to journalists, therefore, is to uphold the ethics of their noble profession and direct all their energies to helping to build up a virile democratic, peaceful and prosperous Nigeria. Journalists must in their investigative approach, expose

288

the enemies of the country and protect good citizens. They must, with the power of the pen, discourage any future military rule and nurture democracy to survive in our dear country, Nigeria.

We must assure the public that we are responsible enough and can operate fairly in an atmosphere of freedom and justice. We can retrieve the lost ground by convincing the nation that we are patriotic citizens capable of displaying a great measure of maturity in our duties.

Press freedom implies the right to obtain, impart, or convey ideas or information through the medium of the Press and other mass media without let or hinderance. However, it does not give us an absolute freedom to use such right to the deteriment of the nation or its people. This right has to be exercised according to law.

And that law demands that for such right to be exercised judiciously, there should be some codes or ethics which will have to be jealously guarded by us all.

To be precise, a free press does not defame the good name of people or disparage their reputation. It does not incite hatred or promote feelings of ill-will and hostility or promote discontent or disaffection among the citizens of the country.

The press is not free to impugn the integrity of government, distort news and information, disclose official secrets or publish obscene matters. There are laudable objectives for the Nigerian Press to pursue.

Therefore, under Nigerian laws and procedures, the press is expected to exercise our freedom to publish, subject to the laws relating to tort, criminal libel, slander, sedition, obscene publications, official secrets, contempt of court, and so on.

(ii) *To Trade Unions*

The labourer is worth his pay. The producers of the country's wealth should share in it. Every regime in Nigeria, army or civilian, revolutionary or benevolent, a little to the right or a little to the left, all appear to favour capitalism. The entrepreneur may hold the capital, but he cannot produce without labour. The government may set up a secretariat, but it cannot function without the work-force. For labour to get the best from the vine-yard, it must organise itself into a responsible patriotic force. Government-sponsored trade union is an aberration. Employers'-guided trade union is a misnomer.

Trade unions, I urge you to rise to your responsibilities. Protect the interest of your members and of the Nation. Go on strike when you must, but obey the laws of the land. Raise your productivity that you may justify a rise in wages. Always take time to study the economy of the country and see where and how you fit in. Only a proper appreciation of your role and responsibility can ensure an egalitarian society.

(iii) *To Professional Bodies*

You are the salt of the earth. The standard of achievement of the members of the professional bodies is the guage for measuring the height of a nation's greatness. Some thorny edges of the country's laws would not be blunted without, for instance, the protests of the Bar Association. Until the different Unions of the teaching staff at every level of our educational institutions rise to improve their lot, their pay would still be reserved "in heaven" hereafter. The Nigerian Medical Association should not only care for the welfare of the members, but should alert the government that hospitals (teaching or specialists or general) are becoming consulting clinics without the drugs to cure. The same role of service to members and to the general public is expected from very many other professional bodies, too numerous to mention.

My word for you is that you use your forum not only for agitating for your welfare, but for contributing to the general growth of the nation. Continue educating your members. Be proud to join the scientific and technological race and show the nation what new input you make to the progress of mankind. The democratic selection of your officers should be mirrowed in the democratic elections of the rulers of the country.

(iv) *To Traditional Rulers*

I respect and uphold culture and tradition. Ours is a heterogeneous society. There must therefore be the custodians of our variegated culture and traditions. The status and influence of Traditional Rulers vary from ethnic group to ethnic group, and from community to community. The early British administrators, in keeping with their system of indirect rule, strengthened the authorities of the Emirs in the North, the Obas in the West and the Eze, Obis, Obongs and Amayanabos in the East. The joltings of nationalism, the pangs of democracy and the barrels of the gun have not much changed the respect given to traditional rulers. Infact, more and more effort is made to accommodate them within the constitution of the land and more roles given to them at their local government areas.

A responsible and respected traditional ruler is insulated from partisan politics, but he should watch and encourage democracy to grow and tacitly discourage any military *coup d'etat*. This is why he merits the honour of being addressed as "father" of the community. This status imposes a grave and dignified responsibility.

(v) *To the Women*

Educate a man, you educate a single individual, educate a woman, you educate a nation. So we are told. And it is a truism. The Nigerian womanhood has come of age. Women have competed favourably with their men counterparts in the professions, business, social life and even in politics. The era of relegating the woman to the background and the kitchen is history. Given equal opportunity women have shown they will succeed.

A woman, Professor Alele Williams, is the Vice Chancellor of the University of Benin. A woman, Chief (Mrs) Kufuriji-Olubi was the Chairman of the United Bank for Africa. During the Second Republic, women were elected Senators, Representatives and Assemblymen. A woman President for Nigeria is no idle dream, for on the world scene, a woman, Mrs

Corazon Aquino, is the President of the Phillipines, Mrs Bhutto was Prime Minister of Pakistan, the longest ruling Prime Minister of Britain (Mrs Margret Thatcher) is a woman. India was ruled for many years by Mrs Indira Ghandi. Why can't a woman aspire to be President of Nigeria?

I am proud of the Nigerian woman. Their role in rural development is significant. Their organisation is dynamic. Considering their higher proportion of our population, no ruler, military or civilian, can ignore them. No candidate seeking for votes can push them aside.

As mothers they should take good care of the type of upbringing they give the children. They should start early to discourage criminal tendencies in the youth and inculcate in them an abhorence for hard drugs. Children should start early in life to be drilled in the tenets of patriotism and respect for family life, so that homes will be the bastion of peace, unity, and respect for one another. These traits carried to the national level, will produce an enduring peace and harmony in the country.

We have witnessed enough of jolts in our national leadership of recent. They do not make for confidence in the future of our dear country. Therefore, women must join hands with men to elect good government, so that coups will end.

(vi) *To the Religious Leaders*

Man is a compound of body and spirit. While the political leader strives to cater for the earthly wellbeing of society generally, the religious leader concentrates on the spiritual wellbeing. The constitution of the Federal Republic of Nigeria provides for a secular state, one in which the political leader is not also the religious leader, and in which situation government does not favour one mode of religion as against the others.

Religious belief is a very sensitive issue and any interference with it often sparks off disturbances. This is where a government in a secular state should not give the impression that the religious beliefs of any section of society enjoys a special favour and patronage of government.

All religions believe in, and respect one Supreme Being, the Creator of the universe. All religions preach love, kindness and tolerance. These qualities which they tell us have their source from God, if practised, will make for harmonious co-existence of God's people on earth. This is why we pay attention when religious leaders speak. Their words, therefore, should always be a guide and not an incitement for the people.

My note to the religious leaders is to urge their adherents to practise the virtues taught them, and carry these to the service of the nation. No religion teaches spilling of innocent blood in a putsch for change of government.

I believe there is God. He is merciful. He is kind. He will hear us when we pray. I urge you religious leaders of all faith to pray to God/Allah for wisdom and protection on the part of the rulers, and patriotism and love of neighbours on the part of the ruled. Only so, can this nation be blessed, be peaceful and be prosperous.

vii)   *To the Youths*

"Child is father of the man." So says the great play-wright, William Shakespeare. This underlies the often repeated truism that the youths are the leaders of tomorrow, and I add, Nigeria's greater tomorrow.

Wars to stem injustice, aggression and territorial encroachments are often waged with the blood of the youths. Youths have spontaneoulsy risen against bad government policies and have changed the course of events.

Therefore, realising the potentialities of the youths, and what the future holds for them, it becomes imperative for me to address a few words of hand-over to you.

First is patriotism. Was it not Sir Walter Scott who said that "he is dead who never turns to say, this is mine, my native land". For your country Nigeria, you have an abundant and deep well of inspiration to draw from the heroes of your land, past and present in patriotism and zest for a united Nigeria.

A future united and prosperous Nigeria depends on wh: attitude the youths of today hold on issues like tribalisn religious bigotry and ethnic chauvinism. Though, some of you fathers may not be completely absolved of these vices, the nevertheless recongised that they should be eschewed. The prepared the grounds for you to succeed in doing so. Th Nigerian Youth Service Corps is a Government programm aimed at achieving nationalism and patriotism. Th establishment of many universities and unity secondary school is an opportunity given Nigerian Youths to integrate and break the walls of language and social barriers. These and other goal: should be encouraged.

Government, on its part should discourage the evil of statisn and allow every eligible youth to take up employment in any State of the Federation of his choice and make a career and a living there.

My other charge to you, the youths, is to be a responsible group. Youths' idealistic proposals should be made to the authorities in a constitutional manner, using the avenues that will not rock societal peace, and cause losses of lives and property.

The slogans of self-sufficiency, hardwork, accountability and patriotism should so get into the marrows of your bones that no youth can be heard to ask "what will Nigeria do for me?" but he will rather ask, "what can I do for Nigeria, my country?"

My charge to you is to mobilise against any further military rule in Nigeria. Military rule is an usurpation of power. It is worse than imperialism which we fought. All the type of energy, all the type of resources, and all the type of talent which we employed to fight imperialism, should now be harnessed and directed by you to fight army take-over of government in Nigeria. A coup in Nigeria is no show of patriotism; it is rather a naked show of thirst for power, more easily achieved by the trigger of the gun. Once a ruling junta instals itself the evil of society continues, corruption, nepotism, greed, religious bias, envy and pride. The nation is left to suffer. The Youths, must help to elect a good government. You must not allow yourselves to be used by any group or party or individual to rig elections or to put the wrong person in government. You must not help to create any excuse for any soldier to raise his gun against the people's will.

(viii) *To the Business Community*

The business community cannot be isolated from the overall policy of government in the economic wellbeing and growth of the nation. Infact, the two opposing ideologies of the world are based on the government's relationship with the control of economic factors namely, the production and distribution of the wealth of the nation. Communism emphasises government control while capitalism champions private management of the means of production.

Therefore, no businessman can afford to sit on the fence with regards to the type of government of the country and how it is run, because a tilt to the right or left affects the very livelihood of the citizens and touches the roots of investiment, production and reward.

My handover note to you is first a charge for high productivity which, if well utilised, will result in a higher standard of living for the nation. An improved level of production pre-supposes a high reward for labour. All these are possible in a climate of stability in government, ...aking economic forecast a reality and reliable. One great source of instability is a sudden violent change in government, occasioned by a military *coup d'etat*. It therefore behoves you as individuals and groups to join in discouraging a military rule in our dear country.

Offer no facilities to any coup plotter. Rather, proudly use the power of your vote to instal the popular leader and the government of your choice. Where you have the aptitude, the temperament and the fervour, put yourself up through your political party for any high public office of the land.

(ix) *To the Farmer*

Air, water and food are the daily needs of man, and you, th
farmer provides man with food. Your role, therefore, is o
paramount importance. Additional to food, you supply most o
the raw materials needed by our industries.

Your cocoa, palm oil, groundnuts, cotton, hides and skins
provided the main wealth of this nation before the arrival o
petroleum. Products from your farms today are no less importan
than then. In fact, the Government-imposed Structura
Adjustment Programme (SAP) has more than re-emphasised th
role you play in the national economy.

You feed the teeming and ever growing nation's population
While you can sustain yourself for a few days, the urban dwelle
cannot survive without you. Your maize, yams, plantain, rice
beans, cattle, chicken, fish will disappear from the market, if you
dare go on strike, even for a short period.

You are therefore no inferior to any other group of the
population. On the contrary! Additionally, you have the power of
the ballot to choose or reject any government. This is the reason
why, like any other section of the population, you must join to
reject military rule. Discourage it with all the weapon at your
disposal, so that a peaceful and stable nation will evolve, where
you will take advantage of technology for easier, quicker, and
richer output from your farms.

(x) *To the Artisan, The Labourer, The Self-Employed*

One may earn one's living by being a cobbler, a carpenter, a
tailor or any other craftsman. An able bodied and strong man,
ready on the wings, to render a service for a just pay is also a
happy member of society.

The petty trader, the hawker and the newspaper vendor, all
render invaluable services and contribute to the gross national
product (GNP)

You are a happy lot, independent, self-sustaining and free. I
encourage you to work harder and to graduate from a humble
station to greater heights. Impossibility is found only in the

dictionary of fools. The Great Creator and Guide of the universe has never been known to say to the man who wills: "Thus far and go no further",

It is observed, that you are the first group that take to the streets in jubilation or outrage, if there is a change of government. Instal a government of your choice by the power of the ballot. You are justified to protest when that power of choice is usurped by any individual or group of individuals. Cheer a popular government, elected by you. Make your feelings known when it derails or fails to keep faith with its manifesto, or governs with discrimination. You must use your power of the vote to change such a government at the next election. You will be proud you did.

But never you again welcome, or acclaim or hail any individual or group usurping your right and power in a military *coup d'etat*. Coups have provided the greatest source of instability to the nation and the main obstruction to the evolution of democracy in Nigeria.

Every segment of society must join to discourage a military intervention to the orderly growth, wealth and prosperity in Nigeria. This is my charge and handover to Nigerians.

Epilogue

The new dawn of the Third Republic invokes two imperatives:

    End of Military Rule

    God-send Leader

(1) *End of Militarism*

It is a fundamental creed that this nation, Nigeria, will no longer be ruled by soldiers. We love the soldiers. They are Nigerians. Every Nigerian has rights and privileges of citizenship, and his political aspiration is to a great extent dictated by his profession. The military man is a professional, not a ruler.

The objective is that there must never again be a two tier citizenship, where the military on the one hand threatens the society and grabs power with the very weapon we asked it to protect us and the nation with; and on the other side is the civilian, reduced to a helpless "second rate" citizen by the power of the gun and the booming of decrees. All these should end, and one Nation, one citizenship and one community emerge.

(2) *God-send Leadership*

The second imperative is a universal prayer for God to send and show us a leader, who by his actions, will shame the military to the barracks. The military cannot go, only for an opportunist nincompoop to take its place. The person of our vision to take the mantle of leadership of Nigeria, will arrive imbued with a patriotic determination to serve.

Anybody who comes with the intention to grab must not rule. Any one who comes with the intention to give, must be given a chance. The people naturally will trust him. They prayed for it. They got him. Then by his words and actions our Leader says to his people, who already have confidence in him "Come follow me. The light is lit, be not afraid." And both leader and follower will march with optimism and glory to the Greater Tomorrow of the Nigerian Nation. Then, the rebirth is complete.

Rebirth Of A Nation
Index

M